J. G. Ballard

Contemporary Critical Perspectives
Series Editors: Jeannette Baxter, Sebastian Groes and Sean Matthews
Consultant Editor: Dominic Head

Guides in the *Contemporary Critical Perspectives* series provide companions to reading and studying major contemporary authors. Each guide includes new critical essays combining textual readings, cultural analysis and discussion of key critical and theoretical issues in a clear, accessible style. They also include a preface by a major contemporary writer, a new interview with the author, discussion of film and TV adaptation and guidance on further reading.

Titles in the series include:

Ian McEwan edited by Sebastian Groes
Kazuo Ishiguro edited by Sean Matthews and Sebastian Groes

J. G. BALLARD

Contemporary Critical Perspectives

Edited by
Jeannette Baxter

continuum

Continuum International Publishing Group

The Tower Building   80 Maiden Lane, Suite 704
11 York Road   New York
London SE1 7NX   NY 10038

www.continuumbooks.com

British Library Cataloguing-in-Publication Data
A catalogue record for this book is available from the British Library.

ISBN: 978-0-8264-9725-3 (hardback)
       978-0-8264-9726-0 (paperback)

Library of Congress Cataloging-in-Publication Data
A catalog record for this book is available from the Library of Congress.

Typeset by Newgen Imaging Systems Pvt Ltd, Chennai, India
Printed and bound in Great Britain by MPG Books Ltd, Bodmin, Cornwall

Contents

Foreword by Toby Litt   vii

General Editors' Preface   xi

Acknowledgements   xii

Contributors   xiii

Chronology or a Version of J. G. Ballard's Life   xv

INTRODUCTION   **J. G. Ballard and the Contemporary**   1
Jeannette Baxter (Anglia Ruskin University, Cambridge)

CHAPTER ONE   **The Geometry of the Space Age: J. G. Ballard's Short Fiction and Science Fiction of the 1960s**   11
Brian Baker (Lancaster University)

CHAPTER TWO   **Disquieting Features: An Introductory Tour of *The Atrocity Exhibition***   23
Jake Huntley (University of East Anglia)

CHAPTER THREE   **The Gothic, the Body, and the Failed Homeopathy Argument: Reading *Crash***   34
Victor Sage (University of East Anglia)

CHAPTER FOUR   **Death at Work: The Cinematic Imagination of J. G. Ballard**   50
Corin Depper (Kingston University)

CHAPTER FIVE   **Mind is the Battlefield: Reading Ballard's 'Life Trilogy' as War Literature**   66
Umberto Rossi (Rome)

CHAPTER SIX   **From Shanghai to Shepperton: Crises of Representation in J. G. Ballard's Londons**   78
Sebastian Groes (Liverpool Hope University)

CHAPTER SEVEN   **Visions of Europe in *Cocaine Nights* and *Super-Cannes***   94
Jeannette Baxter (Anglia Ruskin University, Cambridge)

CHAPTER EIGHT   **Situating the Violence of J. G. Ballard's Postmillennial Fiction: The Possibilities of Sacrifice, the Certainties of Trauma**   107
Philip Tew (Brunel University)

Afterword by Toby Litt   120

Kingdom Come: An Interview with J. G. Ballard by Jeannette Baxter   122

References   129

Index   149

Foreword

Toby Litt

Recently, I caught the wrong bus (a number 21) from Norwich City Centre to the University of East Anglia – where the first International conference on the work of J. G. Ballard, 'From Shanghai to Shepperton' took place, in May 2007. Instead of heading to the campus directly, up the beautifully named Unthank Road, the bus went via Bowthorpe – it also went via Ballard.

Our slow, winding, doubling-back route took in Norwich Research Park and the recently built Norfolk and Norwich University Hospital. A bright low sun reflected off the artificial lakes, at least I assumed they were artificial. Most of the houses we saw, as we crawled along, were on the peripheries of housing estates – facades of pale pink brick and thickly double-glazed windows, lawns which give nothing away and decals on the bedroom windows of suicidal teens. A pregnant woman with a bindi got on; a research scientist I had taken for a student got off. Eventually, the bus arrived at the UEA campus, famous for its unapologetically concrete architecture, especially the stack-box ziggurats in which first-year students are accommodated. We had arrived, also, at Ballard.

Sometimes, when I think about J. G. Ballard the man, I find it hard not to suspect that – somehow or other – he gained access to Google Earth over 40 years ago. His fictional project seems to have been based on a cold assessment of what (apart from woods and fields) takes up most of our country's surface area, what is most obtrusive when viewed from space. Hence, carparks and motorways, airports and their runways, high rise buildings, suburban housing estates, psychiatric hospitals, shopping centres. No other novelist has paid such close attention to the quiddity of where we now live and work – in all its recalcitrant mundanity. The rest of us, for the most part, pass through these spaces with the thought, 'What could *possibly* happen in this emptiness?' The Ballard bluff, or double bluff, has always been that he actually *likes* it here, not least because he sees it not as void but as unbounded plenitude. *Everything* can happen here. At the end of his introduction to *Vermilion Sands* (1971), he mischievously writes of his guess-at-the-future, 'I wait optimistically for it to take concrete shape around me.' This way, or so he insists, is his; the technological, the surface-loving, rather than all the possible others: atavistic, cthonic, nostalgic, theistic.

What we lack in the United Kingdom is any glamour of our present selves. (America, by contrast, suffers from the opposite problem: glamour-dazzle.) But, as an outsider-insider, or an insider-outsider, Ballard manages to see what we can't. He has no interest in our history or, even worse, our heritage. This, in itself, is remarkable.

One of the thought-experiments I play with any British writer is to reimagine them as coming from another country. For example, I refigure Graham Greene as a French writer. How much more seriously he would have been taken, as an existential thinker. Then I move to Muriel Spark and sense how the distance-travelled of translation from German to English would bring her metaphysics so much closer. Then I turn to Ballard. A French Ballard, I think, would be a normalized, de-radicalized Ballard. His characters behave, anyway, more like characters in French art movies than in other British novels contemporary to his own (let alone the ooh-er-missus intersex relations of British cinema 1950–1980). But how about a full-on German Ballard? – with autobahns for motorways, with the motorik regularity of his sentences, with Hitler as an unforgettable erotic backdrop. That has an eerie rightness about it.

As another thought-experiment, I find it suggestive, following Gilles Deleuze and Félix Guattari's approach to Kafka, to speak not of Jim Ballard but of the Ballard Writing Machine (sweet echoes of the Burroughs Adding Machine).[1] This might take away the taint of Shepperton, but it might also take away the tang of Shepperton.

How does the Ballard Writing Machine work? It has a definite predilection for certain formalities. For example, the form of titles, both book and chapter, is very often Definite Article plus Adjective plus Noun (from *The Drowned World* (1962) to *The Atrocity Exhibition* (1970)) although later this becomes Adjective plus Noun (from *Concrete Island* (1974) to *Super-Cannes* (2000)).

It favours a conservative structure. The novels come with numbered, titled chapters. Even the Machine's most extreme production, *The Atrocity Exhibition*, does not deviate from this template.

The contents page of a BWM novel, therefore, manages to suggest something both opaque and transparent. No plot developments are given away, but – if we have encountered the Machine's work before – we already know the parameters of the likely action.

There will be a building-up which is, at the same time, a breaking-down. People collectively will become involved in some regularized mania, within the elaboration of which the actions of the main characters will prove decisive but from which they themselves will remain essentially detached.

The BWM-men will have affairs with the BWM-women. These will start and end abruptly, without great difficulty or regret. Sex will occur but it will be less focused upon, in the writing, than those moments when the dreamworlds of the lovers coincide most closely. The Machine is more interested in the jerky choreography of meeting and parting than the flowing entanglement of hearts. I don't believe any BWM novel features a couple who meet, marry and remain faithful unto death. The lovers are, in a sense, too easily distracted for that; not immoral, just unfocused. Often, it seems almost as if they never come to full consciousness, they are always half-dreaming one another.

But let's stop the Machine and return Ballard's humanity to him, if only for the sake of some slightly less inelegant sentences.

Despite Ballard's insistence upon the parapsychological (see V. Vale's *Quotes* and *Conversations*), it seems to me as though he has no interest in the Freudian subconscious as such. His interchangeable heroes – only a couple of short steps away from the active, square-jawed ciphers of 1950s sci-fi – do not have rich mental lives. But as soon as one takes the external world which they inhabit *as* their subconscious, as soon as one sees sublimation as being replaced by efflorescence, by architecture, then one begins to see Ballard aright. In this reading, there remains no barrier between external and internal worlds.

Ballard is a true Surrealist. But his distance from the originals of that movement is made clearer when you realize how useless a tool automatic writing would be to him. Either all his writing is automatic, or none. And, either way, it accesses the same well-springs.

While reading Ballard, I don't generally feel – as I do with other writers – that this or that passage has come from some deeper place within the psyche. Ballard's explorations are relentlessly horizontal – until, with the internal/external flip, one realizes that they have all along taken the horizontal for the vertical. (Here, he coincides with Warhol.) There follows a moment of vertigo: instead of driving, one has been flying; instead of exploring, one has been perpetually plunging. This simultaneous effacement and enactment of depth is one of Ballard's greatest achievements.

In fact, the post-Warholian displacement of depth, the removal of it as an aesthetic criterion, is one of the qualities most important in Ballard. As far as I'm aware, he did not spend a moment mourning it. Nor does he, like the 1980s Brat Pack writers, allow a satire of vacuity to be deduced by morally sophisticated readers. Patrick Bateman may be the genetic successor of Ballard's emptied heroes, but Ballard is never so obvious as to leave behind a trail of eviscerated bodies. He is, instead, strangely gentle with his characters, even when injuring them – almost, at times, courteous in his approach to their demise.

In Ballard's writing, there are things which are there, which fill pagespace, but which function only to assert their own irrelevance. That the male and female characters are sexually attractive is, after you've read a book or two, taken as a *sine qua non*. This is the libidinal economy within which the Ballardian exchanges take place. It is a post-pill world. No female character can get pregnant, because that would impede the narrative flow; and if any woman does get pregnant, she must have an abortion immediately, silently. Children rarely feature as important characters. What can happen sometimes, without ever mattering, is love. Though it is very likely to be over before it is described as such. All emotions go nowhere, unless they hasten destruction or self-destruction.

In a Ballard novel we expect certain events, and expect them not to bother us particularly; we are instead reading for the rhythm – it is in the wavelength or the pulse of each novel that its true meaning lies. Ballard's periodicity has always been spot on: he leaves out exactly the right things. Technology is central to his vision, but, at the same time, entirely irrelevant to it. The plots of his stories and novels almost never depend upon a recent invention (unless the automobile is recent). It is new conditions rather than new devices which he perceives; services rather than goods.

There is a particular Ballard-sentence. They lead up to and then away from the comma. Very often, the first half of the sentence gets the respectable, necessary job of narration out of the way. There follows a pause, after which the dreamworld of the novel floods through, most often in simile. Each book has its parallel world, from which its comparative imagery is drawn. But also, in some novels, there is a closed-circuit of reference, where a simile in one part of a book (*Crash* is perhaps the strongest example of this) refers or seems to refer to an object or incident at the other end of the book. On a level of similitude, it is emphasized that – from this particular world – there is no escape.

The works of few living writers could withstand the attentions of a two-day academic conference. That, at the end of 'From Shanghai to Shepperton', it still felt as if there was much more to be said, as if we had only started to establish a basic knowledge of the territory, was an indication of the enduring strangeness of Ballard's world.

Note

1. Deleuze, G. and Guattari, F. (1986). *Kafka: Towards a Minor Literature*, University of Minnesota Press.

General Editors' Preface

The readership for contemporary fiction has never been greater. The explosion of reading groups and literary blogs, of university courses and school curricula, and even the apparent rude health of the literary marketplace, indicate an ever-growing appetite for new work, for writing which responds to the complex, changing and challenging times in which we live. At the same time, readers seem ever more eager to engage in conversations about their reading, to devour the review pages, to pack the sessions at literary festivals and author events. Reading is an increasingly social activity, as we seek to share and refine our experiences of books, to clarify and extend our understanding.

It is this tremendous enthusiasm for contemporary fiction to which the *Contemporary Critical Perspectives* series responds. Our ambition is to offer readers of current fiction a comprehensive critical account of each author's work, presenting original, specially commissioned analyses of all aspects of their careers, from a variety of different angles and approaches, as well as directions towards further reading and research. Our brief to our contributors is to be scholarly, to draw on the latest thinking about narrative, or philosophy, or psychology, indeed whatever seemed to them most significant in drawing out the meanings and force of the texts in question, but also to focus closely on the words on the page, the stories and scenarios and forms which all of us meet first when we open a book. We insisted that these essays be accessible to that mythical beast, the Common Reader, who might just as readily be spotted at the Lowdham Book Festival as in a college seminar. In this way, we hope to have presented critical assessments of our writers in such a way as to contribute something to both of those environments and also to have done something to bring together the important qualities of each of them.

Jeannette Baxter,
Sebastian Groes and Sean Matthews

Acknowledgements

I would like to thank the contributors to this volume for their participation and enthusiasm. Many thanks also to my fellow Series Editors Sebastian Groes and Sean Matthews for their helpful suggestions during the preparation of this book, and to Dominic Head for his generous advice at every stage. I would like to thank Anna Sandeman and Colleen Coalter at Continuum for their untiring assistance with editorial queries. I am also extremely grateful to J. G. Ballard for agreeing to be interviewed for this volume. Finally, my biggest debt of thanks goes to Kate Lee; her continued love, support and patience makes it all possible.

Victor Sage's chapter, 'The Gothic, the Body, and the Failed Homeopathy Argument: Reading *Crash*' first appeared, in part, in, Graeme Harper and Xavier Mendelik (eds), Unruly Pleasures: The Cult Film and Its Critics. FAB Press: Surrey, 2000. We gratefully acknowledge the editors for allowing us to reprint material.

Contributors

Brian Baker is a Lecturer in English at Lancaster University and is the author of three books: *Literature and Science: Social Impact and Interaction*, with John H. Cartwright (ABC-Clio, 2005), *Masculinity in Fiction and Film: Representing Men in Popular Genres 1945–2000* (Continuum, 2006) and *Iain Sinclair* (Manchester, 2007). He has also published more widely in journals and book collections in the areas of masculinities, science fiction, and London fictions. He has forthcoming pieces on *Casino Royale*, science and literature, and masculinities and horror, and is working on larger projects concerning space and time in fiction and film.

Jeannette Baxter is Senior Lecturer in English Literature at Anglia Ruskin University, Cambridge and specializes in modern and contemporary fiction. She has published journal articles and book chapters in the areas of literary modernism, post-modernism, Holocaust writing and contemporary British Fiction. She is the author of *J. G. Ballard's Surrealist Imagination: Spectacular Authorship* (Ashgate 2008) and she has forthcoming publications on Ballard, the visual arts and popular culture. She is currently working on a book-length study of the cultural and intellectual legacies of Surrealism in British literature post 1930.

Corin Depper is a Lecturer in the School of Performance and Screen Studies at Kingston University, London. He has written on the work of Ezra Pound and Jean-Luc Godard, and his current research explores the relationship between cinematic space and gallery space in recent film and installation work.

Sebastian Groes is a Lecturer in English Literature at Liverpool Hope University. He specializes in modern and contemporary literature, and representations of cities. His books include *British Fiction of the Sixties* (Continuum, 2009) and *The Making of London* (Palgrave, 2009).

Jake Huntley is an associate tutor at the University of East Anglia, Norwich, where he recently completed a Ph.D. on the representation of genre fiction. He has written articles on science fiction and horror film, principally from a Deleuzian perspective.

Toby Litt was born in 1968. He grew up in Ampthill, Bedfordshire. He is the author of *Adventures in Capitalism, Beatniks, Corpsing, deadkidsongs, Exhibitionism, Finding Myself, Ghost Story, Hospital* and he plays the drums in a band called okay. He is a *Granta* Best of Young British Novelist. His website is at www.tobylitt.com.

Umberto Rossi is an independent scholar, translator, literary journalist and secondary school teacher. He completed a Ph.D. thesis on literature of the First World War at the University of Rome. He has published essays on science fiction, war literature, post-modernist fiction, and J. G. Ballard in Italian and English-language journals. He is currently writing a monograph for Bulzoni Press (Rome) entitled, *Fire Century: Introduction to War Literature.*

Victor Sage is a novelist (*Black Shawl* and *A Mirror For Larks*) and short-story writer, who has also written extensively on the Gothic tradition. His latest monograph on this subject is *Le Fanu's Gothic* (2003). He has edited Charles Maturin's *Melmoth The Wanderer* (2000) and Sheridan Le Fanu's *Uncle Silas* (2001) for Penguin Classics. He is currently working on a cultural history of European Gothic for Polity Press. Victor Sage is Emeritus Professor of English Literature in the School of Literature and Creative Writing at the University of East Anglia, Norwich.

Philip Tew is Professor in English (Post-1900 Literature) at Brunel University, founding Director of the UK Network for Modern Fiction Studies, and Director of the Brunel Centre for Contemporary Writing. His publications include *B. S. Johnson: A Critical Reading* (Manchester UP, 2001), *The Contemporary British Novel* (Continuum, 2004; rev. second ed. 2007), *Jim Crace: A Critical Introduction* (Manchester UP, 2006) and *Re-reading B. S. Johnson* (Palgrave Macmillan, 2007) co-edited with Glyn White. Forthcoming are three books: *Re-Envisioning the Pastoral* (Fairleigh Dickinson UP) co-edited with David James, *Writers Talk: Conversations with Contemporary Novelists* (Continuum, 2008) co-edited with Fiona Tolan and Leigh Wilson, and *Zadie Smith* (Palgrave Macmillan, 2008).

Chronology or a Version of
J. G. Ballard's Life

1930   James Graham Ballard born in Shanghai, China to Edna
            and James Ballard. Ballard's father is the manager of the
            China Printing and Finishing Company.

1930–42   lives at 31 Amherst Avenue, Shanghai, attends the
            Cathedral School. Margaret Ballard born in 1937.

1942–45   interned with his parents and sister in the Japanese
            Detention Centre, Lunghua.

1946–49   sent to England, attends Leys School, Cambridge.

1949–53   studies medicine at King's College, Cambridge. In 1951
            Ballard wins joint first prize in a short-story competition
            with 'The Violent Noon'. Ballard soon abandons his
            medical studies at Cambridge and takes up a place to read
            English Literature at Queen Mary College, University of
            London in October 1951. Ballard leaves Queen Mary in
            1952 without completing his degree; he writes copy for
            the advertising agency, Digby Wills Ltd, works as a
            Covent Garden porter (chrysanthemum department) and
            sells the *Waverley Encyclopaedia* door-to-door.

1953–54   joins the RAF and begins basic training at Kirton in
            Lindsey, Lincolnshire. In 1954 Ballard is posted to the
            RCAF flight training base at Moosejaw, Saskatchewan,
            Canada. Ballard writes his first science fiction story 'Pass-
            port to Eternity'.

1955   marries Helen Mary Matthews, and begins typing up the
            short stories he had written while stationed in Canada.

1956–62   lives in London; first child, James, born in 1956, followed
            by Fay (1957) and Beatrice (1959). In 1956, Ballard pub-
            lishes his first science fiction story, 'Prima Belladonna' in
            New Worlds and visits the 'This is Tomorrow' at Whitechapel
            Gallery, London. Whilst trying to launch his writing career,
            Ballard also works as deputy editor of *Chemistry & Indus-
            try*. In 1960, the Ballard family settle in Shepperton and
            Ballard continues to publish science fiction short stories.

1962   becomes a full-time writer, publishes *Wind from Nowhere*,
            The Drowned World and a short-story collection, *The Voices
            of Time & Other Stories*. Ballard makes his *New Worlds*

	editorial debut with the controversial essay, 'Which Way to Inner Space?'
1963	*The Four Dimensional Nightmare* (short story collection).
1964	Helen Mary Ballard dies of pneumonia during a family holiday in Spain. Ballard brings up his three children in Shepperton. Publishes *The Drought*.
1966	*The Crystal World*.
1967	publishes three short story collections: *The Day of Forever*, *The Disaster Area* and *The Overloaded Man*.
1967–69	'Plan for the Assassination of Jacqueline Kennedy' (1967) is debated in the House of Lords and denounced by Randolph Churchill as a slur on the memory of the dead US President. 'Why I Want to Fuck Ronald Reagan' (1968) becomes the subject of an obscenity trial; charges against Ballard are eventually dropped. These scandals lead Doubleday to withdraw the first American edition of *The Atrocity Exhibition*.
1970	*The Atrocity Exhibition* published in England. Ballard stages an exhibition called 'Crashed Cars' at the New Arts Laboratory, Camden.
1971	*Vermilion Sands*. Ballard stars in a BBC documentary called 'Crash' (directed by Harley Cockliss).
1972	*Chronopolis* (a short story collection).
1973	*Crash*. Ballard survives a car crash.
1974	*Concrete Island*
1975	*High-Rise*
1976	*Low-Flying Aircraft* (short story collection).
1979	*The Unlimited Dream Company* wins the British Science Fiction Award.
1981	*Hello America*.
1982	*Myths of the Near Future*.
1984	*Empire of the Sun* is published to huge success, winning the Guardian Fiction Prize, the James Tait Black Memorial Prize and appearing on the Booker Prize short list. Ballard turns down the CBE and membership of the Royal Society of Literature.
1987	*The Day of Creation*. Steven Spielberg's adaptation of *Empire of the Sun* is released.
1988	*Running Wild*.
1989	*War Fever* (short story collection). The annotated version of *The Atrocity Exhibition* is published by RE/Search.
1991	*The Kindness of Women*. Ballard returns to Shanghai to make a BBC documentary, 'Shanghai Jim'.
1994	*Rushing to Paradise*.
1996	*Cocaine Nights*; publication of a collection of Ballard's non-fiction writings (essays, reviews and articles), *A User's*

Guide to the New Millennium: Essays and Reviews. David Cronenberg's adaptation of *Crash* is released in America but banned by four English councils on the grounds of depravity; the film's release date in the United Kingdom is delayed by 18 months. *Crash* wins a special jury prize for 'originality, daring and audacity' at the Cannes Film Festival.

2000   *Super-Cannes.*

2001   *The Complete Short Stories;* Jonathan Weiss's adaptation of *The Atrocity Exhibition* is released.

2003   *Millennium People.*

2006   *Kingdom Come.*

2008   *Miracles of Life: From Shanghai to Shepperton, An Autobiography.*

J. G. Ballard and the Contemporary

JEANNETTE BAXTER

BALLARDIAN: (adj) 1. of James Graham Ballard (J. G. Ballard; born 1930), the British novelist, or his works. (2) resembling or suggestive of the conditions described in Ballard's novels & stories, esp. dystopian modernity, bleak manmade landscapes & the psychological effects of technological, social or environmental developments.

J. G. Ballard's entry into the *Collins English Dictionary* provides a useful starting point for this collection. The first meaning of Ballardian invokes one of the most significant and challenging writers of the contemporary period. In the course of a career spanning over half a century, Ballard has produced a diverse and voluminous body of work which has courted literary praise and cultural controversy in almost equal measure. While the publication of *Crash* (1973) initiated cries of moral outrage and accusations of wilful perversity from its readers and review-ers, the publication of *Empire of the Sun* (1984) initiated a round of critical acclaim, winning the *Guardian* Fiction and the James Tate Black Memo-rial prizes, and narrowly missing out on the Booker Prize. Subsequent adaptations of these novels to screen by David Cronenberg (*Crash*, 1995) and Steven Spielberg (*Empire of the Sun*, 1987) have gone some way to cementing Ballard's place and popularity within the wider cultural imagination. The same can be said for Ballard's non-fictional writings (essays, reviews) which have appeared in publications as various as the *Times*, *Vogue*, the *Daily Telegraph* and *Playboy*. That Ballard is recognized and valued as a contemporary cultural commentator is evident in Jason Cowley's witty observation that whenever the nation found itself plunged into moments of crisis or trauma (the death of Princess Diana, for instance, or a terrorist attack), the following cry would echo through the *Times* newsroom: 'Call J. G. Ballard' (Cowley: 2001). Apparently, Ballard was seldom at home. Or if he was, he was not answering the phone.

It is precisely this ability to anticipate and give an account of the myr-iad realities of our disturbed modernity to which the second meaning of Ballardian points. Indeed, Ballard, the so-called Seer of Shepperton, has acquired something of a reputation for predicting some of the more unusual shifts within contemporary culture. Most famously in *The Atrocity Exhibition* (1970), Ballard imagined the rise of Ronald Reagan from Hollywood Cowboy to US President. Then, following the death of Princess Diana in a Parisian underpass in 1997, Salman Rushdie wrote a piece for *The New Yorker* in which he suggested how the parameters of the Princess's life and death – a pornographic tale of sex, death and celebrity – had been sketched out, to some degree, in Ballard's *Crash*. A more recent demonstration of Ballard's prescience occurred with the publication of *Millennium People* (2003), a story of terrorist violence which opens with the bombing of Terminal 2 at Heathrow airport. Within months of the novel's completion, anti-terrorist forces rolled into Heathrow Airport in response to a threatened Al-Qaeda attack. Within this context, Ballardian also functions as a kind of trigger for conjuring up a series of distinctive images and landscapes which capture the contemporary condition in all of its violence and ambiguity: murdered celebrities, crashed cars, surveillance technologies, media politicians, gated communities, vast shopping malls; drowned cities, nuclear weapons ranges and testing sites, landscaped business parks. These are just a few of the objects and architectures that make up the world of a J. G. Ballard novel or short story. What is important to bear in mind, however, is that their Ballardian resonance lies less in their straightforward recognizability and more in the way in which these familiar aspects of contemporary culture are rendered strange and unnerving. If the adjective Ballardian is to be understood as providing some kind of mirror on the contemporary world, then it is a mirror which distorts.

At the same time that Ballard's inscription into the English language can be taken as a sign of cultural and literary recognition – a term that has been operating unofficially amongst Ballard readers and scholars for years has finally been authorized and made official – this act of recuperation poses certain problems for a writer like Ballard. Following the commercial and critical success of *Empire of the Sun*, for instance, Ballard was offered a CBE (Commander of the Order of the British Empire) medal which he turned down, saying: 'I just don't want anything to do with all that nonsense, a Ruritanian charade that helps to prop up our top-heavy monarchy' (Ballard cited in Baxter 2004: 35). As the novelist Toby Litt puts it in his Foreword to this collection, this is the voice of J. G. Ballard as 'outsider-insider, or insider-outsider' who remains resistant to the lures of assimilation. We can trace Ballard's disquiet with his adopted country back to the 'shock' which he insists he felt when he first encountered postwar London:

> When I actually arrived in 1946 I found a London that looked like Bucharest with a hangover – heaps of rubble, an exhausted ferret-like people defeated by war and still deluded by Churchillian rhetoric, hobbling around a wasteland of poverty, ration books and grotesque social division. (Ballard 1996d: 185)

To the dislocated expatriate from war-torn Shanghai, England was a foreign country, an imaginary homeland that did not quite live up to the picture-book images which Ballard had been force-fed as a young boy. This is a point which Sebastian Groes picks up and develops in his chapter in this volume. Focusing on Ballard's literary representations of London, Groes places the spatial embodiment of British political, cultural and economic power at the heart of Ballard's imagination in order to examine the author's ambivalent relationship towards England and its capital city. Tracing Ballard's first encounter with London back to the network of signs, stories and fictions which circulated throughout colonial Shanghai and Lunghua camp, Groes reads London as a master narrative which Ballard's writing attempts to dislocate. What Groes's reading illustrates is how Ballard's initial sense of physical alienation soon developed into one of social and psychological estrangement as he began to reflect critically on England's class-ridden system and its allegiance to Empire: 'In short, did the English pay a fearful price for the system of self-delusions that underpinned almost everything in their lives?' The question, he continues, 'played a large role in the difficulty I had settling down here. It fed into my troubled sense of who I was, and encouraged me to think of myself as a lifelong outsider and maverick' (Ballard 2008: 127). No wonder, then, that Ballard flatly refused to become an honorary member of what he perceived to be a political fiction.

It comes as no surprise to learn that, in the same year that Ballard refused the CBE, he also turned down membership of the Royal Society of Literature (Oramus 2007: 267). After all, Ballard has become defined precisely by his decision to operate on the fringes of literary culture. He is, as Roger Luckhurst has argued, one of those 'awkward voices who refuse to play the literary game; their off-centre locations echo their ex-centric, discomfiting writings' (1997: xii). Ballard's authorial ex-centricity is clearly delineated in his initial decision in the 1950s to reject the dominant mode of social realism and the extreme innovations of literary modernism in favour of science fiction. Whilst Ballard considered the stylistic conventions of the social realist novel ('sequential narrative, characters "in the round", consecutive events, balloons of dialogue attached to "he said" and "she said"' (Ballard 1996g: 126)) to be outmoded and imaginatively restrictive in a postwar climate of capitalist expansion and cultural transformation (Ballard 1996g: 126–30), he deemed the experimental aesthetics of James Joyce and T. S. Eliot to be 'alienated', 'introverted' and thus thoroughly inappropriate (Ballard 1996c: 205). Instead, with its long tradition of innovative response to science, technology and rapidly shifting political and cultural climates, Ballard identified science fiction as the only authentic literature of the day:

> At present, science fiction is almost the only form of fiction which is thriving, and certainly the only fiction which has any influence on the world around it. [. . .] In essence, science fiction is a response to science and technology as perceived by the inhabitants of the consumer goods society, and recognises

that the role of the writer today has totally changed – he is now merely one
of a huge army of people filling the environment with fictions of every kind.
(Ballard 1996c: 205–6)

In contrast to the parochialism of mainstream literature, science fiction's
expansive vision promised to respond to the competing vocabularies of
the late twentieth century – science, technology, advertising, capitalism,
consumerism – in a way that just might make sense. This was a process
of intelligibility which also called for a transformed sense of what it
was to be a writer: in a world saturated by fictions of every kind, the
contemporary writer's job was not to overlay these external fictions
with his or her own private fantasies, but to 'invent the reality' (Ballard
1995: Introduction).

Although Ballard's appropriation of science fiction situated him outside of the literary mainstream, his refusal simply to adopt traditional
science-fiction tropes and conventions meant that his ex-centricity was
doubled (see Luckhurst 1997: 1–36). The so-called 'Voice' of the New Wave
science-fiction movement, Ballard published a controversial and provocative manifesto which set out to re-map the trajectories of postwar
British science fiction: 'Which Way to Inner Space?' (1962). Contem-
ptuous of science fiction's generic constraints and hackneyed subject
matter of 'interstellar travel, extraterrestrial life forms, galactic wars
and physical scientific facts' (Ballard 1996i: 197), this polemic called for
a highly innovative form of science-fiction writing which would no
longer look to the skies, but keep a critical and creative eye on the 'alien'
landscapes of the contemporary period. Furthermore, turning its back
on the 'rocket ships and ray guns' (Ballard 1996i: 195) of outer space,
Ballard's renewed and renewable form of science-fiction writing would
set off in search of '*inner* space'; that is a series of shifting and hybrid
imaginative geographies in which the outer world of reality and the
inner world of the psyche fuse in a number of fascinating and startling
ways. This is the imaginative territory which Brian Baker maps in his
wide-ranging chapter. Offering a reassessment of Ballard's early short
stories and novels within the contexts of *New Worlds* and New Wave
writing, Baker explores Ballard's antagonistic relationship towards
genre science fiction in order to set up a series of anti-dystopian readings which insist on the symbolic rather than the social significance
of Ballard's imagination. Focusing on the importance of the Space Age
to the iconography of Ballard's short stories and novels, Baker then
goes on to challenge the extent to which the provocative manifesto,
'Which Way to Inner Space?' (1962), engenders a departure from the
topoi of outer space. He does so, however, in order to demonstrate how
New Wave science fiction in general, and Ballardian science fiction in
particular, constituted a radically experimental form of contemporary

literature which would go on to pose difficult and urgent questions pertaining to time, subjectivity, history and reality.

Most notably, Ballard's experimentalism manifested itself in his transformation of science fiction along visual lines of influence. Specifically, Ballard looked to cinema, Surrealist painting and Pop Art, representational forms, which, for him, had become 'more and more concerned with the creation of new states of mind, constructing fresh symbols and languages where the old cease to be valid' (Ballard 1996i: 197). In contrast to the 'technological pantomime' (Ballard 1996e; 16) which one would find in films such as *Star Wars* (1977), Ballardian science fiction engaged creatively and critically with the contemporaneous French New Wave cinema. In his numerous journalistic writings on European and World cinema, for instance, Ballard foregrounds two innovative and influential works: *La Jetée* (1962) by Chris Marker and *Alphaville* (1965) by Jean-Luc Goddard. A fusion of photomontage (the film is entirely constructed from still photographs), science fiction and 'psychological fable' *La Jetée* is a post-nuclear narrative in which time, space and reality are radically dislocated. As Ballard notes, it is precisely the succession of disconnected images which this short film boasts that creates 'a series of potent images of the inner landscapes of time' (Ballard 1996f: 28). *Alphaville*, meanwhile, draws on the iconography of Pop Art, comic books and film noir precisely in order to place the most alien planet – Earth – under scrutiny. Ballard writes how the alienated landscape of *Alphaville* is utterly indistinguishable from contemporary Paris: 'Godard makes the point that in the media landscape of the present day the fantasies of science fiction are as "real" as an office block, an airport or a presidential campaign' (Ballard 1996h: 19). As Corin Depper argues in his chapter, cinema remains a powerful expression of contemporary culture for Ballard at the same time that if offers new and alternative ways of responding to contemporary culture. Reading *The Atrocity Exhibition* (1970), *Crash* (1973), and *Empire of the Sun* (1984) through their filmic adaptations, Depper illustrates how Ballard's cinematic imagination continues to raise complex questions about form, time, narrative and movement in, and across, written and visual texts. Depper's critical enquiry remains haunted by one persistent question, however, why are three texts which are so intimately bound up with the mechanics, history and spirit of cinema so resistant to their own transformation into images?

Although Ballard has always expressed an eclectic taste for the visual arts, two twentieth-century art movements stand out as particular influences on his writing career: Surrealism and Pop Art. Identifying compatibility between Surrealism's enquiries into the unconscious, Pop Art's obsession with the circulating images and objects of the media and consumer landscapes, and his own abstract and analytical mode of science fiction, Ballard set about constructing a creative and critical analysis of both the chaotic surface realities of contemporary culture and its hidden, unconscious depths:

> The subject matter of science fiction is the subject matter of everyday life: the gleam on refrigerator cabinets, the contours of a wife's or husband's thighs passing the newsreel images on a colour TV set, the conjunction of musculature and chromium artefact within an automobile interior, the unique postures of passengers on an airport escalator – all in all, close to the world of the Pop painters and sculptors, Paolozzi, Hamilton, Warhol, Wesselman, Ruscha amongst others. (Ballard 1996c: 207)

Pop Art's dedication to the aestheticization of everyday objects (cars, celebrities, cans of soup, soap powder boxes, kettles, Coca Cola bottles) combined with its taste for literatures of mass culture (comic books, magazines, advertising brochures) provided Ballard with an ally. Indeed, as early as 1956 when Ballard visited what has commonly been celebrated as the birth of British Pop Art, the 'This is Tomorrow' exhibition (held at Whitechapel Gallery, London), Ballard recognized a keen affinity with Pop Art's revisioning of consumer goods, mass-advertising, and modern communications, and his own personal vision of how science fiction should develop as both an analysis of contemporary culture and an art of the now. Ballard's associations with Pop Art proved to be particularly intense and fruitful during the late 1960s and early 1970s, and some of the most formally experimental and contextually challenging work of this period was carried out in collaboration with Eduardo Paolozzi – sculptor; screen printer; science fiction fan *and* late twentieth-century Surrealist.

Surrealism has shaped the imaginative and critical trajectories of Ballard's writing from the beginning of his career (see Baxter 2009). Its visual and literary influences are evident, for instance, in Ballard's first science fiction short story, *Prima Belladonna*, which was published in *New Worlds* in 1956. Surrealism's drive to dismantle boundaries between the unconscious and conscious, self and object, reason and imagination in order to liberate the mind and spirit from the paralysing sphere of rationalist thought spoke directly to Ballard's non-realist desire to explore 'a heightened or alternate reality beyond that familiar to our senses' (Ballard 1996b: 84). In Surrealism, Ballard not only recognized a common need to dismantle socially constructed notions of identity, subjectivity, and reality in order to open art, literature, history and politics to new ways of seeing, but he also recognized an aesthetic practice that was particularly appropriate to the post-Second World War era: 'The techniques of surrealism have a particular relevance at this moment when the fictional elements in the world around us are multiplying to the point where it is almost impossible to distinguish between the '"real" and the "false"' (Ballard 1996b: 88). For Ballard, the significance of Surrealist aesthetic practices (such as collage, montage, psychic automatism) lay in their ability to penetrate the sub-texts of the contemporary consumer landscape and to expose the network of unconscious energies and insidious psychologies at work within it. It is this Surrealist aspect of Ballard's writing which Jake Huntley sets out to illuminate and interrogate in his essay. Reading *The Atrocity Exhibition* as a radical textual experimental which is still in process, Huntley explores questions of characterization, narrative time and form, and textual (re)composition in relation to Ballard's literary Surrealism. Revised, rewritten and extended with additional stories, authorial notes, illustrations and photographs, the latest version of *The Atrocity Exhibition*, Huntley suggests, may be read as a contemporary Surrealist performance.

Beyond its aesthetic innovations, Surrealist art and literature also provided Ballard with complex and often ambiguous ways of (re)thinking and re-presenting contemporary history. With their hidden perspectives and concealed energies, the time-saturated landscapes of Salvador Dali, Max Ernst and Paul Delvaux (among others) offered up alternative and provocative historical indexes. For Ballard, the confrontation with 'past traumas and experiences' and the 'discharging of fears and obsessions' (Ballard 1996: 146) which preoccupied Surrealist painting confirmed its historical and psychological significance in the age of Auschwitz and Hiroshima. Following the Surrealists' visual investigations into latent and manifest forms of historical violence, Ballard's writings have staged a series of complex, and often ethically challenging, enquiries into contemporary representations of historical atrocity. As a result of this work, a tenacious critical perception of the author has become established which pictures him as a nihilistic and solipsistic historical voyeur whose writing is emotionally detached and morally vacuous. This is a historical picture of J. G. Ballard which many of the essays in this collection confront and challenge. Indeed, responding to the current (re)turn to history in contemporary literature and criticism, the contributors to this collection offer critical perspectives which reread Ballard's work as complex and controversial engagements with history, memory and trauma.

One consequence of this step towards historicizing Ballard's work is that it reveals the inadequacy and inaccuracy of the second meaning of Ballardian which places his work within a rigid framework of dystopian loss. This is far too simplistic and reductive a way of thinking about how Ballard's writings engage with twentieth and twenty-first century histories. While texts such as *The Atrocity Exhibition* and *Crash* are in thrall to contemporary representations of war, death and mutilation, the waning or 'death of affect' produced by the texts' relentlessly violent energies also sets up exigent discussion about the erosion of moral and critical distance within contemporary culture. This is an area for critical discussion which Jeannette Baxter pursues in her chapter. Challenging dystopian readings of Ballard's European fictions, Baxter rereads *Cocaine Nights* (1966) and *Super-Cannes* (2000) as nightmarishly utopian in impulse. In the absence of history, morality and memory, she suggests, the 'nowheres' of Ballard's postwar Europes emerge as dangerous breeding grounds for neo-fascistic forms of power, violence, and aestheticized racism. Yet at the same time that the process of reading these texts challenges us, the readers, to immerse ourselves in their deviant logics and emerging psychopathologies, it also forces us to confront some rather unnerving questions about our own complicity in the criminal horror of contemporary European culture and history.

Ballard's postmillennial fictions continue to explore disquieting issues of historical guilt, amnesia and complicity by exhibiting repeated acts of meaningless violence and perversion. This is an ambiguous fictional trajectory which Phil Tew charts in his chapter. Drawing on René Girard's work on violence, sacrifice and community, Tew explores what he sees as a homicidal compulsion at work in *Super-Cannes, Millennium People* (2003) and *Kingdom Come* (2006). Evaluating representations of compulsive violence in Ballard's recent fictional phase and the earlier novels of *Crash* and *Concrete Island* (1974), Tew considers the sense of communal unease and violent aggression that dominates these postmillennial fictions in relation to complex questions of ritual, sacrifice and trauma. As Tew's reading of the evil and redemptive possibilities of Ballardian representations of sacrificial violence suggest, ambivalence is a key word when thinking about Ballard's writings. Ballard is fascinated by both the creative and the destructive nature of violence; his work records the eradication of historical reality within contemporary visual culture at the same time that it sets out to recover it; he carries out cool and analytical dissections of contemporary culture which are fiercely emotional, ethically engaged and highly amusing. This latter, and much neglected, dimension of Ballard's writing is one which Victor Sage gives focus to in his reading of *Crash*. Paying close attention to the parodic textures of Ballard's pornographic language, Sage explores the ways in which Ballard's deadpan humour emerges as a primary medium for Gothic effects. The force of this kind of rereading lies in its move to confront the ambivalent and unnerving mixture of horror and humour in *Crash*: replete with gothic jokes and grotesque metaphors, Sage suggests, *Crash* can be read as a radical and ambivalent encyclopaedia of imaginary perversions which are rich in satirical and social critique.

It is this sense of Ballard's work as a prolonged experiment in the representation of tensions and ambiguities inherent in contemporary history, culture and language which renders the very existence of the definition 'Ballardian' distinctly odd, even redundant. In some ways, Ballard's entire literary project can be seen as an unrelenting challenge to the very systems of order, classification and knowledge which texts such as dictionaries and encyclopaedias put in place. Highly innovative short stories such as 'Notes Towards A Mental Breakdown' (1976) and 'The Index' (1977) flaunt an irreverence to the authority, coherency and veracity of linguistic systems. 'Notes Towards a Mental Breakdown' consists of an 18 word headline in which each word is explained in a series of footnotes that are laid out in textual blocks. What quickly emerges in the process of reading, however, is that the text's footnotes contradict and undermine one another at every turn. Instead of offering a continuous and complete scientific report on the mental health of an anonymous Broadmoor patient, Ballard's story functions as a parody of realist forms of documentation which lay claim to certainty. Fittingly, the story ends on a paradoxical note: 'It seems possible that although the synopsis conceals a maze of lies and distortions, it is a simple and incontrovertible statement of truth' (Ballard 1976: 855). 'The Index' continues in this manner, taking the form of a 'found document' which the reader is encouraged (by an attached 'Editorial note') to interpret as the index to 'the unpublished and perhaps suppressed autobiography of a man who may well have been one of the most remarkable figures of the 20th century [. . .] Henry Rhodes Hamilton' (Ballard 1977: 940). Again there is no single, coherent narrative to be made from these partial fragments of alphabetized knowledge. The reader may be seduced into attempting to forge narrative links by cross-referencing certain events or personalities recorded in the Index, but such attempts are ultimately rendered futile: just as the life of Henry Rhodes Hamilton (whomever he may be) cannot be contained or ordered within this particular linguistic system neither can it be decoded and made intelligible.

It is in the contexts of definition and categorization that we can return to the first meaning of the word 'Ballardian' in order to problematize it further. As a number of the commentators in this collection argue, Ballard's repeated interrogations into the unstable nature of identity and subjectivity through fictionalized versions of himself not only raise complex issues of textual authority, authorial reliability and the ethics of life-writing, but they also pose the question: who is J. G. Ballard? This is an intricate and elusive line of enquiry which Umberto Rossi follows in his chapter. Tracing the interpenetration of factual and fictional histories across three versions of Ballard's life, *Empire of the Sun*, *The Kindness of Women* (1991) and *Miracles of Life* (2008), Rossi explores the intertextual nature of these works within the specific context of war literature. By insisting that Ballard's texts should be read as generically distinct from one another, Rossi focuses on the ways in which specific textual features and narrative techniques encourage a simultaneous engagement with, and disengagement from, complex narratives of historical violence, trauma and memory. At the same time that each literary rendering of Ballard's life invites the reader to make connections between the author and his fictional selves, he suggests, any straightforward manoeuvre to locate coherency and consistency in and across Ballard's war narratives is rendered redundant.

Although the question – who is J. G. Ballard? – remains a compelling one, it is ultimately hollow because, in a sense, there is no one J. G. Ballard to be found. As Toby Litt suggests in his Afterword, all critical moves to capture, know and 'explain' J. G. Ballard and his work are fraught with ambiguities, paradoxes and, ultimately, uncertainty. But perhaps this is, in part, what makes J. G. Ballard (whomever he may be) a contemporary writer. In much the same way that the contemporary is a mutable and renewable cultural category which evades easy categorization, so J. G. Ballard and his work continue to elude definition.

The Geometry of the Space Age: J. G. Ballard's Short Fiction and Science Fiction of the 1960s

BRIAN BAKER

Chapter Summary: Taking Ballard's *New Worlds* manifesto, 'Which Way to Inner Space?' as its starting point, this chapter explores the implication of time, space and psychology in Ballard's early fiction. Baker traces the connections between Ballard's early novels and the development of his short fiction and attempts to map out the different phases of his exploration of the *inner* space age.

Key Words: *The Drowned World*; *The Drought*; *The Crystal World*; science fiction; inner space; space-time continuum; psychology; space age; fugue states; short story form; *New Worlds*; 'Which Way to Inner Space?'; evolutionary biology

The relationship between J. G. Ballard and the genre of science fiction (sf) is an unusual one. Ballard was first published in the British sf magazine *Science Fantasy*, one of several edited by E. J. 'Ted' Carnell in the 1950s. Ballard's first novel, *The Drowned World*, was serialized in another of this stable, a magazine called *Science Fiction Adventures* in 1962, and many other stories were published in the most famous of this group, *New Worlds*. Edited by Carnell until 1964, when Michael Moorcock assumed the editorship, *New Worlds* was the most important British sf magazine in the postwar period until the cessation of its monthly publication schedule in 1970 (it has since been revived by Moorcock and others in a variety of formats). Carnell and then Moorcock oversaw the rise to prominence of a generation of British sf writers that included Moorcock himself, Ballard, John Brunner and Brian Aldiss.

In the *Encyclopaedia of Science Fiction*, John Clute and Peter Nicholls describe *New Worlds* as at first providing 'a stable domestic market for the leading UK writers [and] encouraged a species of sf more sober in tone than much US material [which] began a shift in emphasis towards psychological and existential sf' (Clute and Nicholls 1999: 868, col.1). Under Moorcock's editorship from 1964, *New Worlds* would become the home of the 'New Wave' in sf, a late flowering of Modernist *topoi* and textual practice in the science fiction genre. The archetypal New Wave sf story was textually experimental and formally and/or generically self-conscious; alienated from the mores and conventions of contemporary mainstream culture (and mainstream 'literary' writing); often influenced by models of depth-psychology with regard to its protagonists; and with a cynical, dystopian or counter-cultural political flavour, quite often symbolized in the generic use of the scientific concept of entropy.

Ballard is a central *New Worlds* and New Wave writer. His story 'The Terminal Beach' (1964), which narrates, in a series of titled paragraphs, the journey to the nuclear-testing site island of Eniwetok of an alienated protagonist called 'Traven', treats of the images and ideas of the Cold War in an oblique and disturbing way. The story can be seen as offering a kind of template for Ballard's own later career (the 'T-' character is central to the 'condensed novels' later collected in *The Atrocity Exhibition* of 1970) and even of New Wave short fiction as a whole (one thinks of Moorcock's 'Jerry Cornelius' sequence of stories and Pamela Zoline's seminal 'Heat Death of the Universe' (1967)). Ballard's textual practice, and his ideas and manifestoes such as the guest editorial in a 1962 edition of *New Worlds* later collected as 'Which Way to Inner Space?', were crucial to the development of New Wave sf in the 1960s, but his connection to mainstream sf has always been problematic, even more so than the New Wave in general. In the *Encyclopaedia of Science Fiction*, Clute and Nicholls underscore this tension by noting that Ballard has never won an award from within the sf community for his work, and his Nebula Award nomination for 'The Drowned Giant' in 1964 was for a text which is untypical of Ballard's work as a whole.

In this chapter, I want to explore Ballard's problematic association with mainstream sf. Specifically, I chart the ways in which Ballard's fictions of the 1960s move away from postwar models of sf writing, characterized by the US dystopian tradition and the peculiarly British tradition of the 'disaster novel', towards a new and idiosyncratic form of sf writing which is marked out by processes of physical and psychological transformation which are both ambiguous and ambivalent. Although Ballard's early fictions have been attacked for not being overtly interested in the kinds of social and political critique which certain literary critics expect and value, it is my contention that Ballard's fictions are not entirely dislocated from the socio-cultural landscapes of the postwar period. As the title of my chapter indicates, it is not the Cold War but the Space Age (partly concurrent but definitely not coterminous) which regulates the imaginary and iconography of Ballard's early fiction, and is at the same time abstracted, made strange. Through a series of close textual readings, I explore the ways in which Ballard subverts sf tropes and conventions in order to produce a different kind of 'space fiction', namely one which explores the deep implications of time, space, psychology and evolutionary biology in order to dismantle anthropocentric narratives and, in turn, open up alternative ways of experiencing, and conceiving of, contemporary human subjectivity.

Towards a poetics of transformation: rereading Ballard's 'space fiction'

In order to fully understand Ballard's significance it is necessary to contextualize the British sf scene in relation to that of the USA. Brian Aldiss (1973) and Roger Luckhurst (2005), in their respective histories of sf, locate a 'twin tradition' at work within the history of English-language sf: the British tradition of the 'scientific romance', inaugurated by H .G. Wells and inherited by John Wyndham, John Christopher, and in his early career, Ballard himself; and the US 'pulp' tradition, from Hugo Gernsback's *Amazing* (from 1927), to John W. Campbell's *Astounding Science Fiction* (from 1937), to H. L. Gold's *Galaxy Science Fiction* (from 1950). These crucial magazines and editorships shaped the development of North American sf and the careers of such canonical sf writers as Isaac Asimov, Robert Heinlein and Frederik Pohl. This tradition encompasses the kind of 'hard sf' that is based upon scientific and technical knowledge, and in the case of the Campbellian interest in ESP or 'psionics', at least the rigorous exploration or extrapolation of such a 'novum' (see Darko Suvin's (1971) term for an invention or innovation from which the sf world is extrapolated) upon the world created. In the 1950s, US sf turned more towards the dystopian, sociological and satirical mode, probably in reaction to the Cold War and the corporate, consumerist, suburban and conformist imperatives of the Eisenhower years. Classic dystopian sf, such as Vonnegut's *Player Piano* (1952), Ray Bradbury's *Fahrenheit 451* (1953) or Pohl and Cyril M. Kornbluth's *The Space Merchants* (1953), offers satirical visions of a world of superabundance, of a material plenty that masks an underlying totalization of political and cultural life. These consumerist dystopias were much praised by Kingsley Amis in his *New Maps of Hell* (1961), an early critical essay on sf for a mainstream audience (and first given as a series of lectures at Princeton). Amis also praised Ballard's early work: on the back of the 1965 Penguin edition of *The Drowned World*, he is quoted as declaring 'Ballard is one of the brightest new stars in post-war fiction.' This enthusiasm waned as the 1960s drew on and Ballard began to publish his *Atrocity Exhibition* texts. As Ballard himself has commented, Amis was no fan of the political radicalism and literary experimentation of the New Wave with its 'shock tactics, tricks with typography, one-lined chapters, strained metaphors, obscurities [and] obscenities' (Ballard 1996b: 190).

However, it is clear to see why Amis might have been attracted to Ballard's early work, particularly that which is in a dystopian vein: 'The Concentration City', published in 1957 (set in a vast, literally endless urban accretion) and 'The Subliminal Man' of 1963 (in which the protagonist discovers that subliminal road signs are driving the furious energies of consumerism) can certainly be seen as variants of the 1950s American vein of satirical, dystopian sf, though both of these stories were published in *New Worlds* rather than in an American magazine. The ultimate failure of the protagonist to resist the pressures of consumerism in 'The Subliminal Man', however, marks Ballard's subtle difference from his US counterparts (who usually offer some kind of moment of suspended possibility of change at the end of the text), and points towards the embracing of catastrophe that is found in *The Drowned World* and elsewhere. It has also brought critical opprobrium down upon Ballard's head. H. Bruce Franklin, in his essay 'What Are We To Make Of J. G. Ballard's Apocalypse?' (1979) is highly critical of Ballard's 'failure' to offer a sustained critique of the capitalist imperatives that drive his human subjects towards alienation, dislocation and ultimately possible psychological fragmentation. Franklin argues about Ballard's reliance on depth-psychology:

> My criticism is that Ballard does not generally go down far enough below the unconscious to the sources of the alienation, self-destruction, and mass slaughter of our age. He therefore remains incapable of understanding the alternative to these death forces, the global movement toward human liberation which constitutes the main distinguishing characteristic of our epoch. (Franklin 1979: 93)

Ballard's work is characterized by Franklin as 'ultimately a literature of despair, negation and death' (Franklin 1979: 93), and he reserves his praise only for 'The Subliminal Man', which is much closer to the kind of critical and dystopian works one finds in 1950s American sf. Franklin reproduces a common critical trope in considering Ballard, the tendency to attack him not for what he does, but for what he does *not* do: offer a left-oriented critique of contemporary capital, and the possibility of resistance to its determinations.

Ballard has demonstrated very little overt interest in the ideological premises of the world he lives in, or the worlds he creates. Later texts such as *Running Wild* (1988), *Super-Cannes* (2000) or *Kingdom Come* (2006) indicate an interest in the control of social (and particularly privatized) space which is of considerable contemporary political urgency, but it is also possible to see these texts in similar terms to the psychological narratives he produced in the early and mid-1960s. The thematic interest in space is apparent in such early stories as 'The Concentration City' (1957), where the search for 'free space' (Ballard 2001: 25) leads to an ultimately circular journey around a globe now encased in urban 'build-up' (Ballard 2001: 27). More typically, in stories such as 'Manhole 69' (1957), a group of postoperative patients (whose need for sleep has been surgically excised) find themselves trapped in a consensual hallucination of collapsing space: 'The gymnasium was shrinking. Inch by inch, the walls were moving inward . . . As they shrank towards each other their features altered' (Ballard 2001c: 60). In 'The Enormous Space' (1989), meanwhile, the first-person narrator retreats to smaller and smaller spaces, finally climbing into a freezer cabinet which contains his dead wife, where 'a palace of ice will crystallise around us' (Ballard 2001a: 1138). As with most of Ballard's early fictions, the physical world of 'The Enormous Space' is an exterior manifestation of a psychological landscape; as Andrzej Gasiorek puts it, the events 'depicted exteriorise psychological adjustments and transformation' (2005: 32). Space is psychologized, and so the boundary between inner and outer worlds becomes blurred.

Ballard's main self-declared sf antecedent is Ray Bradbury, whose own relations to sf, fantasy and mainstream literary fiction are almost as problematic as Ballard's own (See Ballard 1996a: 205–7). Ballard is usually understood to be writing out of a peculiarly British mode of sf: the 'disaster novel' of John Wyndham and John Christopher, what Brian Aldiss characterized as the 'cosy catastrophe' in which a group of men and women survive in an apocalyptic scenario and comfortingly (even heroically) retain a grasp on conventional social and cultural values (See Aldiss 1973: 294). The 'cosiness' of the catastrophe is a product of the *unchanged* state of subjectivity produced by the events of the novels. With the exception of *The Wind from Nowhere* (1962), Ballard's first published (and later disowned) novel, written at speed to break him into professional writing, Ballard's early novels and short stories depart radically from the formula of the British disaster novel. Indeed, finding in it a liberation from the subjectivity constructed by social and cultural institutions, Ballard's protagonists are only too eager to embrace the transformative possibilities of the disaster, even if this is at the cost of personal dissolution. David Punter indicates Ballard's interest in challenging conventional encodings of human subjectivity, an argument which runs counter to Franklin's assessment of Ballard's 'despairing, death-oriented' narratives:

> The long tradition of enclosed and unitary subjectivity comes to mean less and less to him as he explores the ways in which person [*sic*] is increasingly controlled by landscape and machine, increasingly becomes a point of

intersection for overloaded scripts and processes which have effectively concealed their distant origins from human agency. (Punter 1985: 9)

This critique of human agency, most manifest in the seemingly 'passive' ways in which the protagonists of his fiction react to disaster, suggests a much keener edge to Ballard's writing than Franklin allows. It is not that Ballard fails to move 'below the unconscious' to the determining ideological base, but that he focuses upon subjectivity itself as a crucial and constitutive framing of human experience. Perhaps, as Gregory Stephenson insists, there is a thirst for transcendence in Ballard's fiction, a move, that is, towards an 'absolute, authentic being . . . an ontological Eden' (1991: 49), but it is subjectivity itself, *and* its corollary and condition, time, that first must be dissolved.

Dissolving time, space and subjectivity: or how to escape the contemporary

Ballard's recurrent interest in the Space Age is perhaps curious considering his 1962 *New Worlds* guest-editorial-cum-manifesto, 'Which Way to Inner Space?', which called for an sf not of rockets and naïve futurology, 'robot brains and hyper-drives' (Ballard 1996c: 195), but one that would take place on Earth; 'it is *inner* space, not outer, that needs to be explored. The only true alien planet is Earth' (Ballard 1996c: 197). Ballard nonetheless returned repeatedly to the icon of the astronaut in stories from 'A Question of Re-Entry' (1963) to 'The Object of the Attack' (1984), indicating the significance of the space programme to his concerns. In 'A Question of Re-Entry', he writes:

> The implication was that the entire space programme was a symptom of some inner unconscious malaise afflicting mankind, and in particular the Western technocracies, and that the space-craft and satellites had been launched because their flights satisfied certain buried compulsions and desires. (Ballard 2001g: 453)

The Space Age and the NASA programme is not in itself crucial: as elsewhere in Ballard's work, it makes manifest latent or unconscious ('buried') human desires that underlie and precede the conscious, and the structuring of subjectivity. Underlying Ballard's use of the icon of the astronaut is the sense that the NASA programme is a biological, or evolutionary, mistake, a kind of grand transgression against nature which produces unforeseen psychological consequences. In 'Memories of the Space Age' (1982), one of three connected stories from the early 1980s which return to similar ideas and images (the others being 'News from the Sun', 1981 and 'Myths of the Near Future', 1982), the protagonist Mallory, a doctor in the NASA programme, confesses to his unconscious complicity in the first orbital murder. He had allowed a borderline-disturbed astronaut named Hinton to go into space, where he had murdered one of his colleagues. This act produces a kind of 'space-sickness' of fugue-states and loss of temporal awareness that is centred on Cape Canaveral: 'he had torn the fabric of time and space, cracked the hour-glass from which time was running' (Ballard 2001d: 1049).

The disaster is an evolutionary one, a hubristic giant leap out of the biological scheme, and out of time. This is made explicit in 'News from the Sun': 'By leaving the planet and setting off into outer space man had committed an evolutionary crime, a breach of the rules governing his tenancy of the universe, and of the laws of time and space' (Ballard 2001f: 1019). For Ballard's protagonists the consequences are liberating as well as catastrophic. In his early-1980s trilogy of stories, as well as in 'The Illuminated Man' (1964), time is spatialized, coagulating like the jewelled forest of *The Crystal World*. This itself has an interior, psychological root: slowing or freezing time is connected to the 'fugue' states which the protagonists of these fictions increasingly experience. The symptoms of this 'sickness' are outlined in 'Myths of the Near Future':

> At first touching only a small minority of the population, it took root like a lingering disease in the interstices of its victims' lives, in the slightest changes of habit and behaviour. Invariably there was the same reluctance to go out of doors, the abandonment of job, family and friends, a dislike of daylight, a gradual loss of weight and retreat into a hibernating self. (Ballard 2001e: 1064)

These symptoms are in fact the very model of the paths to alienation taken by Ballard's protagonists in many of his fictional texts. What the Ballardian protagonists embrace is the transformative possibilities of the 'disease' that is a rupture in the fabric of space and time, but whether it is time itself or the protagonists' experience of time remains unresolved. Inner and outer worlds are again blurred. In inhabiting 'fugue time', the protagonists become something other, yet are still themselves – perhaps a more full version of themselves, with linear time collapsed into spatial dimensions, onto their own bodies:

> A ruby light glimmered around Sheppard . . . He looked down at his wrists, at his incandescent fingers. The sun was annealing plates of copper light to his skin, dressing his arms and shoulders in a coronation of armour. Time was condensing around him, a thousand replicas from the past and future had invaded the present and clasped themselves to him. (Ballard 2001e: 1074)

If time is the fourth dimension, then the jewelled armour that the crystallized subjects wear (a concretized version of their past and future selves encrusted on their limbs) in *The Crystal World*, (Ballard 1985a: 97, 98) or the dazzling figure of the decrepit Elaine revivified by her young self in 'Myths of the Near Future' (Ballard 2001e: 1067–8), are in a sense four-dimensional beings. (One of Ballard's early short story collections was called *The Four-Dimensional Nightmare*.) When, in *The Atrocity Exhibition*, Dr Nathan explains to Margaret Travis about the 'chronograms' of Etienne-Jules Marey, which he describes as '"multiple-exposure photographs in which the element of time is visible"' (Ballard 1985: 10), he is also revealing the master-image of Ballard's sf texts. In *The Crystal World* or 'Myths of the Near Future', we see time played upon the very material being of the characters.

The evolutionary emphases of these three stories explicitly connect Ballard's later short fiction with his 1960s disaster novels. In fact, 'Myths of the Near Future' recapitulates the beginning of *The Crystal World*: in both, the protagonist travels into the heart of the 'psychic disaster area' (Ballard 2001e: 1068) where time has come to a stop, called by a letter received from a former wife/lover who imprecates 'wish you were here' (Ballard 2001e: 1068), this wife/lover being subject to a fatal disease which will be cured by the phenomenon through an escape from linear time. Where Sheppard's wife Elaine in 'Myths' is wasting away through the onset of the 'space sickness' (Ballard 2000: 1064), in *The Crystal World*, Suzanne Clair has contracted the leprosy that she and the protagonist Sanders were attempting to minister to in their 'leproserie' (Ballard 1985a: 37). The 'nodular lumps all over her face and in the lobes of her ear', the 'leonine mask' which is one of the symptoms of leprosy (Ballard 1985a: 126), echo the encrusted, bejewelled world of the forest:

> The process of crystallization was more advanced. The fences along the road were so heavily encrusted that they formed a continuous palisade, a white frost at least six inches thick on either side of the palings. The few houses between the trees glistened like wedding-cakes, their white roofs and chimneys transformed into exotic minarets and baroque domes. On a lawn of green glass spurs a child's tricycle glittered like a Fabergé gem, the wheels starred into brilliant jasper crowns. (Ballard 1985a: 75)

The connection between leprosy and crystallization underscores the foundational importance of the *biological* in these fictions. David Pringle suggests that the vegetation and self-immolated characters in *The Crystal World* become 'embalmed in eternity' (Pringle 1979: 32). Certainly, the bejewelled forest, itself a symbol of Heaven or the City of God, and the scenes where Father Balthus bestows the gem-encrusted cross onto Sanders to aid his survival (at the same time embracing his own crystallization) does seem to support a spiritual or religious reading of the text. Perhaps, though, the catastrophic zone can be more properly typed as paradisal, the return to a lost psychical or evolutionary Eden, before the onset of human 'civilization'. In 'News from the Sun', the infantile babble of the fugue-state is revealed as a kind of lost pre-lapsarian language: '"Leave Trippett . . ." Franklin tried to speak, but the words slurred on his tongue' (Ballard 2000: 1035). Reverse evolution and the idea of a return before a 'fall' into language, culture and time are repeatedly overlaid.

Even *The Drought*, the novel of the 1960s which least falls into this pattern, shares this rhetoric of reverse evolution, when Lomax tells the protagonist Ransom, pointing 'to the dusty villas along the river . . . "They look like mud huts already. We're moving straight back into the past"' (Ballard 1985b: 46). In fact, in *The Drought*, a novel that falls into three unequal parts (the onset of the drought and the journey from Mont Royal to the beach; a period some years later when Ransom clings on to a precarious beach-zone existence with his formerly-estranged wife; and the return journey, having abandoned his wife, back to the city of Mont Royal), the suggestion is that Ransom has not moved back in time enough in the middle section, a kind of false hiatus in the long trajectory towards deep or symbolic time that characterizes all Ballard's novels of this period. The strange children of Quilter and Miranda Lomax that Ransom encounters at the end of the novel also suggest mutation or transformation, the next generation being better adapted to the coming world, even if the spots of rain at the end of the novel – not felt by Ransom – suggest that the world is changing again (Ballard 1985b: 188).

The evolutionary dynamic is most explicit in *The Drowned World*. Bodkin, the scientist who, like the protagonist Kerans, refuses to evacuate the flooded, tropical London they had been sent to investigate and map explains to Kerans the underlying biological or evolutionary dynamic at work:

> Everywhere there's been the same avalanche backwards into the past . . . Everywhere in nature one sees evidence of innate releasing mechanisms literally millions of years old, which have lain dormant through thousands of generations but retained their power undiminished . . . I am convinced that as we move back through geophysical time so we re-enter the amniotic corridor and move back through spinal and archaeopsychic time, recollecting in our unconscious minds the landscapes of each epoch, each with a distinct geological terrain, its own unique flora and fauna, as recognizable to anyone else as they would be to a traveller in a Wellsian time machine. Except that this is no scenic railway, but a total re-orientation of the personality. (Ballard 1965: 43)

This long quotation requires a little unpacking. Note the insistent re-insertion of humankind into the biological realm. There is no sense that humans can stand outside evolutionary processes and pressures, observing and retaining the mental landscapes of 'civilization' (as in the 'cosy catastrophe'). The human is a biological entity, and as such is as much affected by the changing world as are the lizards or the vegetation. Interestingly Ballard uses the biological ideas of phylogenesis and ontogenesis (that the development of the human foetus in the womb 'recapitulates the entire evolutionary past' (Ballard 1965: 43)) to displace human beings from an assumed place at the top of the evolutionary tree. As Ballard put it in conversation with Brendan Hennessy, 'I wanted to look at our . . . whole biological inheritance, the fact that we're all several hundred million years old, as old as the biological kingdoms in our spines, in our brains, in our cellular structure'. Ballard continues, 'our very identities reflect untold numbers of decisions made to adapt us to change in our environment, decisions lying behind us in the past like some enormous largely forgotten journey (Ballard cited in Hennessy 1971: 164). Ballard's sf is immersed not only in Freudian depth-psychology but, like the science fiction of H. G. Wells to which he refers, also in a modern evolutionary biology that fatally undermines the idea of human dominion over the Earth.

The adaptive determinism of natural selection (the best-adapted species variations survive) feeds the seeming 'passivity' of the Ballardian protagonist. Ballard's protagonists embrace the catastrophe because they accept the logic of evolutionary change. In 'Myths of the Near Future', Sheppard tells his companion Anne Godwin:

This space-sickness – it's really about time, not space, like all the Apollo flights. We think of it as a kind of madness, but in fact it may be part of a contingency plan laid down millions of years ago, a real space programme, a chance to escape into a world beyond time . . . Our sense of our own identity, the stream of things going on around us, are an optical illusion. Our eyes are too close together. Those strange temples in the forest, the marvellous birds and animals – you've seen them too. We've all got to embrace the sun. (Ballard 2001e: 1078)

As I suggested above, subjectivity itself is bound up with time, and this is what must be discarded to enter the 'archaic Eden' of non-time, where '"[e]verything that's ever happened, all the events that *will* ever happen, are taking place together"' (Ballard 2001e: 1078). The Ballardian escape from contemporary conditions is less bound to an economic critique of the social, then, than a willed transformation out of consciousness, the conditions of subjectivity, into a state which is at the same time transcendent and profoundly bodily and biological.

This is particularly evident in both *The Drowned World* and in 'News From the Sun'. In *The Drowned World*, Kerans refuses to go back to the temperate polar stations which are the last institutional refuge of contemporary 'civilization' (and here we must decode this as the contemporary 'developed' world), and instead yields to the biological logic of change. At the end of the novel he heads away from the lagoons of London:

So he left the lagoon and entered the jungle again, within a few days he was completely lost, following the lagoons southward through the increasing rain and heat, attacked by alligators and giant bats, a second Adam searching for the forgotten paradises of the reborn sun. (Ballard 1965: 171)

In 'News from the Sun', Franklin, who is able to move and to communicate in the fugues, attempts to save the elderly astronaut Trippett at the end of the story and is himself trapped among the solar mirrors of the Soleri II community, awaiting rescue:

> Franklin waited for her to fetch him, glad that she had learned to feed herself. He knew that he would soon have to leave her and Soleri II, and set off in search of his wife. Happy now to be free of time, he embraced the great fugue. All the light in the universe had come here to greet him, an immense congregation of particles. (Ballard 2001f: 1036)

The word 'congregation' here, and the reference to Adam in *The Drowned World*, very clearly open the possibility of a quasi-religious reading of these texts: that 'transcendence' is a shedding of the material world, a release of the spirit from the body (see Stephenson 1991: 1). ('Myths of the Near Future', 'News from the Sun' and 'Memories of the Space Age' are pervaded by images of flight.) In 'Myths' the ending sees a revivified Elaine rather than death, however in *The Crystal World* to conjoin with the jewelled forest is not to immolate oneself, but to enter a physical realm where material substance achieves full consummation:

> Above the banks the foliage glowed like painted snow, the only movement coming from the slow traverse of the sun . . . he passed the half-crystallised bodies of men and women fused against the trunks of the trees, looking up at the sun. Most of them were elderly couples seated together with their bodies fusing into one another as they merged with the trees and the jewelled undergrowth. (Ballard 1985a: 163–4)

Transformation, the key to the imagery of the 1960s novels and the short stories, is extended not only to the Ballardian protagonist, but also to landscape, to the physical world itself.

In his Introduction to the 2001 *The Complete Short Stories*, Ballard argues forcefully for the importance of the short story form: 'Short stories have always been important to me. I like their snapshot quality, their ability to focus intensely on a single subject. They're also a useful way of trying out the ideas later developed at novel length' (Ballard 2001b: ix). This process of revisiting, or even rewriting, can be seen most clearly in the relationship between the 'The Illuminated Man' (1964), and the novel *The Crystal World*. Large parts of the story are cannibalized and appear verbatim in the novel, although the setting has been changed (the location of disaster switches from Florida to West Africa) and the characters altered. The fundamental narrative remains intact, however. This constant reworking of images, themes, ideas and narratives has led to Ballard's work being characterized as 'obsessional', but it does at the least provide a remarkable consistency to his body of work. Strangely, his short story writing seems to have come to a halt; his last published collection was *War Fever* in 1990. Perhaps this can be ascribed to the most mundane of reasons: the availability of publishing outlets. Ballard's first period of creativity in the short story, publishing consistently between 1957 and 1969, can be connected to his prominence in the Carnell stable of sf magazines and particularly in *New Worlds* in the 1960s. He had a short story renaissance in the later 1970s when many of his stories appeared in the literary magazine *Bananas. The Complete Short Stories* collection contains only 17 stories written since 1980, and none since 1992, but his novel writing has continued undimmed. Indeed, since that time, his 'literary' reputation has grown in stature considerably. Clute and Nicholls, in the *Encyclopaedia of Science Fiction*, argue that Ballard has stopped writing sf altogether; certainly, his current fictional interest in the psychopathologies of gated communities, science parks and shopping malls is oriented away from the generic sf and short story forms of which he is an undoubtedly highly skilled, and genuinely original, practitioner.

CHAPTER TWO

Disquieting Features: An Introductory Tour of *The Atrocity Exhibition*

JAKE HUNTLEY

Chapter Summary: Focusing on the formal complexities of *The Atrocity Exhibition*, this chapter considers how one is to proceed with reading this most innovative and elusive text. Huntley explores the influence of Surrealism on Ballard and the impact of the distortion of time on the text.

Key words: *The Atrocity Exhibition*; science fiction; literary experimentation; popular culture; subjectivity; identity; Surrealism; repetition; collage; juxtaposition; temporal and narrative distortion; paratext; reader-response.

Chic and hard and gleaming

Following a cycle of novels that, on the surface at least, share resemblances with conventional science fiction, J. G. Ballard's writing shifts into a harsher and more experimental phase in the late 1960s and early 1970s, one that is more grimly apocalyptic than exuberantly speculative. While the counter-culture swirls around him, shaking off recent memories of austerity with psychedelic and psychotropic abandon, Ballard seems to take a more epistemic turn, reappraising his approach and the genre with an apparent dash of optimism:

> A whole new raft of science fiction writers had come along who had read their Kafka, their James Joyce; they were aware of the larger world of the

twentieth-century experimental novel [. . .] [science fiction] seemed so chic and hard and gleaming, like a brand-new showroom radiator grille. There was a hope that science fiction could take a great leap forward and transform itself into a more sophisticated kind of fiction altogether. (Ballard quoted in Self 1996: 349)

The transformation in Ballard's work is indeed sophisticated and the book resulting from the period between 1966–70, *The Atrocity Exhibition* (1970), is perhaps his most innovative piece of prose, replacing, as Angela Carter once put it, drowned cities, vast desert landscapes and crystallizing jungles with something as 'jagged as broken glass' (Carter quoted in Vale 1984: 140). As Ballard explains in the introduction to *Crash* – that subsequent (and now infamous) novel which grew out of the condensed 'Crash!' (1969) chapter – the question of literary invention needs to be comprehensively re-examined:

'What is the main task of the writer? Can he, any longer, make use of the techniques and perspectives of the traditional 19th century novel, with its linear narrative, its measured chronology, its consular characters grandly inhabiting their domains with ample time and space?' (1985: 8).

For Ballard, the answer is emphatic: no, he cannot. And he has no wish to do so. Traditional linear narrative, enervated, exhausted and redundant, is almost the wrong medium entirely in which to be operating. Ballard's response, after all, is a celebration of the brand-new radiator grille as it is subjected to Warholian repetition, examined from epochal distance and in forensic detail, presented at its most defamiliarized and abstracted. Radical, explicit and experimental, *The Atrocity Exhibition* is a jarring montage of jump-cut prose – narrative rather than novelistic, convoluted by repetitive free-association – which is probably more accessible to an audience familiar with frenetic, unrelenting modern media than to the text's contemporary readership, whose nearest touchstones might have been Luis Buñuel's *Un Chien Andalu* (1929), Maya Deren's *Meshes of the Afternoon* (1943), or Alain Reisner's *Last Year in Marienbad* (1961). Rather than displaying 'ample time and space', *The Atrocity Exhibition* is constructed from blocks of hard, gleaming prose assembled into 15 chapters that are concentrated, condensed and compressed, randomized bursts triggered from a faulty space–time continuum, so that they read more like the field notes for some wayward medical research than a novel. Moreover, on a quotidian note, Ballard offers a caveat: 'You've got to remember that the individual pieces that make up *The Atrocity Exhibition* were written independently – virtually as short stories – and published independently, all of them in various magazines. So a certain element of inconsistency crept in' (Ballard quoted in Vale 2005: 258). It is, consequently, a text that both resists and entices readerly response, frustrating exposition and scuttling summarizing inclinations as it exhibits a psychologically-inflected landscape where conflicting media exist simultaneously and characters are reduced to mere pools of identity, as precarious as mercury.

Another face

The Atrocity Exhibition presents a markedly fraught, harried or jeopardized version of sundered subjectivity. The central figure of *The Atrocity Exhibition*, variously named Traven, Travers, Talbot, Talbert and Travis, is the most acute expression of the slippage of identity that occurs throughout the text. Just as the naming process hovers around a small, closed linguistic circuit without settling definitively, so the restless figure of the doctor-patient traverses a series of repeated, reworked backdrops, urgently attempting to establish the conditions under which he intends to '"revolt against the present continuum of time and space"' (Ballard 1990: 12) and destroy the '"imbalance of an asymmetric world"' (Ballard 1990: 14) – in short, to declare World War III on the psychological plane. At least, this is Dr Nathan's initial diagnosis. Latterly – alternately – Nathan refines his case notes: '"What the patient is reacting against is, simply, the phenomenology of the universe, the specific and independent existence of separate objects and events"' (Ballard 1990: 34). As if faced with a galloping pathology, Nathan ultimately reassesses the patient, suggesting Travis is also trying to use car crash scenarios, psychological responses to 'atrocity' and the 'alternate' assassination of President Kennedy to somehow save the victims of the Apollo disaster: '"Trabert will try to reintegrate space and so liberate the three men in the capsule. For him they still wait there on their contour couches"' (Ballard 1990: 48). Perhaps the fullest view of the Travis diagram is that presented retrospectively, by Captain Webster, who explains the aftermath of a crashed landing:

> "He was alive when they got him out, but at one point in the operating theatre his heart and vital functions failed. In the technical sense he was dead for about two minutes. Now, all this time later, it looks as if something is missing, something that vanished during the short period of his death. Perhaps his soul, the capacity to achieve a state of grace. Nathan would call it the ability to accept the phenomenology of the universe, or the fact of your own consciousness. This is Traven's hell. You can see he's trying to build bridges between things – this Kennedy business, for example. He wants to kill Kennedy again, but in a way that makes sense." (Ballard 1990: 36)

Travis's instability is perpetual, somehow existing within the tension of irreconcilable contradiction: '"was my husband a doctor, or a patient?"' (Ballard 1990: 12) asks Margaret Travis. Instead, Travis, collectively, is trapped in a temporal suture, a 2-minute stitch in time. He is caught in a compulsive process of change and transformation that has no purposeful end-point and cannot be resolved in a way that makes sense. This leaves him flickering through the passages in a series of ghostly afterimages, more an entropic sloughing of selfhood than a diagrammatic projection. In the latter stages of the text he seems to fade out, or perhaps diffuse, entirely. There only remain the chrysalis husks, exhausted and abandoned at the end of each chapter, from which the subsequent instalment of Travis has emerged.

In an alternative reading, Roger Luckhurst refers to Travis as the 'T-Cell', suggesting that he acts as a contagion, multiple in the manner of bacilli, which infects the narrative (1997: 86). If this is the case, then his peripatetic nature is strategically vital in inaugurating World War III, revolting against time and reintegrating space, his movements *carrying* instability until it reaches pandemic proportions. Travis's hell then becomes other people's.

Variously aligned conscripts

Sundry characters are drawn into the orbit of Travis's plans. Some, such as the pilot with inchoate features, the woman with radiation burns ('couriers from his own unconscious?' (Ballard 1990: 11)) and the 'Watching Trinity' (Ballard 1990: 45) of Kline, Coma and Xero, are strange, haunting presences, externalized symptoms of Travis's psychopathology who seem to drift through the empty car parks, corridors and desert spaces in his wake. In his marginalia for the Re/Search edition of *The Atrocity Exhibition*), Ballard calls the latter trio 'shadows projected from Traven's unconscious' (Ballard 1990: 32), rather as if they were negatives to his luminescent positive. It is part of the palimpsestic operation of the text that these figures are as present as some of the staff of the unnamed clinic such as Dr Nathan and Dr Catherine Austin; shadows apparently as substantial as the people casting them. Certainly, on a textual level, the reliance on impersonal pronouns heightens this effect: it is quite impossible, at times, to decide which 'he' is looking at which 'she'. This flattening of independent, autonomous identity can also be seen in the way (pre-empting *Crash*), Nathan, Austin, Webster and Karen Novotny are all presented at points in the text as mannequins or posed figures, and are nearly all subject to repeated, 'conceptual' deaths: 'Once again Karen Novotny had died, Talbert's fears and obsessions mimetized in her alternate death' (Ballard 1990: 57). Unwilling performers in Travis's strategic manoeuvres, they are frequently 'staged' in ways that contradict linear narrative, and their lines intersect not only with each other but with alternate versions of themselves. Thus, an effect may be concurrent with, or even precede, its cause, and a character's death may not be their *telos*: Novotny, for example, is confronted with adverts and other reminders of the film depicting her 'sex-death'; Dr Nathan, Webster and Austin all 'die' in the first chapter, the trinity of corpses creating 'a small tableau by the bunkers' (Ballard 1990: 17). In Travis's attempts to overhaul time and space, lifelines become hopelessly tangled, their 'real' presence may be overlaid with images generated anywhere from deep spinal memories to posthumous synaptic bursts.

These interactions throughout *The Atrocity Exhibition* may be tricky to follow, tangling and looping, binding and bordering. The effect is an interwoven structure, or surface, where 'lines' (characters, events) may cross, meet in opposite directions or become folded. Frequently related to inanimate artefacts, the characters come to stand as a sort of 'furniture' of the exhibition and, as such, could be treated as analogues with the mysterious collection left by Travis for Dr Nathan to solve:

> He peered at the objects on the tray offered to him by the nurse. 'So, these are the treasures he has left us – an entry from Oswald's Historic Diary, a much-thumbed reproduction of Magritte's 'Annunciation,' and the mass numbers of the first twelve radioactive nuclides. 'What are we supposed to do with them?' Nurse Nagamatzu gazed at him with cool eyes. 'Permutate them, doctor?' (Ballard 1990: 31)

As the ramifications of Travis' assault on the space–time continuum become apparent, these characters are patched throughout the chapters, caught within the shuffling structure and subject to the exhibition's recursive properties. The 'correct' angle from which to see these figures is unclear – the perspective is equivocal, the focal point somehow askew. Rather, in the manner of the clinic's annual exhibition of patient's paintings where it is uncertain whether the art or the artists are the true subject of the display, the line appears indiscernible, the margin of a mirage.

Exploded view – astronomical perspective

Elsewhere, Ballard's dismantling of identity is more explicit – and prosaic. Karen Novotny is bluntly reconfigured as simply a quantifiable set of sensory stimuli: '"In a sense," Dr Nathan explained to Koester, "one may regard this as a kit, which Talbert has devised, entitled 'Karen Novotny' – it might even be feasible to market it commercially"' (Ballard 1990: 54). The 16 items, ranging from manufactured body parts to medical notes, swabs and speech samples, create '"an adequate picture of a woman, who could easily be reconstituted from it"' (Ballard 1990: 54). Recalling the Surrealist automata of Hans Bellmer (a surrealist figure who also repeats throughout the text), 'Karen Novotny' is brought to life through an arrangement of inanimate pieces, the scattered data accumulating to manufacture a perverse Golem. This mechanical reproduction is an example of the 'liberation of sexual and machine libido' (Ballard 1990: 99) that rebounds throughout the text.

In the Re/Search edition, directly opposite 'The Sex Kit' is one of a series of 'medical illustrations' by Phoebe Gloeckner, a cross sectioned image of oral sex that bears some relation to the text (Ballard 1990: 55). The picture is labelled (glans being 'a'), although the 'key' is missing and one of the inserts corresponds to the '"nipple marked by a small ulcer"' (Ballard 1990: 54) mentioned in the kit. Only with the illustration of an appendix (to accompany the four additional chapters, naturally enough) (Ballard 1990: 110) do the text and illustrations achieve full synchronicity, albeit on the level of a visual pun. Most of the anonymized pictures of dissociated body parts seem to be in arbitrary collision with the text or, in a more appropriate formulation, these visual interpolations are flung viscera, evidence of the explosive propensities of the text. The body, just as much as identity, is liable to be enrolled in this particular theatre of conflict.

It is not just Karen Novotny who is left in pieces. In a bid to draw Travis out or distract his plans, Dr Nathan arranges for a series of photographs of Margaret, Travis's wife, to cover the numerous billboards furnishing *The Atrocity Exhibition*, casting her as *casus belli* and neutralising agent. These vast displays of photographically enlarged body parts, '"an immensely magnified portion of the skin over the iliac crest [. . .] a segment of lower lip, a right nostril, a portion of female perineum"' (Ballard 1990: 15) are pasted across 500 billboards screening off the hospital so that Margaret Travis's fragmented form comes to contain and shield the entire building, the architecture 'housed' within her body. Yet the images of Margaret Travis are so radically distanced from the 'reality' of the woman that it requires a helicopter pilot to supervise the operation, much as the Gloeckner illustrations featuring isolated body parts or cellular views become abstracted and mysterious

Billboards characterize the landscape, displaying depersonalized body parts for spectators and creating connections across strata or pathways for those touring *The Atrocity Exhibition*. Despite the extreme realignments that occur, some figures retain a coherence or integrity unachievable by others: '"the multiplied body of the film actress [becomes] one of the few valid landscapes of our age"' (Ballard 1990: 56). Celebrity proves the most resilient of connective tissue, allowing Elizabeth Taylor, Marilyn Monroe, Ronald Regan, John F. and Jackie Kennedy to endure the fractures, distortions and compressions of the text. The famous maintain a persistence of vision, stabilized in a way that cannot be imitated, casting them as fixed points within the kaleidoscope and allowing everyone else to navigate by the stars.

Little psychological machines

In conversation with Graeme Revell, Ballard states:

> In a sense, I'm assembling the materials of an autopsy, and I'm treating reality – the reality we inhabit – almost as if it were a cadaver, or, let's say, the

contents of a special kind of forensic inquisition. *We have these objects here – what are they*? (Ballard quoted in Vale 1984: 42)

Part of the fragmentary effect of *The Atrocity Exhibition* is achieved through the many lists of random and unconnected artefacts that are scattered throughout the text. Medical samples, discarded bric-a-brac, recovered material, detritus, parts detached from a whole, they represent beached items, churned towards the shoreline by the acute and localized psychological turbulence. For Dr Nathan and others these *found objects* are oblique clues to Travis's mental state and warning of his intentions: they are the debris cast backwards from the assault on the continuum, temporally displaced shrapnel. For the reader they are continual eruptions of enigmatic free-association, sharing the same quixotic cipher as Comte de Lautréamont's famous foundational Surrealist assemblage: 'the fortuitous encounter upon a dissecting-table of a sewing machine and an umbrella!' (1966: 263).

The question of decoding is addressed in the text, yet in a way that merely highlights the incompatibility of the scrambled semiotics: 'What language could embrace all these, or a least provide a key: computer codes, origami, dental formulae?' (Ballard 1990: 64). Such patterns occlude any attempts at discerning the meaning. It is a Surrealist collage, a jarring collision of signifiers yoked into unrealizable metonymic signification, a composition akin to that of *bricolage*, an apparently random assemblage teasingly denying even as it affirms the possibility of an author or originating engineer. Ballard deems as 'idealistic' Travis's 'dream of a perfectible world – a better world, in a moral sense – where everything will make sense'. Ballard continues: 'He wants to assassinate Kennedy again, he says somewhere, but he wants to do it *in a way that makes sense*! He accepts the event, but wants to re-make it in a more meaningful way' (Ballard quoted in Vale 1984: 45). The meaning is not to be found in a key to a transcendent or unifying truth.

Indeed, Ballard frequently seems disparaging of occult phenomena or paranormal revelation, at pains to point out: 'I certainly didn't mean 'magic' in the usual witchcraft sense; I'm totally uninterested in that. I meant it in the ordinary imaginative sense of the word. I'm interested in the way any sudden revelation can transform experience' (Ballard quoted in Vale 2005: 170). Instead of a common, sensible fixed meaning, it is a desire for the fresh angle, the chance of obtaining a sharper focus upon reality itself and its composition. Ballard is in search of a greater perceptual awareness of the marvellous difference between unique artefacts, be they wrecked cars, grossly magnified spinal images or used contraceptive wallets. It is closer to rhizomic thought as opposed to arborescent thought, as Gilles Deleuze and Félix Guattari term it: The tree imposes the verb 'to be,' but the fabric of the rhizome is the conjunction, 'and . . . and . . . and . . . ' (1991: 25). Indeed, the rhizome, as Bill Ashcroft explains, 'is a botanical term for a root system which spreads across the ground (as in bamboo) rather than downwards, and grows from several points rather than a single tap root' (Ashcroft 1999: 116). Emergence from several points is precisely how Travis is manifested throughout *The Atrocity Exhibition*, and the lateral spread of the character continuously produces these clusters of disparate matter.

In this way, Dr Nathan's continual impulse to decode can only prove a fruitless exercise, his attempts to impose meaning across Travis's various assemblages smother any chance to identify the meaning between the fragments in a manner that makes (generates) sense.

> A book like *The Atrocity Exhibition* is a whole set of complicated formulae, in which the characters are obsessed with building little psychological machines that will generate new possibilities out of everything. Even the most humdrum things, like the angle between two walls, become a kind of psychological machine, a device for opening up possibilities. (Ballard quoted in Ronnov-Jessen 1984: 30)

Synthetic landscape

One of the most compelling, and consistent, possibilities within *The Atrocity Exhibition* is the contiguity between the characters and their environment. At its mildest, this is the identification between bodies and buildings, such as the process which allows Margaret Travis's reconfiguration within the landscape surrounding the clinic. It can also be seen in the merging of organic and inorganic, the bodily samples listed alongside sundry items, described above, or the fusing of biological and mechanical attributes, as in the chapter 'Crash!', where 'the car crash is seen as a fertilizing rather than a destructive experience' (Ballard 1990: 99). At its most extreme distortion, however, *The Atrocity Exhibition* reduces identities to mere formulae, simple shapes within the overall complex pattern, where one definitional equivalent can be substituted for another. As Ballard 'explains' in his authorial marginalia: 'In "You: Coma: Marilyn Monroe" the characters behave as if they were pieces of geometry interlocking in a series of mysterious equations' (1990: 41). Within the confines of their apartment, Tallis and Karen Novotny both inhabit and interact with the architecture:

> He watched Karen Novotny walk through the rooms, relating the movements of her thighs and hips to the architectonics of floor and ceiling. This cool-limbed young woman was a modulus; by multiplying her into the space and time of the apartment he would obtain a valid unit of existence. (Ballard 1990: 40)

As if scrupulously balancing the formula, Novotny 'watched his [Tallis's] tall figure interlocking with the dimensions and angles of the apartment' (Ballard 1990: 40). The basic incompatibility between these two axes creates an accelerating tension and eventually the sum of this particular cogito can only become wholly unbalanced: 'After a few seconds her presence became an unbearable intrusion into the time geometry of the room' (Ballard 1990: 42). When Coma finds Novotny's body Tallis says, 'She was standing in the angle between the two walls' (Ballard 1990: 42) to excuse, through the 'geometry of murder' (Ballard 1990: 42), yet another alternate death.

Incompatible geometric figures which somehow exist within a common pattern may see 'You: Coma: Marilyn Monroe' crystallize the stylized narrative framework of the surrounding chapters. While this may make it synecdochic, this is not to suggest it is some sort of key. Whatever synthesis between time, space and identity may be achieved in 'You: Coma: Marilyn Monroe', it does not extend across the entire *Atrocity Exhibition*. The interlocking presences only have a regional meaning, the geometric patterns lost amid the shifting dunes surrounding the apartment.

Ballard's synthetic landscape is not a topology produced through mathematics. In his story 'The Terminal Beach' (1966) Ballard defines a particular form of landscape extending from psychology that seems closer to that inhabited by the cast of *The Atrocity Exhibition*:

> "This island is a state of mind," Osborne [. . .] was later to remark to Traven [. . .] Despite the sand and a few anaemic plants, the entire landscape of the island was synthetic, a man-made artifact with all the associations of a vast system of derelict concrete motor-way. Since the moratorium on atomic tests, the island had been abandoned by the Atomic Energy Commission, and the wilderness of weapons, aisles, towers and blockhouses ruled out any attempt to return it to its natural state. (There were also stronger unconscious motives, Traven recognized: if primitive man felt the need to assimilate events in the external world to his own psyche, 20th century man had reversed the process; by this Cartesian yardstick, the island existed, in a sense true of few other places). (1966: 137–8)

The exhibition space is mutable, the internal walls and other furniture something that can be reconfigured and reorganized according to need. Thus, it is not just a confusion of bodies and body parts integrating with the landscape, but a re-mapping of the external world by the internal, an unfolding of consciousness across the clinical space and beyond. Within the fragmented and competing psyches of *The Atrocity Exhibition*, however, there is a fundamental mismatch: it quickly becomes apparent that no one is able to coordinate on any agreed scale.

The mean time

In 'The Year 2000 Has Already Happened', Jean Baudrillard suggests that the pace of modernity is capable of propelling us from our ontological grounding and flinging us into space (1988: 38–9). From a free-floating position within *The Atrocity Exhibition*, time might be viewed rhizomically – that is, a spreading network of simultaneity rather than a steady, linear progression – or in a sense of federated, autonomous time zones (another export USA, perhaps,) that cause a perpetual, jetlagged disorientation. Unlike the spatial paradoxes, however, Ballard specifically addresses the operation of narrative time in *The Atrocity Exhibition*, both in the main text and in his paratextual commentary.

Travis's strategy for his assault on the space–time continuum, for example, is not to achieve escape velocity, but to extract and isolate temporality itself:

> "Marey's Chronograms are multiple-exposure photographs in which the element of time is visible – the walking human figure, for example, represented as a series of dune-like lumps [. . .] Your husband's brilliant feat was to reverse the process. Using a series of photographs of the most commonplace objects – this office, let us say, a panorama of New York skyscrapers, the naked body of a woman, the face of a catatonic patient – he treated them as if they already were chronograms and *extracted* the element of time." (Ballard 1990: 12)

While his methodology for this procedure remains unexplained (and is not really the point), the results seem to have even more convulsive consequences than Baudrillard's accelerating hyperreality, causing a dehiscence of clock time that scatters effects throughout the text (perhaps mutating and metastasizing Luckhurst's notion of the T-cell). The impact on Travis is profound, although the shock waves appear far-reaching. Close to the centre, Karen Novotny endures 'time-invaded skin' (Ballard 1990: 46), as though it is a percussive blast. In 'You and Me and the Continuum', the mortal remains of the anonymous pilot (presumably another Travis-fragment) are thrown to a footnote in a psychiatric journal published 30 years earlier (Ballard 1990: 81). His parents, moreover, are revealed in the following manner: 'his mother was a 65-year-old terminal psychopath in Broadmoor, his father a still-unborn child in a Dallas lying-in hospital' (Ballard 1990: 84). The perplexed Dr Nathan is in a position to develop a fresh field of medical study into the effects of this schizo-time, surrounded as he is with so many patients presenting with a kind of temporal motion sickness.

The paratextual commentary appended to *The Atrocity Exhibition* some 20 years later further convolutes the text's timing. Similar to Martin Gardiner's *The Annotated Alice*, this paratextual mistletoe clings to the parent text, emerging, rhizomically, from numerous points. While sparse, obfuscatory and cryptic, the commentary goes some way, as Jeannette Baxter observes, to 'taming' – that is, imposing upon – the original (2009: 64–89), yet its predominant feature is to problematize its own performance. Ballard's marginal presence intervenes authoritatively, colloquially, autobiographically, historically, retrospectively, speculatively and equivocally – a one-man show of mythically engineered *bricolage*. At points, the marginalia offer the 'clarification' which is promised to us in the introduction: 'Here, as throughout *The Atrocity Exhibition*, the nervous systems of the characters have been externalised' (Ballard 1990: 44). Elsewhere, however, the prefatory claim of 'amplification' seems more appropriate, particularly when Ballard resorts to expanding upon lines within the original text (elucidating the background or contextualizing a reference), attaching quotes from fresh sources (such as the Goncourt Brothers and Sigmund Freud) or filling the 20-year gap between the two writing events. Most striking, however, are the instances where such recuperation fails. This is where the playful nature of the marginalia is least apparent and the 'present' text merges osmotically with its predecessor, the line between them being breached: 'I forget the significance of frame 230' (Ballard 1990: 27) Ballard admits, referring to the Zapruder footage. 'I can't remember the significance of 11:47 am on a June day in 1975, then some eight years ahead' (Ballard 1990: 47) he continues, in a queasy interzone between prolepsis and analepsis.

Ballard's annotations form a parenthetical frame that is present alongside all the other chapters, paradoxically helping to sequence them while being two decades 'late'. Perhaps the paratext could best be thought of as *The Atrocity Exhibition*'s 16th chapter. It is the most fragmented, certainly; and on occasions the most baffling and oblique, although it maintains its consistency, adhering to an internal logic.

Admission – non-refundable

> I had a very strange sensation, actually: when I recently wrote the annotations to *The Atrocity Exhibition*, I suddenly for the first time – after an interval of 25 years – felt I understood what *The Atrocity Exhibition* was about. It was like understanding a dream.
>
> (Ballard quoted in Vale 2005: 258)

Ever the good Surrealist, Ballard expresses the paradox that to understand *The Atrocity Exhibition* is precisely to misunderstand *The Atrocity Exhibition*. His own 'understanding' is only that of dream logic: tantalizingly indecipherable, uncannily familiar. Any attempt to fix the meaning of this magnificently lubricious text, to pin an explanatory statement alongside the piece (of course, what *The Atrocity Exhibition* is *really* all about . . .) is futile. Something will always fail to fit within the definitive explanation; escaping, creeping, just like the rhizome.

CHAPTER THREE

The Gothic, the Body, and the Failed Homeopathy Argument: Reading *Crash*

VICTOR SAGE

Chapter Summary: Approaching the Baudrillard/Ballard relationship from a new angle, this chapter revisits *Crash* as a site of Gothic horror and humour. Sage argues how Baudrillard's essentially metonymic reconstruction of *Crash* overlooks the impact of Ballard's deadpan use of language which is also full of lurking metaphor.

Key Words: *Crash*; Gothic; the Body; the 'Other'; the Double; Homeopathy; transparency; metaphor; metonymy; humour; 'death of affect'; car crash; sex; perversion; technology; David Cronenberg; Jean Baudrillard.

My starting point is the argument of Jean Baudrillard in *The Transparency of Evil* (1990, trans. 1993) about the state of contemporary culture. On the face of it, this book seems an absolute blueprint for the Modern Gothic. Baudrillard represents contemporary Western culture (which means the late 1980s, but it is the broadest implications of his diagnosis which seem its most significant contribution) as having exorcized its Other and having co-opted evil in the 'transparency' of consensus. This is presented as a nightmare. We are left alone with ourselves: instead of a horrific confrontation with the opacity of the Other, he argues, we are left with the 'hell of the Same': the viral and the virtual go hand in hand, they reflect the fact that we have exhausted all means of self-transcendence – aesthetic, sexual, political, religious – and have substituted for them an inertial and endless proliferation of ourselves.

He puts it in a way that has an instant resonance with the Gothic tradition of the Double, and yet Baudrillard's argument about contemporary culture seeks to go beyond this kind of 'heroic' narrative, regarding it as a structure of consolation that belongs to the past:

Ours is rather like the situation of the man who has lost his shadow: either he has become transparent, and the light passes right through him or, alternatively, he is lit from all angles, overexposed and defenceless against all sources of light. We are similarly exposed on all sides to the glare of technology, image and information, without any way of refracting their rays; and we are doomed in consequence to whitewash – whitewashed social relations, whitewashed bodies, whitewashed memory, – in short to a complete aseptic whitewash. Violence is whitewashed, history is whitewashed, all as part of a vast enterprise of cosmetic surgery at whose completion, nothing will be left but a society for whom all violence, all negativity, are strictly forbidden. (Baudrillard 1993: 44–5)

Traditionally the Gothic horror tradition has thrived on the imaginary confrontation, often horrific, between the Self and the monstrous or threatening Double, the representation of the Other which is banned whether by the informal taboo created by Enlightenment theory, or by the formal proscriptions of Protestant Christianity. The story of the loss of one's shadow is a narrative that belongs to this romantic and popular tradition, because, to lose one's shadow is to lose one's self (or, alternatively, soul). Baudrillard uses here a Gothic metaphor which is already a motif in popular tradition. Consider, for example, the following passage from a German romantic novella of the early nineteenth century, *Peter Schlemihl's Remarkable Story* (*Peter Schlemihls Wundersame Geschichte*), in which the narrator, who has just sold his shadow to a mysterious man in a long grey coat, begins, as he tries to return to the town and lose himself among the crowds, to learn what he has done:

At the gate I was obliged to hear immediately again from the Guard: 'Where has the gentleman left his shadow?' and straightaway again from a couple of women: 'Jesus Mary! The poor fellow has no shadow!' That began to vex me and I avoided very carefully walking in the sun. But this was not entirely successful, for instance in Broadstreet, which the next minute I had to cross, to my misfortune at the very moment the boys were coming out of school. A damned hunchbacked tyke, I see him still, twigged immediately my shadow was missing. He betrayed me with a loud shout to the collected literary pack of street urchins of the suburb who immediately began to review me and throw mud: 'Decent people are careful to take their shadows with them, when they go in the sun.' To get them off my back, I hurled two handfuls of gold in amongst them, and jumped into a cab to give ease to my suffering soul.

As soon as I found myself alone in the moving coach, I began to weep bitterly. (Chamisso 1980: 24)

The tone of this passage shuttles between the comic and the anguished. But note that as early as the early 1800s, there are also satirical and social possibilities in the allegory of the loss of the shadow. The passage reveals, in a comic set of encounters which anticipate Pip's manic persecution by Trabbs' boy in *Great Expectations* (1861), the angst and shame caused to Schlemihl (whose name means, roughly, 'unfortunate one') by the realization of his loss and his sudden exposure in the sunlit street at noon as a shadowless creature to the taunting eyes of any Gerd, Dirk or Dieter. The horror is fairly obviously a satire on the connection between the Enlightenment (the German inflexion of which, Die Aufklarung, has connotations of 'clearing up') and the tyrannical organization of the 'modern', daylight bourgeois state, in which the shadow is a symptom, not of the death of the individual, as it is in other Uncanny romantic traditions, referred to by Freud and Otto Ranke, but of his 'normality'. The shadow traditionally from Plato onwards (ambiguously, through its own insufficiency as a representation) implies its original, the substance, and the joke here about 'decent people' gives away this connection between self-identity and the 'transparency' (i.e. the surveillance) of the individual subject created by the Aufklarung-fuelled 'new' Prussian state. The shadow here has been co-opted by the population and pressed into service as a mobile identity card, and the losing (let alone the selling) of it is a mock-Faustian transgression which causes a breach in the image of the three-dimensional individual, a breach in the system of self-reflection that supposedly guarantees the stability of the subject under the pressure of angst or desire.

The other aspect of the Gothic tradition's anticipation of Baudrillard's metaphor for the 'transparency' of Evil in contemporary culture is the replacement of the shadow by a technological fantasy of prosthetics, and the consequent loss of the Other through reproduction of the Self. Picking up an eighteenth-century motif in the thought of the French Enlightenment writers, the German Romantics were quite obsessed with the horrors of automata and the replacement of the self by a machine, a theme which they (following Diderot's anti-Cartesianism) treated with a variety of responses that included irony and satire. The most obvious example of this Uncanny reversal of values is E. T. A. Hoffmann's 'The Sandman', in which the narcissistic romantic poet-protagonist, Nathaniel, after having shouted at his sensible, but outspoken girlfriend, Clara: 'You lifeless damned automaton!', falls in love with Olympia, a machine created by Professor Spalanzani, who can play the pianoforte and dance. Nathaniel interprets her dancing as superior to his own, which he sees suddenly as full of minute errors. Here is the passage which persistently links the uncanny and the horrific with comedy and satire:

> Although he now found himself in quite another world, it suddenly seemed to Nathaniel that here below at Professor Spalanzani's it had grown noticeably darker: he looked about him and was not a little startled to see that the two lights left in the room had burned down and were on the point

of going out. The music and dancing had long since ceased. 'Parting, parting !' he cried in wild despair; he kissed Olympia's hand, bent down to her mouth and his passionate lips encountered lips that were icy-cold ! As he touched Olympia's cold hand, he was seized by an inner feeling of horror, and he suddenly recalled the legend of the dead bride, but Olympia pressed him close to her; as they kissed, her lips seemed to warm into life.

Professor Spalanzani walked slowly through the empty room, his steps echoing hollowly, and his figure, played about by flickering shadows, had an uncanny, ghost-like appearance.

'Do you love me? Do you love me, Olympia? Say but that word. Do you love me?' Nathaniel whispered, but as she rose to her feet Olympia sighed only: 'Ah, ah!' (Hoffmann 1990a: 155)

The satire of romantic male egotism is presented in the same breath as the uncanny effect of the scene: 'Ah, ah !' is all that Olympia can ever say, but to Nathaniel's fevered narcissism, the exclamation is interpretable in an infinite variety of tones, all of them exhibiting shades of difference. The automaton for him is not visible, because it is shrouded in a counterfactual dream of female perfection. That dream, however, is inseparable from the idea of the woman not answering back. For Nathaniel, the Other has disappeared into a sexual prosthesis, the desire for which is so strong that it overcomes the traditional horror of the Spectre Bride's coldness. The resurrection, instead of striking in him the shudders of impotence because it insists on the conditions of the grave, is a form of warm technology that flatters the ego with the delusion of full acceptance.

Baudrillard alludes to a traditional motif. The dream of a dismissal of the Other is a powerful motif in Chamisso's classic and in Hoffman's famous tale, and forms the basis of Mary Shelley's nightmare of a technological autoparturition in *Frankenstein* (1818). At times this tradition is an explicit parody of vulgar Enlightenment thought, becoming part of modern consciousness through Freud's re-appropriation of Hoffman's 'uncanny', and perhaps, as Terry Castle (see Castle 1995) and Helene Cixous (see Cixous 1976) have forcibly (and quite differently) argued, recuperating in a paradoxical fashion an Enlightenment taboo on the Irrational.

Equally, from Walpole to Ann Radcliffe and Mary Shelley's *Frankenstein*, the narratives of the Gothic are often shaped by the threat of a profane Resurrection of the Body, an explicit taboo reinforced in the Christian (Protestant) credo, which recommits itself during the nineteenth century (after Hume's sceptical challenge in the mid-eighteenth century) to a pre-emptively spiritualized interpretation of the Pauline doctrine of the Resurrection of the Body. The obvious offence against these proscriptions is the ramifying associated myth of the Undead, popular fascination with which dates also from the eighteenth century.

Baudrillard's argument represents this tradition of horror with ironic nostalgia. Those were the days. Evil was the limit of ourselves: the subject relied on these heroic confrontations with the Other to define itself. Think of Poe's 'William Wilson' in the 1830s, the story of a Self who kills his Other and thus takes its place, imprisoning himself in his own narrative in a hell of repetition, at the point of the crime. But in the post-revolutionary period since the 1960s, we (whoever 'we' finally includes) have carried out, Baudrillard argues, a relentlessly successful assault on all the oppositional aspects of the Other, with results as banal as they are horrifying. In the process, the representation has hunted down the original, the represented. And in particular the Body (including the Body Politic in the environment of global capitalism) has been displaced into its own systems of disease and, in the very success of its defences, attacks and destroys itself:

> The uninterrupted production of productivity has a terrifying consequence. Whereas negativity engenders crisis and critique, hyperbolic positivity for its part engenders catastrophe, for it is incapable of distilling crisis and criticism in homeopathic doses. Any structure that hunts down, expels or exorcizes its negative elements risks a catastrophe caused by a thoroughgoing backlash, just as any organism that hunts down and eliminates its germs, bacteria, parasites or other biological antagonists risks metastasis and cancer – in other words, it is threatened by the voracious positivity of its own cells, or, in the viral context, by the prospect of being devoured by its own – now unemployed – antibodies. (Baudrillard 1993: 106)

This shadowless nightmare is our new reality argues Baudrillard, in which the homeopathic doses of negativity provided by the presence of a tabooed Other are no longer possible. The dream of a whole line of Gothic explorers, mad scientists, unalloyed by irony or satire, has come true and we are living in that dream. As Angela Carter once famously said: 'We live in Gothic times' (Carter 1974: 133).

Ballard: 'biomorphic horror' versus 'transcendental geometry'

Baudrillard's argument in *The Transparency of Evil* looks as if it fits Ballard. But there are some qualifications to be made. On closer inspection, the reader's position, the question of interpretation, the nature of our grasp of Ballard's texts at the rhetorical level, is not so simple. Horror and laughter both arise in Ballard out of his deadpan tone and this fact complicates the schematic nature of his effects.

Let us take what is perhaps his most challenging text, *The Atrocity Exhibition*. The utopian nature of the project of Ballard's characters is counterfactual, countersensory. The 'factual' I refer to is presented by them as a prison from which they propose to liberate humanity. The central restriction becomes visible in the construction of our sexuality, our idea of which is neurotically formed by the imperatives of biology, and the battery of repressed unconscious drives identified by Freud, which lead to our death, policed by a collective fiction of 'normality'. We have to reject this nineteenth-century teleology. Freedom from this bourgeois puritan horror of a biological form to which our desires are tied, argues Dr Nathan, one of Ballard's scientists, offers itself in perversion, or 'transcendental geometry', Freud translated into Euclid. But in Ballard's text, the reader is placed in the position of active 'translator', always at the junction of this dialectical opposition, not already its end point. Consider the reader's dilemma over the presentation of the following dialectic:

> **Biomorphic Horror**. With an effort, Dr Nathan looked away from Catherine Austin as she picked at her finger quicks. Unsure whether she was listening to him, he continued: 'Travers's problem is how to come to terms with the violence that has pursued his life – not merely the violence of accident and bereavement, or the horrors of war, but the biomorphic horror of our own bodies, the awkward geometry of the postures we assume. Travers has at last realized that the real significance of these acts of violence lies elsewhere, in what we might term 'the death of affect'. Consider all our most real and tender pleasures – in the excitements of pain and mutilation; in sex as the perfect arena, like a culture bed of sterile pus, for all the veronicas of our own perversions, in voyeurism and self-disgust, in our moral freedom to pursue our own psychopathologies as a game, and in our ever greater powers of abstractions. What our children have to fear are not the cars on the freeways of tomorrow, but our own pleasure in calculating the most elegant parameters of their deaths. The only way we can make contact with each other is in terms of conceptualizations. Violence is the conceptualization of pain. By the same token, psychopathology is the conceptual system of sex. (Ballard 1970: 93–4)

The passage begins with a joke: it may be that Catherine just is not listening to the lecture, as Nathan tries to explain the peculiarities of Travers, her lover, whose bizarre activities have become 'a deliberate summoning of the random and grotesque' (Ballard 1970: 94). Travers is trying to get beyond the 'awkward geometry' of our current sexual life which belongs to biomorphic horror. Hence its place in the list, as a parallel, for it is only when we can reach a 'transfinite' or 'transcendental' geometry that we can be free of this horror. Hence the famous 'death of affect' is supposed to be the opposite of the biomorphic horror. But look at the affective contradiction of the word 'tender' in the next sentence – 'Consider all our most real and *tender* pleasures' (Ballard 1970: 93). It is a pun on love, affection, emotional generosity, on the one hand, and bruising, on the other, challenging Catherine, if she is listening, and the reader who certainly is, in a joking Sadeian fashion, to convert the one to the other. The term 'real' doesn't mean anything after this, except to the Sadist-reader, who will nod in recognition of what he or she has always known. For me, horror has appeared on both sides of the dialectic.

Likewise in the next sentence, the apparent definition of sex as 'the perfect arena, like a culture bed of sterile pus' (Ballard 1970: 93), surely chosen for the maximum impact of Swiftian disgust, is to be understood as a countersensory analogy: 'pus' is usually not sterile, quite the opposite. But here, it seems it is. However, the 'unfortunate' choice of metonym (sex is a 'bed') crosses over the dialectical gap again and defeats the apparent neatness of the speaker's intention. The intended insult to 'biomorphic horror' is the sentence beginning: 'What our children have to fear' (Ballard 1970: 94). This seems to depend on the cliché that biological 'self-transcendence', the traditional consolation for mortality, is expressed in the getting of offspring. But, it is argued, increasing numbers of them will be randomly murdered by us, their parents, in the accident statistics of the motor car which we currently bequeath to them. Let's throw off this empirical horror and actually *design* their deaths! The only thing they have to fear is our pleasure in the geometry, which is purely conceptual after all and will not in the least affect the fact that they will be killed anyway, except they will be killed *better*.

This argument, far from transparent, is opaquely mad and terrifying, unless understood in its dialectical context as an imaginary project in the sense of Jonathan Swift and Daniel Defoe. The same goes for the two apothegms about 'violence' and 'psychopathology' which finish the paragraph, and which purport to state a law, but take the form of slogans. In the self-conscious, self-parodic context of this paragraph, these read more like William Blake's proverbs of Hell than flat 'scientific' statements: the copula ('is') in 'Violence is the conceptualization of pain' (Ballard 1970: 94) is rhetorical, for the reader; it has the force of speculation, not the authority of law. But this distinction creates the interpretative ambiguity and creates the ground of metaphor. It is not surprising that Catherine, meeting an aggressively excited Travers at an exhibition, learns to calm him down by reading him passages from the catalogue about 'Bernouli's *Encyclopedia of Imaginary Diseases*' (Ballard 1970: 94).

The final sentence of this passage lets us see the strategic perversity of a deadpan rhetorical effect:

> A curious aspect of Bernouli's work, and one that must not be overlooked, is the way in which the most bizarre of his imaginary diseases, those which stand at the summit of his art and imagination, in fact closely approximate to conditions of natural pathology. (Ballard 1970: 95)

The perfect form of the counterfactual is when it can be mistaken for the factual.

Crash: the survival of imaginary perversion

In his now much debated reading of Ballard's novel, 'Crash' (Baudrillard 1991: 111–20), Baudrillard also gives us a thematic conspectus for the relation between David Cronenberg's cult film *Crash* and Ballard's *The Atrocity Exhibition* of 1970, from which the narrative of his 1973 novel *Crash* was selected and extended, and Cronenberg's film elaborated.[1] But again I'm going to argue that it is only at a thematic level that his argument seems to map. *The Atrocity Exhibition* anticipates much of Baudrillard's argument by 25 years, but there is a whole other dimension of *Crash* (the book and the movie, which derive from it), that remains unrepresented by Baudrillard's argument.

Before getting on to *Crash*, a few remarks about genre and form which a comparison with *The Atrocity Exhibition* reveals. Ballard's earlier text takes the form of an encyclopaedia of conceits about postwar history and politics from Hiroshima to Vietnam, about psychohistory and psychopathology, art, sex, technology and particularly Science – hard science, not just computer science. Its 15 sections form a romance of documentation, its narrative conveyed in a style of paragraphing which plays between encyclopaedia entries (each paragraph in the entire book is headed in bold type) and the kind of 'objectivist' poetic style of the immediate postwar French novel of Alain Robbe-Grillet. There are also lurches into recycled surrealist motifs from painting and drama (Marcel DuChamp, Max Ernst, Salvador Dali, Alfred Jarry). We do not know therefore whether we should be reading in a linear fashion and connecting up paragraphs, or whether the relation between them is random and we always have to start again. It is a strange mixture of the two, which wrong-foots the reader all the time: conventional linear narrative does not survive this process of defamiliarization. People die before and after they are dead. Death is conceptual, not historical:

> **'Not in the sense you mean.'** Dr Nathan covered the exhibits with a sheet. By chance the cabinets took up the contours of a corpse. 'Not in the sense you mean. This is an attempt to bring about the "false" death of the President – false in the sense of coexistent or alternate. The fact that an event has taken place is no proof of its valid occurrence'. (Ballard 1970: 42)

'Elizabeth Taylor', for example, is reported as dead at one point like Marilyn Monroe, John F. Kennedy and Albert Camus. These deaths are 'notional', even the ones that have happened. The fragmented plot takes places half-in and half-out of the minds of a number of bomber and helicopter pilots from the major scenes of postwar catastrophe who are trying to 'recreate' what are referred to as 'alternate' (Ballard 1970: 70) histories.

The format is a parody of scientific report or learned argument, its images posing and acting, as examples, and, at the same time, trashy and popular, full of deadpan jokes, not 'high' and experimental like the French novel at all. The solipsism which is the Beckettian thematic context of the latter is nowhere to be seen, except as *mutual* solipsism, though traces of it remain in Cronenberg's film. Ballard's world is madly collective, madly 'social', that is a world of analogy in which everything is an analogy for everything else. Freud is turned inside out and grafted onto Euclid: any historical event therefore has an unconscious, but it is free of the binarism of latent and manifest content, its unconscious nature visible in its 'geometry': Karen Novotny's body is a 'modulus' (the term drawn from Le Corbusier). The identifications of paranoid-schizophrenics with public figures (Jacqueline Kennedy, Ronald Reagan) are codified into 'experiments', like Ralph Nader's road-safety accident recreations. Some of these are as extreme and dislocated – jokes in wonderfully horrible bad taste – as anything contained in *Crash* – either Ballard's novel or Cronenberg's narrative selection. For example, Cronenberg retains rear-end crash as an explicitly sexual joke about sodomy, but one cannot think of the following embroidery of this conceit in the narrative decorum of his film:

> Subjects were required to construct the optimum autodisaster victim by placing a replica of Reagan's head on the retouched photographs of crash fatalities. In 82 percent of cases massive rear end collisions were selected with a preference for expressed faecal matter and rectal haemorrhages. (Ballard 1970: 149)

The subjects here are not young and beautiful – as Cronenberg's are, – but 'paretic': that is, in the terminal stages of tertiary syphilis.

The point about Ballard's *Crash* (1973) is that it acts out one small bio-graphical strand of *The Atrocity Exhibition*'s programme of providing the reader with an encyclopaedia of postwar history, as a catalogue of 'imaginary perversions'. The genre of both books and of Cronenberg's movie is mock-utopian, mock-apocalyptic ('autogeddon', an apocalyptic pun which brings together narcissism and the motor car). I stress the 'imaginary', which in the rhetoric of the 1973 novel becomes a persistent source of metaphor, of the counterfactual. Baudrillard's version of *Crash*, however, is relatively flat and humourless:

> The Accident, like death, is no longer of the order of the neurotic, of the repressed, of the residual, or of the transgressive; it is the initiator of a new manner of *non-perverted* pleasure (contrary to what the author himself says in his introduction when he speaks of a new perverse logic, one must resist the moral temptation of reading Crash as perversion), of a strategic reorgani-sation of life beyond the perspective of death. Death, wounds, mutilations

are no longer metaphors for castration – it's exactly the reverse, or even more than the reverse. Only fetishist metaphors are perversion: seduction by the model, by the interposed fetish, by the medium of language. Here, death and sex are read straight from the body, without fantasy, without metaphor, without phraseology. (Baudrillard 1991a: 314)

'Perversion', as Baudrillard rightly says, is not a *moral* motive in Ballard's writing – it is (what he doesn't say) an aesthetic one. The morality is, however, part of his characters' beliefs: Dr Nathan, in the quotation earlier from *The Atrocity Exhibition*, refers (blackmailingly) to 'our moral freedom to pursue our own psychopathologies as a game' (Ballard 1970: 93–4). Baudrillard's quotations from the novel manage to get rid of the impact of Ballard's prose, the suppressed giggle of excitement, concealed under a po-faced listing of terms. At the level of language, the absurdly nautical word 'binnacle', for example, a term which describes projecting bits of dashboard instrument housing, which no one ever uses except in automobile brochures, is repeated in the novel at every opportunity, until it regains a new metaphorical force. The *OED* traces the first usage to 1750 and gives the original meaning as: 'A box on the deck of a ship near the helm, in which a compass is placed'. Ballard picks up the archaic word at the point of its maximum debasement into brochure currency for 'styling', and uses it again and again in a parody of the use of anatomical terms in pornography. Here, the narrator 'Ballard' is with a young prostitute, who could be forgiven for not noticing the nature of his excitement:

> As she brought my penis to life I looked down at her strong back, at the junction between the contours of her shoulders demarked by the straps of her brassiere and the elaborately decorated instrument panel of this American car, between her thick buttock in my left hand and the pastel-shaded binnacles of the clock and speedometer. Encouraged by these hooded dials, my left ring-finger moved towards her anus. (Ballard 1973: 62)

It pops up again with the dreadfully injured Gabrielle, who is, at this stage, almost aware of it: 'as if she realized that the twisted instrument binnacles provided a readily accessible anthology of depraved acts, the keys to an alternative sexuality' (Ballard 1973: 100).

Vaughan's photographs of sexual acts feature a system of visual puns in which, 'sections of radiator grilles and instrument panels, conjunctions between elbow and chromium window-sill, vulva and instrument binnacle, summed up the possibilities of a new logic' (Ballard 1973: 106). The trained reader can even pick up the pathos of the following, apparently 'innocent' use: 'Vaughan was holding passively to the rim of his steering wheel, staring with an expression of defeat at the fading passport photograph of an anonymous middle-aged woman clipped to the ventilation duct of the instrument binnacle' (Ballard 1973: 137). A final example (there are many others). The absurd self-parody of Vaughan's speculations surfaces in the following: 'Monroe masturbating, or Oswald, say – left- or right-handed, which would you guess? And what instrument panels? Was orgasm reached more quickly with a recessed or overhanging binnacle?' (Ballard 1973: 183). I defy the reader not to laugh at this last question. Bathos is somehow wonderfully present. The parody is evidently of the language of pornography and, at the same time, of automobile design research. But this is also meant to be Vaughan's (admittedly, by this time, deranged and explicitly 'self-parodic') expression of 'transcendental geometry'. The comic variations of Vaughan and 'Ballard's' binnacle-fetish make the word stand out as an item of vocabulary that has assumed a bizarre figurative life of its own but which make it (as a programmatic code of the countersensory) unconvincing to the reader. The word in the text will not obey the programme of the characters: the erotic charge of a 'binnacle' is actually – nil.[2]

Metaphors abound in this text, because the premise of Ballard's narrative is the 'imaginary perverse'. Baudrillard's quotations from the novel are all out of context; his first, the death of the minor actress (Baudrillard 1991a: 111), for example, occurs as fantasy in the mind of the narrator 'Ballard' – that's part of the joke. But Baudrillard reads it off literal-mindedly as socio-pathology, as a symptom of a general postmodern 'style' in which 'mutilations are *no longer* metaphors for castration' (Baudrillard 1991a: 113). This is a purely thematic account of Ballard's writing, which is actually an encyclopaedia of jokes about a new application of imagined drives: narcissism, fetishism, coprophagia, sado-masochism, etc. The point is to imagine the logic, the state of desire in which this perversion has taken place. Take Ballard's first act of sex with Helen Remington for example (the name mingles ludicrously an out of date typewriter with the face that launched a thousand ships):

> Seizing me with her body in this arbour of glass, metal and vinyl, Helen moved her hand inside my shirt, feeling for my nipples. I took her fingers and placed them around my penis. Through the rear-view mirror I saw a water-board maintenance truck approaching. It moved past in a roar of dust and diesel exhaust that drummed against the doors of my car. This surge of excitement drew the first semen to my penis. Ten minutes later, when the truck returned, the vibrating windows brought on my orgasm. (Ballard 1973: 80)

The point about this passage is that it is a logical set piece, another insult to 'biomorphic horror': it is counterfactual, mock-erotic. We know this from the phrase 'arbour of glass' (a narcissistic contradiction) which recycles a thousand such seduction scenes in 'arbours' from Renaissance poetry to Victorian pornography's summer house, a genre which itself is expert in spreading sexual anatomy, metaphorically, into an environment. The idea of a 'water-board maintenance truck' actually being a material and motive part of protagonist Ballard's desire in an erotic encounter is at first sight so improbable – read the deliberate realism of the dull descriptive phrase out, and you almost burst out laughing – that the reader is challenged to imagine the state of mind in which such excitement would be possible. The verve of the writing is a triumph: it is the metaphorical logic of imaginary perversion, an imaginary taboo broken, not a reflection of a historically new state of affairs:

> This small space was crowded with angular control surfaces and rounded sections of human bodies interacting in familiar junctions, like the first act of homosexual intercourse inside an Apollo capsule. (Ballard 1973: 80)

There may indeed by now be a sociology of the space capsule in which sex has become banal – among astronauts – but the excitement of desire is in the analogy (the 'first act', not the ten thousandth), for the erotic encounter of 'Ballard' and Helen Remington in their 'arbour'. Baudrillard's thematic account tends to remove the difference between the reader's point of view and the protagonist's, suppressing metaphor and replacing it with metonymy, and converting analogy into reflection, rendering the impact of Ballard's carefully organized writing as passive and symptomatic.

Baudrillard also quotes the laboratory car-crash from the novel (Baudrillard 1991a: 117), without registering the contradiction that it is riddled with anthropomorphic fiction: the mannequins are referred to in the narrative discourse *as if* they were real. A bizarre poetry of metaphor is made out of this; the figures are perversely animated, the language hyperbolic, laced with mock-heroic exaggeration, full of an incongruous mixture of comedy and desire:

> The mannequin, Elvis, lifted himself from his seat, his ungainly body at last blessed by the grace of the slow-motion camera. Like the most brilliant of all stunt men, he stood on his pedals, legs and arms fully stretched. His head was raised with its chin forwards in a pose of almost aristocratic disdain. (Ballard 1973: 126)

'Ballard' here has just begun to see what Vaughan sees, and Vaughan has just leaked into his trousers at the sight. The theological allusion in the first sentence 'blessed by the grace') is to the counter-gravitational (i.e. counterfactual) 'grace' of Kleist's puppets, an idea which in its turn is compared, metaphorically, to the fiction of transcendence created by the 'slow-motion camera'. This perverse anthropomorphism is pursued and energized by allusion and metaphor and embedded analogy, alternate logics to the functional. Baudrillard, anxious to foreground on a thematic level the question of representation, reduces this passage back to a 'hyperfunctionalism', which gets rid of the clear distinction between fiction and reality which the inversion of these terms is based on. In 'Simulacra and Science Fiction', he writes, 'In *Crash*, there is neither fiction nor reality – a kind of hyperreality has abolished both' (Baudrillard 1991a: 127). That is the project of Vaughan and 'Ballard', not Ballard's text.

For all its almost-fatal aestheticism, Cronenberg's movie has faithfully translated the perverse logic of the novel into visual form: it too is a solemn, witty, reversed-premise *bildungsroman* that uses the format of pornography. The main story is the encounter between 'James Ballard' and Catherine, both of them already beginning to experiment in perverse and prosthetic erotics, and the violently bisexual car-crash addict Vaughan, who shows them how much further the erotics of the car crash can go.

There are two quite distinct sexual codes: the languid bourgeois eroticism of James and Catherine at home is cut with brutal and dispassionate (in the visual context, very 1950s) lust, the briskly animal encounters of James in the car, with the other victim of the car crash, Dr Remington, whose husband – to add to the spice – was killed. Suddenly, we feel James has discovered a whole new world of sexual perversion. The car, not as mere site, but erotic instrument. And he proceeds to introduce Catherine to it, who has already, independently, made a mild beginning for herself with an aircraft engine cowling (Cronenberg 1996).

In this simpler logic, fucking equals crashing and the ultimate orgasm – the little death – is Death. The compromise, which retains consciousness and therefore enjoyment, is extreme mutilation. Vaughan – already mutilated – in Cronenberg's film cannot wait, and drives off the road, over the rail and onto a tour bus. James and Catherine's murmured joke is, 'Maybe next time . . .' (Cronenberg 1996) which ranges precisely from the comfortable bourgeois desire for absolute sexual bliss, to its reverse – absolute mutilation. In a comic parody of the main plot, Vaughan's friend, Gabrielle, so badly mutilated she cannot walk, reduces a car sales man to erotic jelly, a scene which is expanded from one dead-pan line of the novel:

> She provoked a young salesman on the Mercedes stand to ask her to inspect a white sport's car, relishing his embarrassment when he helped her shackled legs into the front seat. Vaughan whistled in admiration of this. (Ballard 1973: 174)

Unlike the novel, the film ends with James performing consolatory anal intercourse on a doll-like Catherine, still in her post-accident position, as she masturbates against the blunt knife-edge of the car's window frame (Cronenberg 1996).

The premise of sexual initiation is consistently reversed and the pornographic story told the wrong way round in Cronenberg's film; and there is some ingeniously represented 'biomorphic horror'. Cronenberg creates what in Ballard is 'abstraction', meaning the process of conversion of objects and bodies into conceptual analogy, by the use of extreme stylization within a skeletally linear narrative frame: he relies (to marvellous effect, it should be said) on statuesque pacing, whispered dialogue, derelict musical cadences and the alienated way in which the camera dwells on aspects of the (posed) body. After Vaughan has violently (i.e. 'abstractly') copulated with Catherine, an activity regulated by the cycle of a car wash sequence, James and Catherine are lying on the bed together at home. Ballard's inverted logic is brought out more clearly in the movie than in his own novel in this scene. Catherine's bruised and torn body is posed very carefully to resemble a corpse, the raised pubis and the hipbones and the impossibly concave belly mocking the conventions of the ideal (i.e. the magazine-created) live body to give a perfect, ghoulish form to the erotic code. This is rigorously logical reversal by stylization, a visual pun, which translates the 'analogy' and 'mimetization' of *The Atrocity Exhibition* into other, more naturalistic conventions.[3] These conventions are at least as far away from naturalistic narrative and more Gothic than Ballard's own *Crash* at this point, which relies on the voyeurism of 'Ballard', the protagonist, 'mimetizing' with the head of his penis (using it like an invisible marker-pen) the wounds of her raped and torn body (Ballard 1973: 166). Cronenberg by contrast hands the paradox straight to the viewer by means of an enigmatic tableau.

Nor, finally, at the level of representation, is Ballard's 'mimetization' (an obsessive item of the rhetoric of *The Atrocity Exhibition*, but not of his *Crash*) equivalent to Baudrillard's famous 'simulation'. Ballard's term hovers between replication and miniaturization; but it contains no whiff of nostalgia for the notion of an 'original', as Baudrillard's notion of the 'perfect crime' of simulation does, however ironically. We've hidden the Body, i.e. the Original. For Ballard and Cronenberg their appropriation of Gothic style requires no concept of an Original.

For Ballard in the late 1960s and early 1970s, real twentieth-century history is an imaginary perversion, the horrific invention of the Other; for Baudrillard, in the late eighties, it is a kind of post-Hegelian loss, the loss of the Other, and of all means of self-negation and 'self-transcendence' (which apparently includes orgasm). Cronenberg, in the late 1990s, who has his own visceral Gothic obsessions with the human body, stomach cavities, etc, is interested, too, in the *biography* of imaginary perversions, but not in a Fall from Grace as a representation of contemporary culture.

Of course, there are some obvious points of symmetry between Baudrillard the critic, on the one hand, and Ballard and Cronenberg, the artists, on the other – otherwise the critic's argument would not be so seductive. Baudrillard states the programmatic aspects of the writing quite clearly. Ballard is concerned indeed to explore loss of affect (he invented the phrase, the 'death of affect', in *The Atrocity Exhibition*, in 1969), and he is also interested in replication, and prosthetics, but that deadpan style is a primary medium of Gothic effects, an ironical way of representing a transcendence of the horrors of our biomorphic psycho-history, not simply or primarily a metonymic reflection of the prison of technology. He, like Kurt Vonnegut or early Joseph Heller, is concerned with ways of representing the unrepresentable limits of mass human insanity. But Baudrillard replays Walter Benjamin's famous loss of 'aura' (i.e. twentieth-century art's loss of the ideal of a unique original through the technology of mass reproduction) as a way of describing 'our' post-evolutionary banalizing of Evil, 'our' descent into irreversible metonymy. For Ballard and Cronenberg, and their 'autogeddon', there is no trace of an absent 'authenticity' in their Gothic jokes, and they prove it to us by the grotesque, hyperbolic energy of their metaphors.

Notes

1. Cult is clearly a semantic vortex. I am assuming throughout this essay that cult is what is sometimes called the 'defining other' of taboo. The banning of Cronenberg's *Crash* in the United Kingdom converted a director working in an established popular tradition (Gothic horror), into a cult director, just at the point when he was making a nod to a literary source of the 1970s. This is the way I see the irony (and boredom) of the film's reception: its 'moment' is a titanic-sized iceberg, most of which lies below the surface of post-modern orthodoxy. I am aware that one could argue the case the other way round: that Cronenberg was a cult (meaning 'minority', even 'elite') director already, who was lunged into the mainstream by being banned. But for me the term 'cult' is not simply a socio-economic label that implies the mechanism of supply and demand; it is also the sign of an alteration in the chemistry of expectation.
2. Strictly speaking, 'binnacle' appears to have the grammatical form of the metonym, not the metaphor. This is why Baudrillard reads the main rhetorical system of the text as fetishistic and metonymic ('hyperrealist'). But 'transcendental geometry' (i.e. the capacity to 'see' (conceptualize) the analogy which allows the sexual excitement encoded by the 'binnacle' to take place), requires a metaphorical grasp *before* metonymic extension can happen. One might say the cubism of the text takes place as a result of its surrealism, not the other way round. Cf Jakobson on similarity and contiguity in the visual arts: 'A salient example from the history of painting is the manifestly metonymical orientation of cubism, where the object is transformed into a set of synecdoches; the surrealist painters responded with a patently metaphorical attitude'. See Jakobson, R. and Halle, M. (1956; 1971). *The Fundamentals of Language*. Mouton: The Hague and New York, p. 92.
3. This neologism 'mimetized' is interesting, drawing in 'mimesis' (imitation) and mimicry (caricature), as well as 'miniaturization'. For example, 'the mimetized disasters of Vietnam and the Congo recapitulated in the broken fenders and radiation assemblies'. Not in 'these broken fenders', but in their 'contours': the process is the 'geometry', the abstract relation, not the concrete objects. We no longer care about the objects, because they could be anything, even things which are objects of knowledge, but not objects in the common sense at all, like 'the Vietnam war'. This makes it more than a Baudrillardian 'simulation' which is like a kind of 'trompe l'oeil', a confidence trick disguising the loss of the object. Or, consider what a difference the term makes to the following sentence, which is very Baudrillardian until we get to the awkward business about Ralph Nader: 'Planes intersect: on one level the tragedies of Cape Kennedy and Vietnam serialised on billboards, random

death *mimetized* in the experimental auto-disasters of Nader and his co-workers (Ballard 1970: 67; italics mine). ('Auto's also playfully literalised: 'Young Virgin auto-sodomised by her own chastity' (Ballard 1970: 67): a good example of an imaginary perversion). So to 'mimetize' doesn't just equal 'virtualize', if we define the term 'virtual' as 'Not physically existing, but made by software to appear to do so' (OED concise) because one is talking about what is self-consciously presented as simultaneously subjective fantasy and 'historical event' (Originally published in 'Unruly Pleasures: The Cult Film and its Critics', Xavier Mendik and Graeme Harper (eds), FAB Press, England, 2000, ISBN 9781903254004).

CHAPTER FOUR

Death at Work: The Cinematic Imagination of J. G. Ballard

CORIN DEPPER

Chapter Summary: Exploring *The Atrocity Exhibition* (1970), *Crash* (1973) and *Empire of the Sun* (1984) through their filmic adaptations, this chapter addresses the complexities and idiosyncrasies of J. G. Ballard's cinematic imagination. Depper demonstrates how Ballard's work raises questions about form, time, narrative and movement in, and across, literary and cinematic texts.

Key Words: *The Atrocity Exhibition; Crash; Empire of the Sun*; Cinema; adaptation for screen; time; image; narrative; Gilles Deleuze; Francis Bacon; Edweard Muybridge; Jonathan Weiss; Steven (Spielberg); David Cronenberg.

The bal(l)ade of J. G. Ballard

J. G. Ballard's fiction has long maintained a fascination with cinema: the peculiar mutability of the film studio operating, along with the ever-present airport, as one of the quintessential architectures of his work; the one facilitating a literal transit between places, and the other defined by its essential transitoriness, its capacity to be transformed into a universe of possibilities. But the cinema is not just an industry for Ballard, or even merely the embodiment of twentieth-century mass culture: it is also a form that has allowed for the very refiguring of both experience and narrative; one that permits new modes of thinking and being to emerge. In his short story, 'The 60 Minute Zoom' (Ballard 2001 [1976]) the narrator watches his wife's adultery through the lens of a movie camera only for us to realize, in the moment of her climatic murder, that rather than simply recording the unfolding event, the narrator is in fact replaying the footage of his crime. Ballard's narrator is transformed into a murderer before our eyes: film has been both his accomplice and his witness, splitting the temporality of the narrative as the narrator metamorphoses from cuckold to killer. For Ballard, then, the cinema has become a key element in his attempt to explore what amounts to a pathology of narrative.

Given this focus, it is not entirely surprising that his work has attracted the attention of filmmakers, with (to date) three feature films adapted from his novels, and it is these books that will provide the focus of this chapter. The chronology of the adaptations runs inversely with the publication date of the novels, so that Jonathan Weiss's adaptation of Ballard's 1970 work *The Atrocity Exhibition* was completed in 2001; *Crash* from 1972 was filmed by David Cronenberg in 1996; and Steven Spielberg's film of *Empire of the Sun* was released in 1987, just 3 years after the book in 1984.

Despite being written over a span of nearly two decades, I intend to view the three books as a loose trilogy, or rather triptych, united not merely by their status as works chosen for adaptation, and suggest that they can be seen as presenting a significant development in Ballard's thinking about the history and ontology of cinema. Although my central focus will be on *The Atrocity Exhibition*, the other two works present a counterpoint to the main discussion, and in several instances are explicit about elements buried within Ballard's earlier writing.

In this respect, the work of the French philosopher Gilles Deleuze provides a useful framework for a discussion of Ballard's cinematic engagement. Like Ballard's fiction, which took a markedly experimental turn in response to the shifting cultural landscape of the late 1960s, Deleuze's philosophical project became galvanized (and popularized) in the intellectual climate of France in the years following the events of May '68. While not 'officially sanctioned' by Ballard in the manner of Baudrillard, Deleuze's work has the potential to initiate a more complex exploration of the intellectual underpinnings of his writing.[1] While it is beyond the scope of this chapter to delineate a full account of the connections between Ballard and Deleuze, the two volumes of Deleuze's *Capitalism and Schizophrenia*, co-written with psychologist Félix Guittari and subtitled *Anti-Oedipus* and *A Thousand Plateaus* (2004, 2004a), represent attempts to construct new models of thought and history structured around a radically decentred form dubbed the 'rhizome' that operates against linear and dialectical ideas. This is mirrored in the formal structuring of the books as a series of seemingly disconnected sections, which force the reader to abandon earlier experiences of reading philosophy in favour of a radically decentred process, almost inevitably skipping across sections and creating new pathways of meaning. In their endlessly shifting patterns of influence these two works could easily be seen as companion pieces to Ballard's *The Atrocity Exhibition*, which proffers a similarly unstable ground on which new notions of history and identity are endlessly being constructed and destroyed.

Furthermore, Deleuze has written two books on the history of cinema, drawing on the work of the early twentieth-century French philosopher Henri Bergson, (the publication of whose book *Matter and Memory* (1896) was synchronous with the Lumière Brothers first demonstration of the *Cinématographe*), and establishing several new paradigms along the way. In these books, Deleuze makes a key historical distinction between cinema pre- and post-World War II. He argues that for its first half-century, cinema was essentially defined by its capacity to capture movement. That gives way, in the aftermath of the trauma of the war, to a more self-reflexive mode of filmmaking, heralded by Italian Neorealism (a movement that married an attempt to use cinema to record the harsh realities of postwar life with an aesthetic utilizing real locations and non-professional actors), that sees cinema shifting focus to an observation of the passage of time, and which for Deleuze is encapsulated in what he refers to as 'the time-image' (1992: 211–15).

Writing in *Cinema 2: The Time-Image*, Deleuze describes the development of postwar narrative by fusing together the French words for trip, 'balade', and ballad, 'ballade', to create the portmanteau 'bal(l)ade' (1989: 3) to describe the loosening of earlier classical narrative chains and the emergence of a newly anecdotal form epitomized by Roberto Rossellini's films with Ingrid Bergman such as *Europa 51* (1951, Italy), Michelangelo Antonioni's quintessential work in *l'Avventura* (1959, Italy) and Jean-Luc Godard's *Pierrot le fou* (1965, France). For Deleuze, such films present both new ways of considering the types of stories that can be told in the postwar world and suggest the emergence of a new type of cinematic image that is capable of registering its own temporal presence. As with Deleuze's wider philosophical project, his approach to cinema offers a radical attempt to break with earlier models of film history, and to present a vision of cinema that is about the re-colonization of spaces rendered derelict and fragmented; of the move against simple linearity (both in historical and narratological terms) in favour of something far more fluid and complex.

Following Deleuze's punning, I would suggest that one may further pun his term into a 'Bal(l)a(r)d(e)' form in order to discuss the new sort of narrative situations that J. G. Ballard begins experimenting with at the end of the 1960s, and which, arguably, characterize the development of his fiction over the next two decades. As with Deleuze's identification of his form with narratives structured around trips (as opposed to quests where the narrative goal is always clear), each book in my Ballardian triptych is characterized by both the necessity of movement – be it the endless parabolas of *The Atrocity Exhibition*, the traversing of

London's periphery by Ballard and Vaughan in *Crash* or the huddled prisoners of war shipped between internment camps in *Empire of the Sun* – and a steadily growing awareness of the futility of these travels. This Bal(l)a(r)d(e)ian form is, I would suggest, a mode of narration that has at its core an essentially cinematic view; of narrative seen as an endless, cyclical tracking shot – yet which, when first encountered in its nascent state in *The Atrocity Exhibition*, also evokes the prehistory of moving images as well.

The Atrocity Exhibition

The Atrocity Exhibition is perhaps Ballard's most formally experimental work and presents the reader with a series of connected narrative situations rather than a simple linear structure (Luckhurst 1997: 83). Divided into 15 'chapters' with such gnomic titles as 'You: Coma: Marilyn Monroe', 'Why I want to fuck Ronald Reagan' and 'The Assassination of John Fitzgerald Kennedy Considered as a Downhill Motor Race,' which are themselves divided into equally curiously titled paragraphs, the book establishes a shifting central character in the figure of a doctor/ patient at some form of unnamed psychiatric institution (Ballard 1993: 1) who is in the care of a Dr Nathan. This patient's identity remains unstable; initially given the name Travis, he transforms into Talbot, Traven, Tallis, Trabert, Talbert, and Travers in subsequent chapters. This shifting nomenclature contrasts with the seeming precision of the scientific presentation of the novel (described by Roger Luckhurst as 'a contemporary psychopathology in its clinical repetitive prose' (Luckhurst 1997: xvii)), with each paragraph labelled like an eccentric anatomical specimen; a nomenclature of the central character's growing psychosis.

The gradual transformations of the central character's name suggest both a movement in time and space, but at the same time a form of stasis, as if the name revolves around a central pivot made up of the letters 'T' and 'A'. This series of dislocations serve to establish a shifting ground where space and narrative are unable to maintain even the most tentative of grips. Ballard has described the book as presenting the psychodramas staged by this central character using whatever materials he could find to hand, and of which he is both the instigator and principle actor (Vale and Juno 1984: 154). The 15 chapters that comprise the book are less a coherent narrative series than individual successive snapshots presenting a single situation at various moments of transformation, like some strange synthesis of the Stations of the Cross and nineteenth century Chronophotography, that precursor of cinema which attempted to record and analyse the nature of movement through a series of photographic images.

Indeed, Ballard has mentioned that an inspiration for the book's method can be found in the work of the late-nineteenth-century French physiologist and photographic pioneer Etienne Jules Marey (Delville 1998: 32), whose motion studies utilized a single photographic plate to show motion as a fluid transformation from one state to another, and whom one finds nestled amongst the first of the numerous lists that pepper the novel:

> The noise from the cine-films of induced psychoses rose from the lecture theatre below Travis's office. Keeping his back to the window behind his desk, he assembled the terminal documents he had collected with so much effort during the previous months: (1) Spectro-heliogram of the sun; (2) Front elevation of balcony units, Hilton Hotel, London; (3) Transverse section through a pre-Cambrian triolobite; (4) 'Chronograms' by E. J. Marey. (Ballard 1993: 1–2)

This is followed a few paragraphs later by Dr Nathan's analysis given to Margaret Travis, the wife of his patient:

> "Marey's chronograms are multiple-exposure photographs in which the element of time is visible – the walking human figure, for example, is represented as a series of dune-like lumps." [...] "Your husband's brilliant feat was to reverse the process. Using a series of photographs of the most commonplace objects – this office, let us say, a panorama of New York skyscrapers, the naked body of a woman, the face of a catatonic patient – he treated them as if they already were chronograms and *extracted* the element of time." Dr Nathan lit his cigarette with care. "The results were extraordinary. A very different world was revealed. The familiar surroundings of our lives, even our smallest gestures were seen to have totally altered meanings. As for the reclining figure of a film star, or this hospital". (Ballard 1993: 6)

This description presents one of the central paradoxes of the book: the minute description of quite unrealizable effects, for Dr Nathan does not elaborate on *how* Travis has *extracted* time from his Chronograms, leaving the mental image on the threshold of the realizable. Furthermore, despite this name-checking of Marey in the text, I would suggest that the book's structure is far more closely aligned to the work of that other pioneer of chronophotography, Eadweard Muybridge, whose photographic technique differed from Marey's in that it presented motion not as a fluid movement but as a decomposition of separate fragments, with each phase of movement isolated as an individual frame. As Rebecca Solnit has pointed out, Marey's work, despite being carried out with far greater scientific precision than Muybridge, steps away from cinema in its blending of movements into a single figure, whereas Muybridge's form of fragmentation moves, seemingly paradoxically, closer towards it as it offers the potential to reconstruct movement from its deconstructed image-series (Solnit 2003: 210). Somewhat surprisingly, Deleuze fails to distinguish between the work of the two Chronophotographic pioneers (1992: 5), when in fact one could go so far as to suggest that in their different approaches, one blurring movement, the other fragmenting it, one finds the prehistory of the distinction between the movement-image and the time-image that is so crucial to a Deleuzian film history.

Muybridge's work on Motion Studies was first undertaken for the American tycoon Leland Stanford in the late 1870s. Muybridge pioneered the development of chronophotography, developing a multi-camera set-up designed to settle the debate over equine locomotion: Stanford had been dissatisfied with earlier representations of horses trotting and sought a scientific means of establishing the position of the animal's legs in motion. Stanford's prize racehorse, Occident, was recorded over a dozen separate images that span a complete cycle of the horse's movements when at a trot (Hendricks 1975: 99–110). Muybridge's research, enthusiastically supported by Stanford, demonstrated the capacity of the camera to be used in scientific enquiry, and encouraged his work on all forms of locomotion, both animal and human, initially exploring such commonplace movements as walking and running, but gradually moving into rather more eccentric actions such as emptying buckets of water and wrestling. Each stage in these motion studies can be seen as a miniaturized psychodrama, the individuals locked for eternity in endlessly repeating cycles of movement; science turned Sisyphean in the blink of an eye. Indeed, the effect of reading *The Atrocity Exhibition* leaves one with a similar sense of quivering stasis, of never quite knowing where the narrative begins and ends, the variously named protagonists never existing long enough for any fixed identity to emerge against which change can be gauged. Perhaps then they are better understood as symbolic positions in a cyclical movement, rather like Muybridge's eternally running Victorian atheles, destined to live out in perpetuity a time of cyclical movement.

Indeed, it was Muybridge who developed the Zoopraxiscope, a means of projecting his photographic studies sequentially, thus transforming them back into a moving form (Solnit 2003: 202; Hendricks 1975: 114–6). This tension then between the individual and the series can be seen to be mirrored both in *The Atrocity Exhibition*'s similar tension between individual paragraphs, and between the shifting identities of the 'Travis' character, referred to by Luckhurst as 'The T-Cell' in reference to the depletion of T-Cells as a measure of the progress of the HIV virus, as if the character has infected the book and is spreading through it (1997: 87; n2 186). Muybridge's illustrated lectures also anticipated in their naked Victorians engaged in increasingly baroque poses that quintessentially Ballardian fusing of science and pornography. This slightly disreputable quality – captured in the rather lubricious 'scientific' illustrations for the Re/Search edition of *The Atrocity Exhibition* (Ballard 1990: 8, 84, 85) combines the coolness of scientific discourse with the heat of a showman who understands the importance of the erotic in entertainment. It is also illustrative of that curious tension at the heart of the cinematic image between an attachment to an 'ethical' capturing of the real, and an acknowledgment of its voyeuristic potential.

Geographically, too, there is a connection between the two men, for Muybridge was born just a few miles down-river from Ballard's Shepperton at Kingston-upon-Thames, and although spending the best part of 40 years away, returned in 1894 to live out the last decade of his life in the town. The Kingston Museum devotes a room (the Eadweard Muybridge Gallery) to the work of its most famous son (although as Solnit has pointed out his birthplace is now a computer store – 'A shell stuffed with California' (2003: 253)) and his archives are also housed in the town. Strange then that Ballard and Muybridge should find one another in this suburbia at London's south-west perimeter: airports in one direction, film studios the other, encircled by the great ring of the M25, a colossal Muybridge Zoopraxiscope disguised as a motorway.

Ballard's additions to the text, written for the 1990 Re/Search edition of the novel and printed at the end of each chapter, pass comment on the more uncanny aspects of the work, its strange historical anticipations of the Reagan era, and function rather akin to a DVD commentary *avant-la-lettre* (something Ballard has provided for Jonathan Weiss's adaptation of the book), adding a further authorial paratext to a text already buckling under the weight of its own allusive power. For example, glossing one of the book's most notorious chapters, Ballard remarks on his perspicacity:

> 'Why I Want to Fuck Ronald Reagan' prompted Doubleday in 1970 to pulp its first American edition of *The Atrocity Exhibition*. Ronald Reagan's presidency remained a complete mystery to most Europeans, though I noticed that Americans took him in their stride. But the amiable old duffer who occupied the White House was a very different person from the sinister figure I described in 1967, when the present piece was first published. The then-novelty of a Hollywood film star entering politics and becoming governor of California gave Reagan considerable air-time on British TV. Watching his right-wing speeches, in which he castigated in sneering tones the profligate, welfare-spending, bureaucrat-infested state government, I saw a more crude and ambitious figure, far closer to the brutal crime boss he played in the 1964 movie *The Killers*, his last Hollywood role. (Ballard 1993: 168)

This additional textual ambiguity, with the commentary further destabilizing any coherence of narrative voice, could be seen as possessing something of the anecdotal quality identified by Deleuze in his bal(l)adic cinema: the laconic voice-over of a film like *Jules et Jim* (François Truffaut, 1962, France) which both undermines and memorializes the melodrama of the on-screen action is rediscovered in Ballard's marginalia, at once melancholy reminiscences and cheerful asides noting the prescience of his vision.

Weiss's adaptation of the book succeeds in transposing the novel's key scenes as much as it fails in an attempt to impose some degree of narrative coherence on the material. Beginning with a voice-over that establishes the film as 'made' by Dr Travis ('The following film was created by Dr Travis of our institution. He referred to it as The Atrocity Exhibition. It is the only trace remaining from his tenure with us. His present whereabouts are unknown and there is some doubt as to whether he is even still alive. The film constitutes a remarkable document of his mental breakdown' (Weiss 2001)), it captures the tone of the book most effectively in its use of found footage, shards of images from pornographic films and science experiments. These sequences are intercut with a retelling of Travis's mental collapse, where the stilted dialogue, although authentically Ballardian, frequently teeters on the edge of absurdity. The shifting allusiveness of Ballard's text never really finds a cinematic equivalent in Weiss's film: aiming for something akin to the decadent *froideur* of *Last Year at Marienbad* (1961), Alain Resnais and Alain Robbe-Grillet's infamous attempt to transpose the *nouveau roman* into cinema, Weiss instead ends up closer to sci-fi B-Movie pastiche.[2]

Ballard himself, however, has welcomed the film, claiming, in two faxes sent to the director and reprinted in miniscule reproduction as part of a DVD sleeve-note, that the film transforms his vision into filmic form more accurately than any other adaptation:

> It's a remarkable piece of work, clearly a great labour of love, and a unique kind of cinema in its allusiveness, poetic imagination and a vast repertory of powerful effects that are freely available to film today, but rejected in favour of the star-driven vehicles that monopolise the highways of the film-going mind. [. . .] How imaginatively, with what I assume were limited resources, did you flesh out the images cited in the book – Duchamp, the periodic table, X-rays, geometric models and so on. (Weiss 2005)

And herein lies the key to *The Atrocity Exhibition*'s paradoxical cinematic frigidity: a novel that seems to draw on the very bedrock of filmic innovation for its structure becomes a curiously inert cinematic experience, its attempt to draw out from the book a study in sexual obsession is undermined by an absolute lack of psychological depth. Some sequences do, however, capture the cyclic quality of the book's singular vision. For instance, the sequence in which the figure of Travis runs in a lengthy parabola away from a parked car, only to return once more to his starting point, and vomit over the car's bonnet, plays as if one of Muybridge's athletes had suddenly turned psychotic in recognition of the absurdity of his plight. The film's opening moments, a succession of near-abstract black and white photographs of Dr Travis, pay evident homage to Chris Marker's *La Jetée* (1962) (a parable of time travel told solely in still images and voice-over and given an enthusiastic review by Ballard in *New Worlds* in 1966 (Vale and Juno ,1984: 101)), also convey something of the novel's uncanny power. Yet the inability of the film to find a successful analogue of 'The T-Cell's' shifting identity means that as a total experience it feels, for one familiar with the book, like an attempt to 'illustrate' the text rather than fashion a work with its own internal coherence. However, the film's intrinsic difficulties also point to the sense that the book's engagement with cinema rests more in an *idea* of cinema as potential form, of cinema as a model of thought, rather than in the fully realized film. As Weiss himself has commented of his adaptation, 'Perhaps it isn't even a film, really, but then I don't know what else to call it' (Weiss 2005).

Indeed, it is possible to suggest that it is through the work of a painter, rather than a filmmaker, that one can begin to develop a more complex sense of Ballard's proto-cinematic engagement. As Marey commented on the work of his co-conspirator in unlocking the secrets of motion: 'So far as artists are concerned it would create a revolution for them, since one could furnish them with true attitudes of movement; positions of the body during unstable balances in which a model would find it impossible to pose' (quoted in Solnit 2003: 200). Marey could hardly have predicted (given the shock felt by the academic painter Messonier whose own equine studies were undermined by Muybridge's work (Solnit 2003: 197)) that the artist whose work would draw most heavily on Muybridge would be Francis Bacon. Significantly, Bacon's work is also a reference point for *The Atrocity Exhibition*:

> In part a confusion of mathematical models was responsible, Dr Nathan decided. Sitting behind his desk in the darkened laboratory, he drew slowly on the gold-tipped cigarette, watching the shadowy figure of a man seated opposite him, his back to the watery light from the aquarium tanks. At times part of his head seemed to be missing, like some disintegrating executive from a Francis Bacon nightmare. (Ballard 1993: 134)

This reference appears to be to a series of paintings Bacon worked on in 1953 called *Three Studies of the Human Head*, depicting a be-suited figure undergoing various unidentifiable but clearly violent actions. The sickly pallor of the man's flesh blurs with the depthless streaked background as unseen forces pull and tear at him. It is not clear how we read this series: as the slow progression of an unfolding incident, three views of the same subject, or three separate but similar individuals undergoing equivalent tortures. Nevertheless, in conversation with David Sylvester in 1962, Bacon has been explicit about the influence of Muybridge on his work (Sylvester 1987: 32), suggesting that his work has served a dual function in influencing his painting. On a more prosaic level, it provided him with source images for his characteristically transmogrified bodies: Martin Harrison notes that Bacon first consulted Muybridge's *Animal Locomotion* at the Victoria and Albert museum in the late 1940s in the build-up to his first one-man show in 1949–50 (Harrison 2005: 97).

As with Ballard's collecting of the wastepaper accrued by his friend Christopher Evans, a computer scientist at the National Physical Laboratory, from which he was able to fashion the characteristic prose-style of *The Atrocity Exhibition* (Vale and Juno 1984: 9), Bacon's co-option of the scientific element in Muybridge allows him to devise a new vocabulary of figurative art that reconnects the representation of the body to a mode of scientific enquiry stretching back to Leonardo. Bacon's use of these photographic studies often takes successive images and transforms them into a single figure; effectively rediscovering stasis out of movement. In his *After Muybridge: Woman Emptying a Bowl of Water and Paralytic Child on All Fours* (1965), he takes two of Muybridge's most famous sequences and combines them in a single painting, the two figures placed on a large circular armature that recalls both a theatrical backdrop and the circular slides of the Zoopraxiscope.

Gilles Deleuze conducted a book-length study of Bacon's art, entitled *The Logic of Sensation*, in which he explores his painting through a complex series of interactions with the history of Western art, describing Bacon as attempting to rescue the figurative from figuration; to find, post-abstraction, new modes of representation. Bacon freezes movement into attitude and gesture, or as Deleuze describes it, the effect of movement on the immobile body: 'heads whipped by the wind or deformed by an aspiration, but also all the interior forces that climb through the flesh' (Deleuze 2003: xi). Deleuze perceives Muybridge's influence on Bacon as playing a significant role in his reworking of the figurative tradition in art at a time when progressive artists were abandoning it for abstraction:

> The most significant thing about the photograph is that it forces upon us the 'truth' of implausible and doctored images. Bacon has no intention of reacting against this movement; on the contrary, he abandons himself to it, and not without delight. (Deleuze 2003: 91).

In Deleuze's description of Bacon's attitude, one can hear an echo of Dr Nathan's account of Travis's manipulations of photography: 'The familiar surrounds of our lives, even our smallest gestures, were seen to have totally altered meanings.' (Ballard 1993: 6). Bacon has also suggested that the influence of Muybridge extended to his development of the triptych or series as a form capable of questioning the interrelations between canvases, so that each work is seen as a unit in a larger project (Sylvester 1987: 31). Hence, perhaps, his insistence on conditional titles such as 'studies towards' that seem to prevent the work ever being seen as fully realized. Again, the section headings in *The Atrocity Exhibition* with titles like 'Notes Towards a Mental Breakdown' and 'The Yes or No of the Borderzone' serve a similar aim of undermining any sense of fixity or completion in the novel.

In his discussion with Bacon, Sylvester characterizes his work as falling into three distinct periods: the first contains a clear distinction between the figure and field of colour behind it; the second, and most significant for the development of the painter, he describes as *malerisch*, with the third synthesizing these two tendencies (Sylvester 1987: 118–20). This term comes from the art historian Heinrich Wölfflin, and refers to the way in which painted forms merge and blend with one another; clear lines and distinctions are overturned in favour of a fluidity of light and shade. Sometimes translated as 'painterly', *malerisch* is more to do with the blurring of the distinction between figure and ground (Murray and Murray 1997: 315), and in Bacon's case further unsettles the relationship between his biomorphic forms and the paint out of which they are shaped. Deleuze builds on the sense of the *malerisch* in Bacon to describe how his work is evocative of this desire to pull figuration out of the canvas. It becomes part of Deleuze's sense of Bacon as a painter of 'sensation'; of attempting to discover how flesh is both shaped and distorted by paint, as if the practice of painting is part of seeing the flesh and coming to some new understanding of it.

One could, therefore, claim that another significant visual source for Bacon is effectively a *malerisch* form of the work of Muybridge: namely the Zapruder footage taken of the J. F. K. assassination which became a crucial primary source for The Warren Commission report. As Margarita Cappock has noted, Bacon's use of a red arrow as a key motif in his paintings dates from the use of just such a device in the analysis of the 8 mm footage (Cappock 2005: 101). Equally then, the obsessive focus on the J. F. K. assassination, and the Zapruder footage in particular, in *The Atrocity Exhibition* can be said to be enacting Dr Nathan's description of Travis's attempt to remove the element of time from his photographic studies. The obsessive slowing down of movement, of bullet into Presidential brain, seems as much an attempt to undo the assassination, as it is to comprehend it.

Crash

Developing this idea, I would suggest that of the Ballardian triptych I am exploring, the second panel, *Crash*, represents a *malerisch* reworking of the clear lines of *The Atrocity Exhibition*. If in the first book, the distinction between chapters and sections is clearly, almost pedantically, delineated, *Crash* blurs its chapters into one another like the coupled cars of an auto-accident. Read consecutively, *Crash* emerges out of its predecessor, elaborating on and developing ideas contained in miniature in its precursor. Indeed, the central figure of Vaughan in *Crash* is quite clearly a development of Travis (his preoccupations with the discourses of medicine and sex are fused into the persona of this so-called 'T.V. Scientist' who spends his time obsessively documenting car crashes and following their victims). One could suggest that in contrast to the shifting names of *The Atrocity Exhibition*'s central character, another *malerisch* element in *Crash* is found in Ballard's decision to give the narrator his own name; a blending of figure and ground every bit as unsettling as a Bacon portrait. This narrator, a director of television commercials, is drawn inexorably into Vaughan's orbit following a head-on car crash in which the driver of the other car is killed and his wife, Dr Helen Remington, injured. After his own recovery, Ballard and Remington become lovers, and as with the previous novel, the boundaries between doctor and patient, subject and object, become increasingly confused.

Furthermore, if *The Atrocity Exhibition* draws on the prehistory of cinema, *Crash* fuses the ontological basis of film with its populist manifestation in Hollywood, at times revelling in its mythology and history, yet this is really the antithesis of the Hollywood Novel – we are a very long way from Southern California. Instead, Hollywood, embodied in the figure of Elizabeth Taylor, has journeyed to the south-west fringes of London, to Ballard's home turf to shoot, not a film, but a commercial. It is in this environment that Taylor becomes the fixation of the psychotic Vaughan who wishes to stage an auto-accident in which their deaths will effect a uniting of those twin emblems of the twentieth century, the automobile and the cinema.

David Cronenberg's adaptation of the novel, infamous at the time of its release and vilified in the British press for its supposed 'depravity', has in the years following its release, come in for some stringent criticism of precisely the opposite persuasion, notably from Iain Sinclair in a book ostensibly devoted to the film, but which becomes detoured into a Ballardian reverie. Sinclair's main animus against the film springs from a perceived timidity in comparison with the novel, arguing that Cronenberg's film tames the unruly quality of Ballard's work into something more closely resembling commercial pornography, stripping it of the subversive charge that made the original such a disturbing work: '[Ballard's] prose is urgent, swarming with a maggoty life that runs counter to the cryogenic elegance of Cronenberg's translation' (Sinclair 1999: 43). Unlike the incoherence into which Weiss's *Atrocity Exhibition* falls, Cronenberg's *Crash* is, surprisingly given its scandalous reputation, too well mannered to convey the novel's radical charge. For Sinclair, it is significant that Taylor is entirely excised: her presence in the novel being replaced by a re-staging of the death of Jayne Mansfield, a knowing parody of Marilyn Monroe who aspired to the brunette-hued tragedy of Elizabeth Taylor and Jackie Kennedy (1999: 114). The characteristic chilliness of Cronenberg's aesthetic would, of course, seem to be a good fit for Ballard's prose: Linda S. Kauffman has asked, rhetorically: 'Were David Cronenberg and J. G. Ballard separated at birth?' (Kauffman 1998: 149). However, his film now seems strangely anaemic: the fashions and the cars are a decade out of date, and its premillennial anxieties, embodied in repeated shots of depopulated Toronto freeways (replacing Ballard's London hinterland), evokes an essentially 1990s vision of the twenty-first century: we notice James Spader's blow-dried coiffure more than the potency of the film's ideas. Here again lies one of the paradoxes of cinema: it has provided Ballard with a model of new modes of thinking and narrative possibilities, yet the actual images of cinema are so suffused with an essentially documentary power that to attempt to purify them into purely abstract ideas is a project almost inevitably doomed to failure. It is this excessive quality of film, something reined in by directors under the aegis of 'a personal style', that seems, ultimately, to upset any attempt to create a cinema of pure affect. Furthermore, one could suggest that Cronenberg succeeded in making far more Ballardian films in *Videodrome* (1982) and his remake of the *The Fly* (1986) a decade earlier. In their grotesque images of James Woods' gut fusing with the mechanics of a VCR (surely embodying Vaughan's 'TV Scientist' more effectively than Elias Koteas' essaying of the character in *Crash*), or of the inverted Baboon (the unfortunate result of one of Jeff Goldblum's scientist's early experiments in teleportation), one sees the potential of a truly *malerisch* cinema. Cronenberg's *Crash* captures something of this quality only in the ultimate encounter between Ballard and Vaughan, their act of copulation less a sex scene in any conventional sense so much as a fusing of identities. In the novel's descriptions of Vaughan, defined by his proximity to blood and semen, he somehow echoes one of Bacon's figure studies where the body is only barely capable of containing the fluids pulsing beneath the surface of the flesh:

> Vaughan loosened his leather jacket, exposing the re-opened wounds that marked his chest and abdomen, a deranged drag queen revealing the leaking scars of an unsuccessful trans-sexual surgery [. . .] I moved my mouth down his abdomen to his damp groin, marked with blood and semen, a faint odour of woman's excrement clinging to the shaft of his penis. (Ballard 1995: 166)

Cronenberg's adaptation stages this encounter in the back of Vaughan's Lincoln, capturing the seamy quality of Ballard's prose in a series of dimly lit images, blurring the bodies of the two actors together (Cronenberg 1996). At such moments, Cronenberg's film feels at its most Baconian as well; the space of the car transformed into something akin to his depthless voids, the figures suspended in a miasma of paint.

Empire of the Sun

Shifting focus once more, the triptych is completed with the addition of the final panel. In many ways *Empire of the Sun* is clearly anomalous within Ballard's oeuvre; his most obviously accessible work, it gave him a wide readership for the first time. And yet, it shows a further development in Ballard's engagement with cinema. The book opens in

Shanghai in the lead up to Pearl Harbor, where the young protagonist, Jim (another of Ballard's fictive identities), is surrounded by images of the already two-year-old European war; a war being waged by a country of which he is a citizen but has never seen:

> Jim had begun to dream of wars. At night the same silent films seemed to flicker against the wall of his bedroom in Amherst Avenue, and transformed his sleeping mind into a deserted newsreel theatre. During the winter of 1941 everyone in Shanghai was showing war films. Fragments of his dreams followed Jim around the city; in the foyers of department stores and hotels the images of Dunkirk and Tobruk, Barbarossa and the Rape of Nanking sprang loose from his crowded head. (Ballard 1985: 11)

Ballard's suggestion that it took 40 years for him to process the events of his childhood before he could write *Empire of the Sun* (Ballard 1996: 271) hints, of course, at the difficulty of re-assimilating history into fiction – a tension which Ballard goes on to explore in the fictionalized account of Spielberg's adaptation of *Empire* in *The Kindness of Women* (Ballard 1992: 331–48). In situating its young protagonist within the context of events whose magnitude he can scarcely begin to grasp, *Empire* demonstrates the necessity of a vantage point far outside the individual in order to convey the sheer weight of what is taking place. That newsreels figure so prominently in the book's opening moments is evocative of this desire to present a documentary past around which the novelist's art can be spun:

> The *March of Time* films were more sombre, in a way that appealed to Jim. Suffocating in a tight cassock, he watched a burning Hurricane fall from a sky of Dornier bombers towards a children's book landscape he had never known. (Ballard 1985: 12)

In this respect, if *The Atrocity Exhibition* is about Cinema's essential mechanics, its ability to render movement and capture time, and *Crash* fuses these ideas with a parable of malignant celebrity, *Empire* unites cinema and history, exploring the failure of film to capture the lived experience of historical events. The newsreels from the European war that Jim watches are intended to serve as a rallying call for ex-pats, but they evoke, instead, the history of an unknown world whose fate seems sealed even before Pearl Harbor. Throughout the novel, images drawn from the world of film recur, from the abandoned open-air cinema where Jim is temporarily detained on his way to the Lunghua camp (Ballard 1985: 108); to the invisible newsreels watched on empty walls by prisoners driven mad by the privations of life in the camps:

> She stared at the whitewashed wall above her son's bunk, as if watching an invisible film projected on to a screen. Jim worried that Mrs Vincent spent too much time watching these films. As he peered through the cracks in his

cubicle he tried to guess what she saw – a home-made cine film, perhaps, of herself in England before she was married, sitting on one of those sunlit lawns that seemed to cover the entire country. (Ballard 1985: 173)

This cinematic consciousness extends from Ballard's book to Spielberg's film, where the silvery glow of the atom bomb witnessed by Jim at the abandoned Olympic Stadium is rendered by the same shimmering light as if it were flickering from a colossal movie projector (Spielberg 1987). It is as if, in this one moment, Spielberg suggests that the history of the twentieth century is predicated on its transformation into images and light. Spielberg's movie necessarily refigures the curious intimacy of the book into a far more epic cinematic register; the young Jim, though presented with a recognizably Ballardian lack of sentimentality, seems a far more innocent figure in the streets of Shanghai and the dusty expanse of the internment camp (Spielberg 1987). In the novel, his feral existence carries the uncomfortable sense that civilization can only ever veneer the true brutality of life; something replaced in the film with a far more Boys-Own account of life at Lunghua – an exciting lacuna to an otherwise comfortable life. What Spielberg's film cannot convey is the failure of cinema to capture the shift in consciousness brought about by the war, and of the new world formed in atrocities of which the newsreels could offer only the most tendentious of approximations.

This sense of cinema as undergoing an ontological shift through the experience of the war has been characterized by Deleuze as marking the emergence of the 'time image'. Cinema, which for its first half-century had been defined by its Muybridgean capacity to present movement, would now fold in on itself and take as its new subject its capacity to render its own temporality (Deleuze 1992: 211). He also describes new geographies that were opened up in the aftermath of the war, and described them as being 'any-spaces-whatever' (1992: 212): shifting locations that were initially produced out of the postwar rubble. Ballard has commented of Shepperton that he doesn't really live there, that 'it's just a sort of grid reference on the map' (Vale and Juno 1984: 14). In this one sees the continued perpetuation of the postwar geography that he first describes as emerging at the end of the war at the camp at Lunghua. Indeed, the geographies of all three works in this triptych are paradigmatically 'any-spaces-whatever': from the clinic and its scorched environs in *The Atrocity Exhibition* to the ring roads and airports of *Crash*, these are all quintessential postwar geographies.

These three works then are drawn together by the spirit of cinema, yet remain as separate entities, much like the triptychs of Bacon that capture the minute shifts of light and shadow that play across the surface of a figure as it turns to and from the light; three works that, in their different ways, are evocative of how cinema has existed in the blind field – that point in the peripheral vision where an object appears to materialize and dematerialize – of Ballard's fiction. This fiction has created a world that, despite an evident debt to cinema, has proven curiously resistant to its own transformation into images. Both Francis Bacon and Jean-Luc Godard have drawn on Jean Cocteau's remark that we witness 'death at work' (Sylvester, 1987: 135/Godard, 1986: 181) in both film and the mirror in front of our faces: in Ballard's refiguring of a cinematic mode of experience we find a writer whose very project seems to be to scrutinize that image with a long, hard stare.

Notes

1. In an interview with Linda Kauffman, Ballard responds to her question as to whether he has read any French theorists with the following statement: 'No, I'm sorry to say. The only French thinker I've read at all is Baudrillard. But only some of him. Some of it is totally impenetrable. He wrote complimentary things about *Crash*, but, having written my own novel, I *still* couldn't understand him!' (Kauffman 1998 : 192).
2. In a lengthy, and occasionally fractious, interview with Simon Sellars of the *Ballardian* website, Weiss explains his intentions in making the film, and goes some way to defend his approach to Ballard's novel:

    > Normally, a script is extremely important, as a film is about characters and you understand them through dialogue and action. *The Atrocity Exhibition* is very different. It is about places, space – meaning architectural space – time, events, unusual forms of consciousness, et cetera. There is no narrative. A non-narrative film . . . People are so thoroughly conditioned in narrative, they will project it ANYWHERE they can. Everyone who watches *The Atrocity Exhibition* will construct a narrative of their own, and I have never heard two that were identical. Some viewers become quickly frustrated by the lack of narrative and think of it as a personal affront, an insult to their intelligence. Since they do not 'get it' because they are looking for 'it' in the wrong place, they become upset and dismiss the film. But others, who just let it flow over them, have reported experiences usually found during serious drug episodes, extended periods in isolation tanks or other attempts to get beyond the purview of quotidian consciousness.' (http://www.ballardian.com/weiss-interview)

CHAPTER FIVE

Mind is the Battlefield: Reading Ballard's 'Life Trilogy' as War Literature

UMBERTO ROSSI

Chapter Summary: Reading *Empire of the Sun* (1984), *The Kindness of Women* (1991) and *Miracles of Life* (2008) as a 'Life Trilogy', this chapter explores Ballard's literary renderings of his own life. Rossi traces the interpenetration of factual and fictional histories across the three texts and considers their intertextual nature within the specific context of war literature.

Key Words: *Empire of the Sun; The Kindness of Women; Miracles of Life;* life-writing; autobiography; fiction; autofiction; Second World War; Shanghai; Shepperton; war literature; memory; trauma; testimony.

J. G. Ballard's life-writings have acquired something of a reputation for echoing each other in ways which are far from straightforward.[1] His latest publication, *Miracles of Life: Shanghai to Shepperton*, is no exception. Take the following authorial assertion:

> In many ways my entire fiction is the dissection of a deep pathology that I had witnessed in Shanghai and later in the post-war world, from the threat of nuclear war to the assassination of President Kennedy, from the death of my wife to the violence that underpinned the entertainment culture of the last decades of the century. (Ballard 2008: 145)

While this quotation identifies, on the one hand, the centrality of violence to Ballard's postwar literary project, it also recalls a significant passage from the *Kindness of Women* (1991), an earlier exercise in life-writing in which the narrator and protagonist, a fictional 'James Ballard', is confronted once more with the nightmares of twentieth-century history:

> After three days to cross a country and a sea, we returned to Shepperton. The long French roads helped me to straighten the perspectives of my mind. The past, on which I had turned my back on the day of my marriage, had rushed up and now stood behind me. Miriam's death joined me once again to all those nameless Chinese who had died during the Second World War. I remembered the dusty dead beside the crushed motor-cars in the Avenue Edward II, and the straining jaw of the Chinese clerk at the rural railway station, first rehearsals for an afternoon at Figueras. Images of the bone-white paddy fields came back to me, like the pearly light that lay over Lunghua after the explosion of the atom bomb in Nagasaki. Kennedy had outstared Khrushchev during the Cuban missile crisis, but American bombers were still parked under the flat skies of Cambridgeshire, and the kingdom of light waited to be born from those concrete aprons among the fens. (Ballard 1992: 164)

Even though this passage reads like the kind of surrealist list of random juxtapositions which one might find in *The Atrocity Exhibition*, it is actually a synopsis (of sorts) of the first half of *Kindness*, a series of key – and not at all random – events in the protagonist's life which are all intimately connected to narratives of historical atrocity, war and death. In this moment of clarity, 'James Ballard' recognizes that his life is strewn with episodes of collective death and destruction, be they the physical and psychological realities of the Second World War and the death of his wife, or the impending imaginary threats of the Cuban missile crisis and the nuclear Armageddon.

Although the more recent critical tendency has been to warn against reading *Empire* and *Kindness* as semi-autobiographical texts which not only 'decode the bizarre and perverse aberrations that had gone before' (Roger Luckhurst 1997: 155) but also claim a transparent and coherent identity 'between J. G. Ballard and the Jamie/Jim figure in the texts' (Luckhurst 1997: 158), the author of *Miracles*, it would appear, is encouraging such a reading by inserting a revised version of a key passage from *Kindness* into the latest literary rendering of his life. The suggestion is that the moment of realization experienced by the fictional James Ballard after the death of his wife also applies, in some way, to the author. Like the author figure of *Kindness*, whose mind is violated and stimulated by the violence of war so as to make him want to reproduce it imaginatively over and over again, J. G. Ballard's exposure to the heinous physical and psychological realities of the Second World War left such deep traces in his mind so as to inform everything he has written since the publication of his first short story, 'Prima Belladonna', in 1956.[2] The suggestion remains that J. G. Ballard's mind – and the minds of his fictional altar-egos – is a battlefield, a complex psychological

landscape of violent images, memories and histories, some of which are
real and some of which are fictional.

Having said this, however, it would be both naïve and reductive to
think that *Miracles* offers a definitive version of J. G. Ballard's life. While
the book casts light on, or one might say even *de-fictionalizes*, some
aspects of the author's life (such as the death of his wife, Mary, who
died from pneumonia while holidaying in Spain), *Miracles* conspicuously ignores other aspects of the author's private and public lives.
Ballard's son, Jim, for instance, is largely absent from the text and he
does not, unlike his sisters, feature visually in a portrait photograph.
Also, with the exception of Ted Carnell, the editor of *New Worlds* from
1949–63, Ballard, the so-called 'Voice' of the New Wave movement,
rather surprisingly makes no individual mention of fellow New Wave
writers Brian Aldiss, John Brunner and Pamela Zoline. At the same
time that *Miracles* does not attempt to fill in all of the gaps in Ballard's
personal and working lives (a move which most readers of an autobiography might expect), neither does it contain a checklist which can be
used to explain away key Ballardian obsessions or repeating motifs such
as drowned cities, crashed cars and dead astronauts, a move for which
some readers must surely have hoped.

Such a traditionally 'realist' approach to reading *Miracles* would lead
us to miss the point of Ballard's latest exercise in life-writing, a point
that is hinted at by its subtitle: 'Shanghai to Shepperton'. This phrase
not only connects two real physical places *and* two imaginary spaces in
a number of complex ways; but it also, metonymically, brings two
worlds, China and Britain, and two ages, pre- and post-Second World
War, into a dialogue with one another. In this chapter, my approach to
reading Ballard's life-writings is to map and explore this *interpenetration*
of fictional and factual histories. Shanghai may well be seen as a projection of Ballard's obsessions – the 'wickedest city in the world' (Ballard
2008: 5) is revealed as a hotbed of violence, sex and glamour – but, at the
same time, the young J. G. Ballard is also possessed by the mythology of
Shanghai, the 'bright but bloody kaleidoscope' which was infinitely
produced, circulated and transformed by the media during his childhood (Ballard 2008: 3–8). This 'mediatization' of reality also extends to
historical violence and, specifically, the endless fictionalization of the
'European War' which Ballard witnessed as a boy in the form of a 'news-
reel war' which 'soon became the dominant weapon [. . .] many of them
screened at night against the side of buildings, watched by huge crowds
of passing pedestrians' (Ballard 2008: 38).

In contrast to the 'real' conflict of the Second Sino-Japanese War
which raged in China from 1937 to 1945 and which the young Ballard
witnessed at firsthand (Chapter 2 of *Miracles*, 'Japanese Invasion', tells
how the Ballard family was forced to vacate their home in the International Settlement due to the 'artillery shells from the rival Chinese and
Japanese batteries [. . .] passing over [their] roof' (Ballard 2008: 26)), the

War in Europe remained an imaginary war, a thrilling spectacle 'taking place on the silver square above my head' (Ballard 2008: 38). Although the young voyeur is protected, in one sense, from the *physical* dangers of the European War, the *psychological* pressure of having to 'find the real in all this make-believe' (Ballard 2008: 38) and thus differentiate the actual from the ideological is revealed to be a constant battle.

Notably, the challenge of differentiating real memories from mediated images is reworked fictionally in another key passage in *Kindness*:

> Within a few days [. . .] my memories of the bombing had begun to fade. I tried to remember the dust and debris in the Szechuan Road, but the confused images in my head merged with the newsreels I had seen on the Spanish civil war and the filmed manoeuvres of the French and British armies. (Ballard 1992: 27)

If Ballard's mind is a battlefield, it is a multi-layered battlefield, a palimpsest of numerous and various narratives of historical violence, ranging from World War I to the Cold War. This is, in part, what marks Ballard's life-writings out as particularly interesting examples of war literature. Analyses of the relationship between literature and war tend to focus on a single conflict (usually the First World War, Vietnam or the Second World War) and on a single national literature. Examples of such monothematic and monolingual studies include Mario Isenghi's *Il mito della grande Guerra* (1970) (The Great War Myth) and Paul Fussell's *The Great War and Modern Memory* (1975). Ballard's war narratives, in contrast, are heterogeneous in their scope. To extend Luckhurst's reading, it *is* a 'mistake to view *Empire* as a novel about World War II' (1997: 161) because *Empire*, *Kindness* and *Miracles* are all to varying degrees about *several* wars. War literature studies is currently moving towards a comparative, transnational approach, as exemplified by A. D. Harvey's essay *A Muse of Fire* (1998), and Ballard's trio of war-related books, with their focus on issues of intercultural relations (four civilizations clash in *Empire*: the Chinese, the Japanese, the British and the USA) provides an interesting case study for this kind of approach.

Reading *Empire*, *Kindness* and *Miracles* within the framework of war literature may also help us to refine the generic status of these complex books (see Rossi 2007: 155–77). One of the most important issues in war literature is negotiating the complex dialectic between fictional creativity and factual testimony. War narratives are often difficult to place on either side of the fiction/autobiography boundary. But this is an issue that may be better understood by taking into account ongoing critical discussions of autobiographical discourse. According to Sidonie Smith and Melanie Watson, for instance, the traditional generic marker of 'autobiography' (realist, monologic) can be usefully replaced with 'life narrative', a term which suggests that any claims to autobiographical truth are fallacious because 'the referential "real" assumed to be "outside" a text cannot be written; the subject is inescapably an unstable fiction; and the autobiography-fiction boundary remains illusory' (Smith and Watson 2001: 186). The interpenetration of fact and fiction in *Empire* and *Kindness* is something on which Ballard has commented in interviews and essays. *Kindness*, he once said, 'is my life seen through the mirror of the fiction prompted by that life. It is not just an autobiographical novel; it is an autobiographical novel written with the full awareness of the fiction that that adult life generated' (Ballard cited in Self 1995: 360).

According to Smith and Watson, there are over 50 different genres of life narrative, and while each genre differs according to the specific textual features and narrative techniques in play (see Smith and Watson 2001: 183–208), no genre of life narrative is necessarily attributed a greater or smaller 'truth value' (Smith and Watson 2001: 12–13). Based on this theoretical framework, I would like to read Ballard's life-writings as moving laterally across three different life narrative genres namely, *Empire* as a novel based on real-life events; *Kindness* as an 'autofiction', that is a 'fictional narrative in the first-person mode' where the author conflates real and fictional elements (Smith and Watson 2001: 186); and *Miracles* as an autobiographical life narrative. Clearly *Miracles* is not an autobiography in any traditional sense: its slim size and selective perspective means that this is yet another *partial* version of Ballard's life. Furthermore, its frequent intertextual nods to Ballard's previous life narratives characterize *Miracles* as a kind of 'auto-biographia literaria'; that is, a literary autobiography which mixes life narrative and metafictional commentary. What is more important to grasp at this stage, therefore, is that Ballard life narratives, which I would like to style a 'Life Trilogy', are not viewed as discrete elements in a series, but as a 'set of ever-shifting self-referential practices that engage the past in order to reflect on identity in the present' (Smith and Watson 2001: 3).

It is interesting to note that, with the publication of *Empire*, *Kindess* and *Miracles*, Ballard's life narratives move from an overtly fictionalized telling of his war experience to an ostensibly more factual, albeit partial, version of events. The first work, *Empire* (which focuses on the historical period from December 1941 to Autumn 1945) boasts a very strong fictional component as real historical events and supposed autobiographical details are refracted through a series of imagined episodes (such as Jim's claim to have witnessed the atomic light from the bombs at Nagasaki and Hiroshima). As Ballard maintains in *Miracles*: 'I have given a general picture of Lunghua Camp in my novel *Empire of the Sun*, which is partly autobiographical and partly fictional, though many incidents are described as they occurred' (Ballard 2008: 81–2). Most notably, *Empire* employs a range of what Andrzej Gasiorek terms 'distancing' narrative techniques (2005: 145), which include a self-conscious prefatory statement in which the author, J. G. Ballard, foregrounds the fictional nature of his war narrative (the above quotation from *Miracles* echoes this prefatory comment); the use of multiple, and often competing, narrative points of view (including an 'unnamed' and 'anonymous narrator who occasionally gives information that Jim would not have known at the time' (Gasiorek 2005: 144)) and the use of third-person narration. This latter, overt narrative manoeuvre, helps to create a distance between the author J. G. Ballard and the 'Jim/Jamie' figure of the text since the latter is locked into his role as the main character in a war novel.

Gasiorek has also noted that *Kindness* offers another 'perspective on the events of the war, mainly by focussing on its consequences for the adult protagonist's life in the post-war period' (2005: 148). He continues:

> Switching from a third-person narration, it ostensibly provides a more 'personal' and therefore more 'truthful' account than that vouchsafed by *Empire* [. . .] but the later text is no less artfully constructed, and its reflections on the experiences of a character called 'James Ballard' are neither straightforwardly autobiographical nor unproblematically veridical. (2005: 149)

Gasiorek is quite correct to offer such a cautious reading of *Kindness*. Although the author figure/protagonist 'James Ballard' is arguably closer to the figure of J. G. Ballard these fictional and real identities do not map consistently or coherently on to one another. The prevalence of dialogue also clearly bespeaks a substantial element of fictional elaboration. Having said this, however, the relative distance between *Kindness* and *Miracles* is arguably reduced. In contrast to *Empire*, *Kindness* covers a much longer period than the 1984 novel, beginning with the outbreak of the Second Sino-Japanese War in 1937 and ending in 1987. Furthermore, it presents a series of vignettes which read like a distorted chronology of J. G. Ballard's life: medical studies at King's College, Cambridge; RAF training at the Moose Jaw NATO air force base in Canada; the death of his wife, Mary (re-imagined as 'Miriam') in 1963; and an imagined account of Steven Spielberg's adaptation of *Empire* which not only takes the fictionalized Ballard back to the Second World War years in a move of dreamlike return but which also echoes Ballard's televised return to the Chinese metropolis in 1991 (Ballard 2008: 265–76). Thus the war and its horrors continue to cast their shadows on Ballard's postwar life: everything begins in Shanghai and returns to the 'terrible city' via the 'virtual reality' projected by Spielberg's film.

In contrast to *Empire* and *Kindness*, *Miracles* boasts a form and structure which is much closer to autobiographical writing. It is especially interesting to note how Ballard has inserted photographs – self-portraits, portraits of family members, images of significant buildings (31 Amherst Avenue; the former F Block Lunghua Camp) – into his text, as if he wanted to offer readers documentary evidence which would support and strengthen this particular version of events. Another conspicuous and significant feature of this book is that Ballard's parents,

James and Edna, are finally delineated and discussed in ways which the former life narratives deny (the Jim/Jamie figures of *Empire* and *Kindness* are famously orphans of war, only to be reunited with family members in peacetime). This gradual shift from a distancing novelistic narrative to an arguably more naked form of life narrative may be interpreted as a movement from a protective, virtual rendering of war to a more faithful statement of how the author really experienced the Second World War and its aftermath. While *Empire* is dominated by the unbridled and often naïve imagination of a boy whose mind is filled with media images and who 'watched a burning Hurricane fall from the sky of Dornier bombers towards a children's book landscape of English meadows he had never known' (Ballard 1984: 12), *Miracles* is engaged, in a process of de-fictionalization as it begins to unearth and exhibit Ballard's most personal experiences, such as his 'gradual estrangement from [his] parents, which [. . .] began in Lunghua Camp' (Ballard 2008: 82).

In *Miracles*, Ballard explains his protracted silence on his Shanghai years in two different, yet related ways. First, he reveals how he 'never talked about [his] life in Shanghai or internment in Lunghua even to [his] closest friends. Too much had happened even for a race of novelists to digest' (Ballard 2008: 130). The first problem appears to be one of comprehension: how can the novelist even begin to understand let alone articulate in some coherent and meaningful way the chaotic and destructive nature of war? As Ballard points out: 'too much had happened to me, and to the boys sitting at the desks around me, in the wartime years' (Ballard 2008: 129). 'Continuous upheavals', he writes, 'had unsettled family life: fathers were away in the Middle East or in the Pacific, mothers had taken on jobs and responsibilities that had redefined who they felt they were' (Ballard 2008: 129). Ballard's gesture to various crises of identity engendered by the radical and violent transformations of war echo Walter Benjamin's inter-war observations in 'The Storyteller' (1936):

> Was it not noticeable at the end of the war that men returned from the battlefield grown silent – not richer, but poorer in communicable experience? [. . .] never has experience been contradicted more thoroughly than strategic experience by tactical warfare [. . .] bodily experience by mechanical warfare [. . .] A generation that had gone to school on a horse-drawn streetcar now stood under the open sky in a countryside in which nothing remained unchanged but the clouds. (Benjamin 1979: 84)

Benjamin's meditations on how the horrors of modern industrialized warfare were too excessive for the limited psychological resources of the 'fragile' (Benjamin 1979, 84) postwar subject resound throughout *Miracles*. But we might also find echoes of them in Jim's musings in

Empire, when he compares the 'real' war of the Sino-Japanese conflict with the European spectacle presented by Pathé and British Movietone newsreels:

> Jim had no doubt which war was real. The real war was everything he had seen for himself since the Japanese invasion of China in 1937, the old battlegrounds at Hungjao and Lunghua where bodies of the unburied dead rose to the surface of the paddy fields each spring. Real war was [. . .] the bloody heads of communist soldiers mounted on pikes along the Bund. In a real war no one knew which side he was on, and there were no flags or commentators or winners. In a real war there were no enemies. (Ballard 1985: 14)

This passage was written in the early 1980s by a 50-year-old professional writer, but such an understanding of the physical and psychological consequences of war was still out of reach of a teenage self who had not yet digested all that he had witnessed. To adapt the war which he had experienced in China from 1937 to 1945 to the ideological frame of reference proposed by the media was impossible. Besides, the teenager who graduated from the University of Lunghua, and who knew what real war was like, also knew that the Americans, the Russians and the Chinese had actually won the war, and that the British Empire was more of an ideological fiction than a political reality. Indeed, the decline of the British Empire is symbolized in *Empire* by the sinking of HMS *Petrel*, which echoes the more famous sinking of the *Repulse* and *Prince of Wales* by the Japanese in December 1941. In *Miracles*, meanwhile, the waning of British Imperial power manifests itself in what is arguably the most iconic of Ballardian images, the drained swimming pool. Having been relocated to the French Concession with his family, the young Ballard encounters this 'mysterious empty presence' for the first time:

> I would walk through the unmown grass and stare down at its canted floor. I could hear the bombing and gunfire all round Shanghai, and see the vast pall of smoke that lay over the city, but the drained pool remained apart. In the coming years I would see a great many drained and half-drained pools, as British residents left Shanghai for Australia and Canada, or the assumed 'safety' of Hong Kong and Singapore, and they all seemed as mysterious as that first pool in the French Concession. I was unaware of the obvious symbolism that British power was ebbing away, because no-one thought so at the time, and faith in the British Empire was at its jingoistic height. (Ballard 2008: 26–7)

Once again Ballard gestures to the obfuscating powers of the media landscape; the ideology of the British Empire, he maintains, was sustained by newsreels, propaganda images and a willing and self-deluded audience who 'genuinely thought that [they] had won the war single-handedly, with a little help, often more than a hindrance, from the Americans and Russians' (Ballard 2008: 126).

Another aspect of Ballard's protracted silence speaks to two intimately related matters: the crisis of historical representation and the issue of literary form. As the following quotation reveals, the aspiring writer was sensitive to the enormous experiential changes which the postwar population had endured: 'People had memories of bombing raids and beachheads, endless hours of queueing and waiting in provincial railway stations that were impossible to convey to anyone not actually there' (Ballard 2008: 130). How does the writer even begin to represent the physical and psychological realities of war? This question, which is infused with a range of other implications (ethical, political, social), also raises the issue of aesthetic form: what kind and structure of language would be most appropriate for engaging with an irrevocably altered human condition? Recalling his attempts in the 1950s to write short stories while working as a travelling salesman, Ballard writes:

> [My] writing was still stuck. I had sensibly abandoned my efforts to go one better than *Finnegan's Wake*, and I knew that I wasn't muscular and morbid enough to emulate Hemingway. My problem was that I hadn't found a form that suited me. Popular fiction was too popular, and literary fiction too earnest. A spate of World War II memoirs and novels were being published, but surprisingly it never occurred to me to write a novel based on my own wartime experiences. (Ballard 2008: 161)

With the absence of a literary model that could respond to the kinds of social, economic, material and psychological changes which war had forced upon the British population, Ballard writes how 'seven or eight years after the war, I had begun to switch off my memories of Shanghai. Very few people had shared my experiences, and the European war was still everywhere around us in a hundred bomb sites' (Ballard 2008: 161). In this context, the 'switching off' of memory cannot just be restricted to a reading of traumatic repression. More practically, it is also a question of audience, or rather what Ballard perceives to be a lack of one for his non-European experiences of war.

Ballard goes on to map out a decisive turn in his literary career when, turning to the genre of science fiction, he sets the course of a postwar literary project that will turn its back on the past and immerse itself (and its readers) in the explosive and constantly shifting realities of the present:

> Here was a form that was actually about the present day, and often as elliptical and ambiguous as Kafka. It recognised a world dominated by consumer advertising, of democratic government mutating into public relations. This was a world of cars, offices, highways, airlines and supermarkets that

we actually lived in, but which was almost completely missing from all serious fiction. No one in a novel by Virginia Woolf ever filled up the petrol tank of her car [. . .] No one in Hemingway's post-war novels ever worried about the effects of prolonged exposure to the threat of nuclear war. (Ballard 2008: 166)

As Ballard goes on to describe, his idiosyncratic brand of science fiction – one which drew specifically on Surrealism and Pop Art as aesthetic and imaginative sources (see Gasiorek 2005: 8–16) – promised to tap into the unconscious landscapes of the 1960s and to uncover 'the pathology that underlay the consumer society, the TV landscape and the nuclear arms race [. . .] Or so I thought, staring at the silent airfield, with its empty runways that stretched into a snow-blanched infinity' (Ballard 2008: 167).

Ballard's double-take is conspicuous in tone and content, implying that the violent past of the Second World War began to resurface long before the publication of *Empire*. To suggest this is not to repeat a reductive critical manoeuvre and fall into the trap of reading *Empire*, *Kindness* and *Miracles* as '"straight" texts which finally [render] the fiction autobiographically comprehensible' (Luckhurst 1997: 155). It is, instead, to accentuate the dialogic nature of Ballard's life narratives whilst also foregrounding the centrality of war to Ballard's entire oeuvre. Consider the following fictionalized account of a real-life event which Ballard appended to 'End-Game' (1963), a short story that was republished in 1968:

> Three weeks after the war ended I walked back to the camp along the Shanghai-Nanking railway line. At the small wayside station an abandoned platoon of Japanese soldiers were squatting on the platform, watching one of their number string up a Chinese youth with telephone wire. Four hundred yards away, on a tank-trap embankment, a group of Kuomintang (Allied) Chinese troops were feeding themselves on the Spam and Nescafe misdropped by the B-29's three miles from the camp. Neither of these groups did more than look at me as I walked past. (Ballard 1968: 80)

Ballard goes on to tell multiple versions of this event across the course of his literary career. In *Kindness*, it is retold in the terms of a slow atrocity exhibition of physical and psychological cruelty that lasts seven harrowing pages (Ballard 1992: 55–62). In 'The End of My War', a short autobiographical piece first published in the *Sunday Times* in 1995, it is collapsed into three very brief paragraphs which are recast in tones of sadness and regret (Ballard 1996: 285). In the context of *Kindness*, the murder of the Chinese clerk becomes an archetypal experience of the brutality and senselessness of war which will affect the protagonist, Jim, for the rest of his life. His friend Peggy observes: 'That terrible afternoon on the railway line near Siccawei – you'd seen dozens of atrocities by

then [. . .] but for once you were too close. A part of it happened to you'
(Ballard 1992: 270). That this real historical incident is not retold in
fictional terms in *Empire* is suggestive of its traumatic nature. Indeed,
it is omitted along with another significant and unsettling experience,
namely Ballard's forced intimacy with, and consequent 'gradual estrangement' (Ballard 2008: 82) from, his parents. Commenting on his reasons
for editing his parents out of *Empire*, Ballard reveals: 'I thought hard
about this, but I felt it was closer to the psychological and emotional
truth of events to make 'Jim' effectively a war orphan' (Ballard 2008: 82).
In *Kindness*, published 7 years after *Empire*, Ballard manages to present
a version of that fateful encounter at the railway station, only this violent tale of torture and humiliation is still retold at some distance: the
'Jim' character of *Kindness* remains, like the 'Jim/Jamie' figure of *Empire*
an 'orphan' of war (Ballard 1992: 33).

It is only in *Miracles* that Ballard's painful estrangement from his
parents *and* his traumatic witnessing of the killing of the Chinese clerk
are finally admitted into the picture and allowed to somehow coexist.
Turning his back on the corpse of the dead Chinese and on the psychologically dead Japanese soldiers (Ballard 2008: 107), Ballard recalls:

> I was badly shaken, but managed to steady myself by the time I had reached
> the western suburbs of Shanghai. Perhaps the war had not really ended,
> or we had entered an in-between world where even on one level it would
> continue for months or even years, merging into the next war and the war
> beyond that. I like to think that my teenage self kept his nerve, but I was
> probably aware of nothing other than the brute fact that I was alive and this
> unknown Chinese was dead. In most respects, sadly, my experiences of the
> war were no different from those of millions of other teenage boys in enemy-
> occupied Europe and the Far East. A vast cruelty lay all over the world, and
> was all we knew. (Ballard 2008: 107–8)

After telling this latest version of events, Ballard does not simply propose it as a 'primal scene' (Delville 1998: 75) which just might help us
to interpret the many and various atrocity exhibitions which he has
staged in the course of his literary career, but he also situates this traumatic event within a specific historical context. He is a representative, of
sorts, of a whole generation of teenage boys in enemy-occupied coun-
tries whose minds have been both warped and shaped by the atrocious
realities of the Second World War. J. G. Ballard belongs to that generation of people whose minds are battlefields, complex and differentiated
psychological landscapes which are scarred by the shocks and traumas
engendered by modern industrialized warfare.

No wonder then if Ballard, who survived the killing grounds of
the Second World War, has written a 'Life Trilogy' which might be
hermeneutically unified by the complex metaphor of the screen

(Cortellessa 1999: 123–9). While the young Ballard used to block out his younger sister's annoyances at the dinner table by hiding behind a 'large plywood screen' (Ballard 2008: 41), the boy also indulged his morbid fascination with historical violence by watching spectacles of war played out large on the cinema screens of Shanghai. Although Ballard's fictions can be read as literary variations on Freud's screen memories – memories which are not necessarily historically accurate but which function in order to repress traumatic experiences – (see Freud 1985: 85), they also resemble the multiple atrocity screens which the protagonist of *Kindness* watches obsessively. As his friend Peggy tells him: 'Your mind was up there, moulded against that screen [. . .] all you wanted to do was sit in the darkness and watch those suicide pilots crashing into American ships' (Ballard 1992: 269). Between traumatic denial and voyeuristic contemplation, the screen may offer a unifying figure for Ballard's 'Life Trilogy': *Empire, Kindness* and *Miracles* can be read as a series of life narratives which selectively screen traumatic memories in order to protect the scarred mind of the writer, but which, at the same time, also screen multiple images of violence, war and death – just like the cinema screens in 1930s Shanghai that so mesmerized an English boy with visions of a war to come.

Notes

1. Following Smith and Watson, I use 'life-writing' as a general term for 'writing of diverse kinds that takes a life as its subject'. This can include biographies, novels, historical writing or an 'explicit self-reference to the writer' (Smith and Watson 2001: 3).
2. The importance of war in Ballard's fiction has already been pointed out by Tamás Bényei, who focused on national stereotypes and metaphors of initiation in *Empire of the Sun* (See Bényei 2000: 255–68), and Dominika Oramus, who devoted a whole chapter (entitled 'Battlefields') of her monograph on Ballard to the significance and representation of war in his fiction (See Oramus 2007: 82–109).

CHAPTER SIX

From Shanghai to Shepperton: Crises of Representation in J. G. Ballard's Londons

SEBASTIAN GROES

Chapter Summary: Focusing on Ballard's literary representations of London, this chapter traces the shifting significance of the English Capital across three phases in his career: the 1960s, 1970s and 2000s. Groes explores Ballard's ambivalence towards his adopted country and reads London as a master narrative which Ballard's writing attempts to dislocate.

Key Words: *The Drowned World*; *Crash*; *Empire of the Sun*; *Millennium People*; London; Shanghai; Shepperton; anti-imperialism; signification; realism; cities; space; place; globalisation; capitalism.

One of the great creative forces behind J. G. Ballard's writing is his antagonism towards cities, and London in particular. Since the beginning of his writing career, the author has drowned it, set it on fire, and blown it up – with highly original and imaginative results. In reaction to the Imperial centre as a repressive, anti-revolutionary instrument, Ballard consciously positions himself in Shepperton, the Thames-side town situated 17 miles to the west of London. Roger Luckhurst has noted how this move is a metaphorical expression of Ballard's preferred position in the literary world: 'the London literary scene and the academy feel discomfited by writers who have chosen the edges of the city. That geographical marginality is either taken as wilful perversity or, more threateningly, as an affront to the pretensions of the centre' (1997: xi). In an illuminating interview with the London-writer Iain Sinclair, Ballard reveals how his decision to operate on the literary and geographical fringes of London relates to his desire to represent modern consciousness:

> There's a huge bias in the English novel towards the city as subject matter and setting for the novel. I take quite the contrary view . . . I regard the city as a semi-extinct form. London is basically a nineteenth century city. And the habits of the mind appropriate to the nineteenth century, which survive into the novels set in the London of the twentieth century, aren't really appropriate to understanding what is really going on in life today.

> I think the suburbs are more interesting than people will let on. In the suburbs you find uncentred lives. The normal civic structures are not there. So that people have more freedom to explore their own imaginations, their own obsessions. And the discretionary spending power to do so.

> There's a sort of airport culture – with its transience, its access to anywhere in the world. Social trends of various kinds tend to reveal themselves first in the suburbs. The transformation of British life by television in the 60s took place, most of all, in the suburbs, when VCRs came in. In the suburbs you have nothing to do except watch TV. (Ballard cited in Sinclair 1999: 84)

I would like to problematize Ballard's antagonistic vision of London by arguing that the British capital occupies a *central* rather than marginal place in Ballard's imagination. I do so because it ties together several levels of signification into a master narrative that his writing attempts to dislocate: physical London, as a dense conglomeration of buildings, streets, squares, theatres and cinemas, forms a city-as-text that allows us to read the history of London as a product of developing capitalism and literary tradition as two distinct, but related forms of signification.

Ballard's texts engage in constant acts of reading and interpreting London's materiality; they respond to the Capital at the level of signs. When psychiatrist Robert Laing moves to a hypermodern tower block in *High-Rise* (1985a), he looks at central London from his apartment, and makes the following distinction: 'By contrast with the calm and unencumbered geometry of the concert-hall and television studios below him, the ragged skyline of the city resembled the disturbed encephalograph of an unresolved mental crisis' (Ballard 1985a: 9) Here, Laing reads London's messy, organic 'structure' as a dense crowding of signifiers which derive their signified from a repressive Victorian era that stifles the creative imagination.

Ballard's fictional autobiographies, *Empire of the Sun* (1984) and *The Kindness of Women* (1991) form a key to his representation of London and Britain. These texts show that a form of cultural schizophrenia operates in his fiction, which emerges from a crisis of signification that Ballard experienced in the International Settlement in Shanghai, China, and in the Lunghua Civilian Assembly Centre. This is because the attempted subversion of London as spatial, economic and literary discourse within his texts locks the author into a relationship with a city whose very being forms the measure of a reality that is itself increasingly unstable. By paying close attention to Ballard's use of London's street names, it becomes clear that his use of proper nouns forms a strategy that appropriates a realist strategy – the magical act of naming – in order to subvert it. This is why the incorporation of Ballard's name into the *Collins English Dictionary* is highly ambivalent: while the entry acknowledges the unconventional and challenging nature of Ballard's writing, his inscription into the English language by one of the official institutes that guards it, robs the author of his subversive power.

Three distinct phases take place in Ballard's writing of London. During his early career in the 1960s, Ballard attempts to block the signification of London as a master narrative altogether. As Ballard's use of real London street names in *The Drowned World* (1962) suggests, his representation of the city does not leave the realm of the mimetic. In fact, Ballard's attempts to rewrite the centre *affirm* rather than subvert London as master signifier, the central expression of cultural values in relation to which all other terms are defined. This leads to a second phase during which Ballard's texts flee towards the peripheral zones around the city, which are unburdened by such constrictive traditions of signification. Although *Crash* (1973) operates a deterritorialization of signifiers aimed at liberating the subject through a free flow of sexual desire and the collapse of social categories, this results in the acknowledgement of new signifying centres of post-modernity – non-space and abstract space such as Heathrow, the tower block, the traffic island and the gated community. This is why in later works such as *Millennium People* (2003), Ballard is able to return to the city he loves to hate: through linguistic and architectural simulation, London is increasingly dislocated from itself and slowly becomes the dispersed sign system that Ballard experienced in his youth.

The Dislocation of 'London' as Centre of Signification

Ballard was haunted by London long before he experienced its materiality at first hand:

> My image of London was formed during my Shanghai childhood in the 1930s as I listened to my parents' generation talk nostalgically of West End shows, the bright lights of Piccadilly, Noël Coward and Gertie Lawrence, reinforced by a Peter Pan and Christopher Robin image of a London that consisted entirely of Knightsbridge and Kensington, where 1 per cent of the population was working-class and everyone else was a barrister or stockbroker. When I actually arrived in 1946 I found a London that looked like Bucharest with a hangover – heaps of rubble, an exhausted ferret-like people defeated by war and still deluded by Churchillian rhetoric, hobbling

around a wasteland of poverty, ration books and grotesque social division. (Ballard 1996: 129–30)

In Ballard's text, London is foregrounded as an overtly fictional city which is reconstructed from an older generation's nostalgic and collective memory, and from his own childhood literary imagination. Ballard first encounters the city as a discursive construct which he perceives retrospectively to be a politically motivated misrepresentation aimed at upholding class divisions. Ballard thus becomes very much aware that the city in general, and London in particular, is an essentially unknowable place partially made up of the myths and fictions which it inspires. Ballard's also understands that the city is preconditioned by the climate and cultural context in which one grows up: Ballard's London is overcoded by a thick coating of his Shanghai experiences.

Ballard's fictionalized self experiences another version of London during his internment in Lunghua camp, a place in which signification breaks down on a more fundamental level:

In his ceaseless journeys around the camp Jim had learned to recognize every stone and weed. A sun-beached sign, crudely painted with the words 'Regent Street', was nailed to a bamboo pole beside the pathway. Jim ignored it, as he did the similar signs enscribed [sic] 'Piccadilly', 'Knightsbridge' and 'Petticoat Lane' which marked the main pathway within the camp. These relics of an imaginary London – which many of the Shanghai-born British prisoners had never seen – intrigued Jim but in some way annoyed him. With their constant talk about pre-war London, the older British families in the camp claimed a special exclusiveness. He remembered a line from one of the poems that Dr Ransome had made him memorize – 'a foreign field that is for ever [sic] England . . .' But this was Lunghua, not England. Naming the sewage-stained paths between the rotting huts after a vaguely remembered London allowed too many of the British prisoners to shut out the reality of the camp, another excuse to sit back when they should have been helping Dr Ransome to clear the sceptic tanks [. . .] And yet the London street signs fascinated him, part of the magic of the names that he had discovered in the camp. What, conceivably, were Lord's, the Serpentine, and the Trocadero? (Ballard 1985: 167–78)

The act of renaming Lunghua camp according to real London street names recreates a synchronically aligned city of the mind. This recycling of names therefore allows those who experienced the material city to disguise the harsh reality of Lunghua with an imaginary London. This renaming is essentially a colonial act that linguistically superimposes one geography onto another (this is reinforced by Ballard's ironic intertextual reference to Rupert Brooke's patriotic First World War poem, 'The Soldier' (1914)). For the Shanghai-born Ballard, however, this imaginative act fails because he has no experience of, and thus no access to, 'the real' to which the signs refer. In fact, for Ballard an inversion takes place whereby the material reality becomes the signified of the London street names, which are associated with imprisonment, hunger, excreta, diseases and death. Ballard retroactively prophesizes that, for him at least, London will always be associated with decline, death and social inequality: 'I feared that the England I visited after the war would be a larger version of Lunghua camp, with all its snobberies and social divisions, its 'best' families with their strangled talk of 'London town' brandished about like the badges of an exclusive club, a club I would do my best to avoid joining' (J. G. Ballard 1991: 35).

Andrzej Gasiorek argues that Ballard's early experience of England in a 'distanced and debased form' (2005: 1) lies at the heart of his writerly imagination:

> Thus despite his alter ego's confident prognostications that Lunghua Camp will provide a key to England, the transition from a colonial and significantly Americanized reality to a parochial and largely decaying English milieu proves that mapping one in terms of the other is fraught with difficulties. The slippage between these two imaginative worlds opens up a creative space in which Ballard's fiction operates. It gives rise to a series of indeterminate, liminal zones that permit the writer to engage in an exploratory, speculative cartography of the contemporary everyday. (Gasiorek 2005: 2)

Ballard's Lunghua experiences certainly form the creative dynamo behind his work, but Gasiorek does not explain *how* this slippage, earlier identified by Luckhurst as an 'interstitial zone' (1997: xv), actually occurs. Gasiorek's critical terminology also obscures the fact that Ballard's narratives never truly leave the realm of mimesis. In Lunghua, Ballard not only discovers his desire for subverting the metropolis as the imperial master narrative, but he discovers that empirical, naturalistic language and realistic naming form a powerful means of challenging conventional sense-making processes.

For Ballard, the inversion of the relationship between London's material reality and the discursive systems that precede it results in the breakdown of conventional forms of signification. Indeed, the proliferation of Londons at the level of signs leads to a dispersal of signifiers, which Ballard experiences as liberating, revealing, and, most importantly, ambivalent: 'In retrospect, I realized that internment helped people to discover unknown sides of themselves' (Ballard 1985: 291). Thus, Ballard is attracted to this suspension of conventional signification because it shows him that the imagination works by exploiting a system of signification.

This rupturing of signification comes about because of the intimate relationship between capitalism and language as systems that produce a knowable external reality. In *The Order of Things* (1966) Michel Foucault analyses the evolution of the monetary system in order to point out crucial changes in the development of capitalism. During the Renaissance money is transformed from being an objective instrument to measure wealth and commodities into a 'commodity like any other – not an absolute standard for all equivalences, but a commodity whose capacity for exchange, and consequently whose value as a substitute in exchange, are modified according to its abundance or rarity: money too has its price' (Foucault 2002: 185). In other words, the absolute relationship between coinage and commodities is substituted for an arbitrary one whereby 'money (and even the metal of which it is made) receives its value from its pure function as a sign' so that '[t]hings take on value, then, in relationship to one another' only (Foucault 2002: 191).

Foucault's reference to the metal of which coins are made leads us to the idea that a similar change takes place in our understanding of language as a system of representation. In *The Coiners of Language* (1994), Jean-Joseph Goux traces the analogy between language and money in the writing of French nineteenth-century novelists. In literature, gold traditionally stands for solidity and truth, and is therefore equated with the idea that naturalist or transparent writing is able to convey reality objectively and empirically. The premise here is that the novel needs to be an accurate and authentic report of human experience mediated through a referential use of language. Gold and realist language are therefore equated: 'As long as gold circulates "in person," we are in the realm of realist literature. When gold is replaced by tokens (of dubious convertibility) we enter the domain of nonfigurative experience' (Goux 1994: 91). However, just as money's value can become relative, as Foucault suggests, in the experimental writing of Modernists such as James Joyce, Samuel Beckett, Mina Loy and Djuna Barnes the fixed relationship between signifier and signified is destroyed in favour of structural play, whereby words are exchanged only among themselves without acknowledging what they are supposed to refer to.

In *Empire of the Sun*, the fictionalized Ballard experiences the collapse of monetary stability described by Foucault. His understanding of value is skewed, for instance, when he and his friend Patrick 'play the untended roulette wheels with Mr Maxted's money [. . .] while Mr Maxted sat in the office with the owner, moving around other piles of banknotes' (Ballard 1985: 27). This suggests that in the supremely wealthy environment of Ballard's upbringing the abundance of money makes it insignificant. This meaninglessness is perpetuated in an inverted way in Lunghua, where money as the system of value is cancelled out altogether and replaced by an exchange of commodities and rationed food stuffs: the prisoners 'spent all day hunting for food' (Ballard 1985: 182) and Jim steals sweet potatoes in exchange for weevils and 'cracked wheat, an animal feed grown in northern China' (Ballard 1985: 183).

The linguistic dislocation of Lunghua-London combined with the suspension of systems of monetary exchange within the camp produce a form of schizophrenia in Ballard's text that is exploited creatively throughout the *oeuvre*. *Empire of the Sun*, for example, foregrounds the doubling of Jim's experience of himself: whereas the Britons protect themselves by creating a fantasy London, the young Ballard survives the horrors of war and imprisonment by means of a

> strange doubling of reality [. . .] as if everything that had happened to him since the war was occurring within a mirror. It was his mirror self who felt faint and hungry, and who thought about food all the time. He no longer felt sorry for this other self. (Ballard 1985: 103)

It is this crisis that Ballard's texts investigate: this splitting of the self shows Jim that he does not need to subject himself to received linguistic systems or ideologies that are not of his own making. Similar to William Blake, whose work is also driven by the need to escape enslavement by creating his own system, Ballard's texts constantly attempt to suspend, destroy or rewrite systems of signification which mainstream politico-economic and cultural powers impose on the world.

Blocking the master signifier: *The Drowned World*

The Drowned World (1962) presents London as precisely the kind of system that seeks to enslave. The scientist Kerans and his colleagues are stranded in a post-apocalyptic city which has flooded as a result of solar radiation. The only character at ease with this new world, Kerans takes up residence in the penthouse suite of the Ritz Hotel, a grand architecture which once embodied Imperial decadence, but which now oozes 'the subtle atmosphere of melancholy that surrounded these last vestiges of a level of civilisation now vanished forever' (Ballard 2008: 9–10).

Within the drowned landscapes of London conventional signification is negated. Money, for instance, simply has no value; this becomes clear when Kerans jokingly offers to 'buy' his colleague, Riggs, 'a drink' (Ballard 2008: 13). In the absence of capitalist production, Kerans's offer remains an impossibility. The capitalist ordering of time has also been suspended ('the meaningless orientation of the clock hands' (Ballard 2008: 61)) along with any semblance of European art and culture (Ballard 2008: 16; 28; 29). Simultaneously, such exchanges show that language, as the reader knows it, has itself become obsolete. However, whereas the instinctive reaction of most characters, and the reader, is to somehow recover the world through conventional forms of signification, Kerans's counterintuitive motive is to push his psychic and linguistic regression 'to a point where a second Adam and Eve found themselves alone in a new Eden' (Ballard 2008: 23). The destruction of the metropolis implies a positive regeneration into a primitive state that sees the reconstitution of man at one with the world because experience is unmediated by systems of signification produced and controlled by others and not dependent on our 'fallen' language. Kerans's aim of achieving a condition *before* conventional signification is an intricate part of his attempt to arrive at a prelapsarian state.

The introduction of the deranged pirate Strangman, a reincarnation of Conrad's Kurtz in *Heart of Darkness* (1904), marks a potential turning point in the novel. The cargo of his boat consists of signs that embody the categories of the world now lost: money, valuables and relics from the Sistine Chapel and the Medici tomb. Bodkin's dismissal of the art – '"[a]esthetically, most of this is rubbish, picked for the gold content alone"' (Ballard 2008: 94) – points out the uselessness of Strangman's project. His need for stable signification, embodied by his Kurtzean lust for gold and treasure, has no value in a world beyond monetary exchange. Although Strangman's desire for money is connected directly to conventional language, his desire to rehabilitate previous systems of signification produces a corruption in his language. He often mimics Kerans, for instance, using 'a pious voice' (Ballard 2008: 98). Moreover, his discourse is riddled with deceit: recall how he uses a cliché to pretend that his alligators, which function as his guard dogs, 'won't hurt' (Ballard 2008: 92).

Strangman continues with his insane postcolonial project by pumping dry a lagoon which contains London's West End. Soon the characters are walking though Leicester Square, with Kerans fighting 'to free his mind, grappling with this total inversion of his normal world, unable to accept the logic of the rebirth before him' (Ballard, 2008: 120–1). However, it is not so much the city, but the city as the literal embodiment of a discourse expressing old categories of thought that Kerans wants to destroy: 'Colonel, you've got to flood it again, laws or no laws. Have you been down in those streets; they're obscene and hideous! It's a nightmare world that's dead and finished, Strangman's resurrecting a corpse!' (Ballard 2008: 159). However, conventional signification has been restored: when Strangman rescues Kerans and Beatrice from one of his alligators, he seduces Beatrice by giving her a rhinestone necklace: '"For you, my dear." Deftly, he strung the strands around her neck, regarding the effect with pleasure' (Ballard 2008: 128). The necklace is not merely an inanimate object with a particular monetary value, but Strangman's pleasure at 'the effect' can only take place because signification has been temporarily restored; in other words, it allows Strangman – whose uncommon name stands in ironic contrast to his desire for common signification – to signify his passion for Beatrice. This restoration is reinforced by the foregrounding of street names: '"Coventry Street, Haymarket . . . " Kerans read off the rusting street signs' (Ballard 2008: 125). The realism inherent in the London street names generates a sense of safety and comfort for the reader while the resurfacing of London exposes that the stabilization of former signifying systems through Strangman's project is tied to London as the central discourse of imperial signification.

Ballard's flaunting of London's street names points to one paradox at the heart of *The Drowned World*. Although the novel wants to confront the reader with this new world, Kerans's nightmare world never expresses itself in the form and language of the novel. The supposed oneiric inner landscape and the characters' linguistic regression are rendered in a language that is safely anchored in the linguistic currency of the reader's world. When Kerans drifts into unconsciousness when diving too deep, we are told how: 'he could see the ancient nebulae and galaxies shining through the uterine night, but eventually even their light was dimmed and he was only aware of the faint glimmer of identity within the deepest recesses of his mind' (Ballard 2008: 110). This passage attempts to render Kerans's inner experiences, yet because the sentences are grammatically intact, and language functions referentially, we remain in the realm of naturalistic representation. What is more, although Ballard's novel overtly reworks characters and tropes from Conrad's anti-imperial *Heart of Darkness*, the psychopathology of the colonial project (which is critically expressed in the oppressive language of Conrad's novella) stands in contrast to Ballard's empirical, naturalistic language. Thus *The Drowned World* conveys Kerans's regression into a prelapsarian, Adamic state (where there is a direct, absolute relationship between language and the world) in a postlapsarian language. Ballard only has a 'fallen' language at his disposal, which inadvertently affirms London as a centre of signification. Because the images of London are rendered discursively, in language, Ballard is arguing that it is not London, but London as a fallen language that he is attempting to destroy.

A cuneiform of the flesh: systems of exchange running wild in *Crash*

To escape the oppressive discourse of the city that operates throughout Ballard's 1960s texts, the fictions of the 1970s attempt linguistic and geographical dislocation by moving to London's periphery. *Crash*, for instance, presents a world in which systems of exchange are running out of control. The novel is narrated by a fictional television producer 'James Ballard', who, after a near-fatal car crash (in which he kills someone else) is unable to work and so operates outside the capitalist system of exchange. Under the influence of Vaughan, a crazed 'TV scientist' who stages repeated car crashes both real and imagined, Ballard awakes to the transcendental nature of the technological landscape surrounding Heathrow airport:

Our apartment house at Drayton Park stood a mile to the north of the airport in a pleasant island of modern housing units, landscaped with filling stations and supermarkets, shielded from the distant bulk of London by an access spur of the northern circular motorway which flowed past us on its elegant concrete pillars. [. . .] I realized that the human inhabitants of this technological landscape no longer provided its sharpest pointers, its keys to the borderzones of identity [. . .] this placid suburban enclave [. . .] faltered before the solid reality of the motorway embankments, with their constant and unswerving geometry, and before the finite areas of the car-park aprons. (Ballard 1995: 48–9)

This passage suggests that, rather than a human-centred production of space, it is the automobile, as the ultimate expression of late capitalist science and technology, that shapes London's peripheral landscape. The spirit of geometry governing the concrete surfaces (runways, motor-ways, the open spaces of the reservoirs) forms an ideal site for Ballard's speculative imagination because it is emptied out of signs and street names that tie the subject to the responsibility of place. *Crash* portrays a landscape in which the driver moves on an 'empty motorway, past deserted filling stations' (Ballard 1995: 16) and arranges *rendezvous* with airport prostitutes in 'multi-storey car-parks – the top decks are empty in the evening' (Ballard 1995: 61). The naming of London and Drayton Park stands in contrast to the homogenized, geometric landscape, which in fact stands opposite to its supposed 'solid reality': whereas in *The Drowned World* the dreamlike state of the characters is temporarily pen-etrated by the real, in *Crash* phantasmagoria corrodes conventional conceptions of reality.

The designification of space is caused by the triumph of the motor car and results, as Richard Sennett's explains in *Flesh and Stone* (1994), in a renegotiation of desire:

The technologies of motion – from automobiles to continuous, poured-concrete highways – made it possible for human settlements to extend beyond the tight-packed centers out into peripheral space. The look of urban space enslaved to these powers of motion is necessarily neutral: the driver can drive safely only with a minimum of idiosyncratic distractions [. . .] streets emptied of street life apart from drivers. As urban space becomes a mere function of motion, it thus becomes less stimulating itself; the driver wants to go through the space, not to be aroused by it. (Sennett 1994: 17–18)

However, Ballard's text operates a counterintuitive effect whereby the homogenization of peripheral space leads to deviant sexual desires: landscape, architecture and the car are expressions of modern technolo-gies that direct human behaviour towards 'perverse' sexual obsessions revolving around the sexual arousal produced by potential crashes. The empty landscape stages new forms of desire by releasing the signifier from its obligation to the signified, a dispersal which allows for a confused rereading of the human body and the motor car in terms of each other:

> I could imagine her sitting in the car of some middle-aged welfare officer, unaware of the conjunction formed by their own genitalia and the stylized instrument panel, a Euclid of eroticism and fantasy that would be revealed for the first time within the car-crash, a fierce marriage pivoting on the fleshy points of her knees and pubis. (Ballard 1995: 99)

The suggestion that such descriptions 'seemed to be a language in search of objects' (Ballard 1995: 35) affirms the dislocated signification within the novel.

Gilles Deleuze and Félix Guattari, who narrate the relationship between the unconscious in terms of the homogenization of space in both *Anti-Oedipus* (2004) and *A Thousand Plateaus* (2002), describe how deterritorialization is accompanied by the emergence of all kinds of 'machines' that release urges and desires from perverse fixations and familial neuroses: 'Schizoanalysis [. . .] treats the unconscious as an acentred system [. . .] as a machine network of finite automata (a rhizome), and thus arrives at an entirely different state of the unconscious' (Deleuze and Guattari 2002: 18). Rather than thinking of the unconscious as a deep structure or three-dimensional space to be mined by the psychoanalyst, Deleuze and Guattari's model emphasizes surfaces: it is this change that describes Ballard's altered representation of human psychology from *The Drowned World* to *Crash*. This mechanism allows for a rereading of the human body in terms of the car, offering a line of escape:

> The whiteness of his arms and chest, and the scars that marked his skin like my own, gave his body an unhealthy metallic sheen, like the work vinyl of the car interior. These apparently meaningless notches on his skin, like the gouges of a chisel, marked the sharp embrace of a collapsing passenger compartment, a cuneiform of the flesh formed by shattering instrument dials, fractured gear levers and parking-light switches. Together they described an exactly language of pain and sensation, eroticism and desire. (Ballard 1995: 90)

In the text, desire is satisfied by bringing fetishized signifiers onto the surface. Ballard's text makes clear that the proliferation of deviating sign systems exposes the danger of reading, which becomes an essentially erotic, sexual activity. The narrator's understanding of 'the real excitements of the car crash' (Ballard 1995: 19), for instance, is a product of discursive arousal, as the many references to textuality suggest: he speaks of the 'language of pain and sensation', 'the translation of wounds' (Ballard 1995: 26) and an 'encyclopaedia of pains and discharges' (Ballard 1995: 39). What is also made clear is that in the late twentieth century it is not the content of what is read that is important, but the form. The architecture and geography of the technologized landscape draw out a behaviour whereby reading occurs *for the sake of reading* rather than for meaningful explorations of the content. The text therefore continually emphasizes stylization and aestheticization, the dangerous destruction of the relationship between signifier and signified:

> Even the smallest movements seemed to be formalized, hands reaching towards me in a series of coded gestures. If one of them had unbuttoned his coarse serge trousers to reveal his genitalia, and pressed his penis into the bloody crotch of my armpit, even this bizarre act would have been acceptable in terms of the stylization of violence and rescue. (Ballard 1995: 23)

However, the point of *Crash*'s reading of sign systems in terms of one another is not that signifiers are floating free into a system of random exchange. 'Ballard' and Vaughan are not experiencing an infinite mobility of desire that allows any sign to be substituted for any other sign. Instead, two specific sign systems are substituted for one another: the human body and the car. This happens because a clear metonymic relationship exists between the body and car, and between sex and the car crash. In both cases two objects collide, penetrate and merge: 'A faded agency picture of the car in which Albert Camus had died was elaborately reworked, the dashboard and the windshield marked with the words 'nasal bridge', 'soft palate', 'left zygomatic arch' (Ballard 1995: 136). In other words, the attempt to escape conventional signification in *Crash* results simply in a new form of signification which has its roots in a literary, poetic technique. Similar to *The Drowned World*, Ballard only has a debased language at his disposal, which forces its user to always think of signs in terms of other signs.

Renaming the Streets: *Millennium People*'s Linguistically Inflated London

Although the advance of Britain into late capitalism causes the decline of the hierarchical structures set up under Empire, this 'progression' destroys the ideologies on which it constructed itself and leaves behind ruins amidst which new centres of order emerge. Ballard's later work focuses in particular on the ways in which gated communities emerge as new pockets of order, which subsequently succumb to the same forces that operate in the peripheral topography of London. This occurs because, as *Crash*'s connection of the human body and cars suggests, a complete dislocation of signification is impossible: new centres, reference points and fixations always take place: the psychopathology of the protagonists moves beyond dislocation to form new signifying connections. In *Crash*, it is Heathrow airport and the motor car itself; hence the narrator's suggestion that Vaughan was a projection of his 'own fantasies and obsessions' (Ballard 1995: 220) reaffirms the real: the narration of the novel forms the cure that re-establishes everyday signification and propels the narrator back into the capitalist system and labour market.

Just as the same power structures governing the human body and the car allow for their becoming interchangeable, so the changes taking place on the urban periphery overtake the city itself. Henri Lefebvre calls this a consequence of the advance of abstract space, which is:

> founded on the vast networks of banks, business centres and major productive entities, as also on motorways, airports and information lattices. Within this space the town – once the forcing-house of accumulation, fountainhead of wealth and centre of historical space – has disintegrated. (Lefebvre 1991: 53)

Lefebvre notes that during late capitalism organic, material spaces that are the product of intense labour are not only replaced by highly artificial, rationalized spaces such as the endlessly sprawling, decentred suburbs of the postmetropolis, but also by an urban phenomenon that Ballard is interested in exploring: the gated community.

Millennium People is Ballard's most overt criticism of the ways in which political power affects the spatial organization of contemporary Britain. The reader is plunged headlong into the now deserted London gated community of Chelsea Marina, where a 'small revolution was taking place, so modest and well behaved that almost no one had noticed' (Ballard 2003: 3). Psychologist Richard Markham becomes involved in this bourgeois uprising, masterminded by the ex-paediatrician Richard Gould, which forms a cover up for a darker campaign of terror against the London-based cultural institutions (such as the National Film Theatre, the BBC's Broadcasting House and Tate Modern) which 'played a leading role in brainwashing the middle classes' (Ballard 2003: 149). The terrorist actions against real institutions and buildings are framed within the oneiric narration of Markham, whose powers of perception, in ironic contrast to his name, are extremely limited.

Chelsea Marina mimics an earlier London by copying its street names from the surrounding, expensive Mayfair and Knightsbridge areas: there is a main thoroughfare (Beaufort Avenue) leading to the central Cadogan Circle beside which stands a seven-storey block of flats, Grosvenor Place, a 'raffish cul-de-sac and a reminder of another, older Chelsea' (Ballard 2003: 7–8) and Nelson Street. The names inscribe the gated community with former imperial mastering narratives (this is ironically affirmed by the name of the development that formed the inspiration behind Chelsea Marina: Chelsea's Imperial Wharf development). Chelsea Marina does not simply copy Chelsea, but it *re-presents* Chelsea by referring to real streets in the district right next to it:

'So this is Chelsea Marina. It feels more like. . .'
'Fulham? It is Fulham. "Chelsea Marina" is an estate agent's con. Affordable housing for all those middle managers and civil servants just scraping by.'
'And the marina?'
'The size of a toilet bowl and smells like it'. (Ballard 2003: 51)

This passage underscores how Chelsea Marina is a marketing ploy based on linguistic inflation: estate agents sell parts of London by masking perception, and thus generate a version of 'London' by means of signs; this is similar to the way in which London was recreated in Lunghua. Thus, another breakdown is taking place whereby, through a synchronic alignment, a new space in London is inscribed with the old street names. The middle-class realization of this linguistic dislocation leads to the revolution in the novel. The revolutionaries' subsequent attempt to rebaptize Chelsea Marina by renaming the streets after radical French filmmakers from the 1960s fails: the political establishment is aware that its power is dependent on their control over the discursive practice of producing space. *Millennium People* repeatedly suggests how the city is shaped by authority whose power lies in its discourse: consider, for instance, a 'megaphone was blaring when I returned to the window, its ponderous message lost on the crowd, orotund phrases bouncing off the the [*sic*] rooftops' (Ballard 2003: 201).

This play with signs indicates an important shift in Ballard's London discourse. Whereas Ballard's earlier work writes London as language of the real in order to subvert it by means of the unreal, here, even outside the superreal narrative framework provided by Markham, London is represented as divorced from itself:

The Thames shouldered its way past Blackfriars Bridge, impatient with the ancient piers, no longer the passive stream that slid past Chelsea Marina, but a rush of ugly water that had scented the open sea and was ready to make a run for it. Below Westminster the Thames became a bruiser of a river, like the people of the estuary, unimpressed by the money terraces of the City of London.

The dealing rooms were a con, and only the river was real. The money was all on tick, a stream of coded voltages sluicing through the concealed conduits under the foreign exchange floors. Facing them across the river were two more fakes, the replica of Shakespeare's Globe, and an old power station made over into a middle-class disco, Tate Modern. Walking past the entrance to the Globe, I listened for an echo of the bomb that had killed

Joan Chang, the only meaningful event in the entire landscape. (Ballard 2003: 180)

Ballard makes a direct connection between the ephemeral nature of money in the late capitalist era and its effect on the physical metropolis. As money has now become immaterial and stripped of its capacity to signify in a simple manner, this dislocated signification expresses itself in simulacral architectural structures such as Shakespeare's Globe, a reconstruction of the original theatre not even built at its original location. One may think here of tourists attraction such as the London Dungeon and, more recently, Dickens World, which was prefigured by Ballard's *New Worlds* colleague Michael Moorcock, whose *Mother London* criticized the Disneyfication of London under Thatcher: '"Have you seen Katherine Dock and round here? It could be a set from *Oliver*." / "Disneyland," Leon agreed. "Or rather Dickensland"' (Moorcock 1988: 391). In other words, late capitalist London is exchanging itself at the level of signifiers without signified. After blowing up the National Film Theatre, smoke and 'a moraine of ash' (Ballard 2003: 141) cover the entire area, including the Hayward Gallery, Waterloo Bridge, the Millennium Wheel, and Markham finds 'the same images of disaster hanging from the kiosks in the Charing Cross Road' (Ballard 2003: 141). A similar process involves the Tate Modern, a museum housed in a former power station. Ballard criticizes this because the original *form* of the building is unsuitable to act out the *function* of a museum because its physical structure does not denote that function clearly enough. This criticism is remarkable: similar disapproval has come from Sinclair, who notes that 'in England many cultural venues have something odd about them. Take Tate Britain, which used to be a prison, the Millbank Penetentiary [. . .] Even now you can actually still feel the spirit of imprisonment. Tate Modern has all the qualities of a hospital' (Sinclair quoted in Groes 2005: 73). However, similar criticism coming from a Londonphobe seems odd: Ballard's critique of inauthentic London presupposes that there is, or once was, an original discourse of London, a 'real'.

Thus a problem emerges because of this shift in this representation of London as simulacrum: London is no longer the master narrative but is itself rewritten by global capitalist forces beyond its control. Narratologically speaking, this weakens the power of realistic naming because the text itself undercuts the reader's emotional and libidinal investment in realistic naming: if Tate Modern and The Globe are not authentic anyway, and Chelsea Marina is a fictional community, why should the reader care? These names as signs fail to evoke the reader's engagement with the city because highly specific processes of naming buildings, institutions and political figureheads, create an aporia that deflates the potential of fiction to imaginatively subvert. This, second, undermines the thrust of Ballard's political agenda: the naming of New

Labour's leadership and cultural institutions emphasizes too much the 'real' at the expense of the fantastical. Whereas Ballard previously represented power as invisible but present – London functioned as an anonymous signifier of power – power is here made visible in figures of political, economic and cultural authority, such as the Home Secretary and Tony Blair. Thus, Ballard's claim for Chelsea Marina as 'a unique republic, a city without street signs, laws without penalties, events without significance, a sun without shadows' (Ballard 2003: 294) is less potent than in his previous work.

J. G. Ballard Square

At the beginning of Ballard's career a terrible irony would have taken place if the London mayor had decided to name a London square after J. G. Ballard: similar to Ballard's incorporation into the English language by the *Collins English Dictionary*, it would mean the recuperation of a writer whose work is aimed at subverting the very signs which voice England's former cultural, politico-economic and imperial hegemony. Ballard's work has evolved together *with* the city, and it traces London's transformation from a post-imperial and posthumous entity to a metropolis that has reinvented itself as a new centre in the global economy. Ballard's early attempts to destroy London in writing have affirmed the city as a central discourse of power, which his texts dislocate by operating a dialectic between, on the one hand, the unreal and fantastical, and, on the other hand, the concretely real. In the recent writing, London's materiality is increasingly unmoored from the real, changing into the dislocated discourse which Ballard experienced in Lunghua. Therefore, naming a London Square after Ballard would be fitting: it would mean the inscription of a radical fictional space into a discursive fabric that is increasingly no longer representative of the British nation, but a confused, post-national language – a multitude of tongues that, for better or for worse, twenty-first century London increasingly speaks. The world, it seems, has caught up with Ballard.

CHAPTER SEVEN

Visions of Europe in *Cocaine Nights* and *Super-Cannes*

JEANNETTE BAXTER

Chapter Summary: Tracing Ballard's literary responses to the shifting landscapes of post-war Europe, this chapter reads Ballard's Europes as a series of labyrinths in which time, space, language and subjectivity are decentred. Baxter explores the absence of history, morality and memory in *Cocaine Nights* (1996) and *Super-Cannes* (2000) and reads these 'nowhere' spaces as nightmare Utopias.

Key Words: *Cocaine Nights*; *Super-Cannes*; postwar Europe; labyrinth; time; space; language; subjectivity; Georges Bataille; 'The Labyrinth'; 'The Psychological Structure of Fascism'; utopia; dystopia; euphemism; neo-fascism.

Ballard's writing has long been engaged with the shifting physical and psychological landscapes of postwar Europe. Published 4 years before the raising of the Berlin Wall, 'The Concentration City' (1957) re-imagines Europe as a vast urban labyrinth of stone walkways, elevated iron staircases, bricked up backstreets and narrow corridors which end 'abruptly in a tangle of ripped girders and concrete' (Ballard 2001: 27). Anticipating the material and ideological partitions which made up real Cold War geographies, Ballard's Europolis is not only a relentless topography of divisions and dead ends, but it is also cruelly inescapable. The Kafkaesque-sounding protagonist, Franz M., boards a 'Westbound' train in search of 'free', 'non-functional' space only to find that, 10 days later, he is returning to the 'East'. Frustrated and disorientated by somehow arriving at his original point of departure, Franz learns that all trains in the City follow a 'curvature', an 'inherent feature of the City'

(Ballard 2001: 36) which no one can delineate or account for. Neither can anyone explain why Franz's journey across the City has transported him back in time. Under interrogation by the State Authorities, the student notices the date on a desk calendar: '12 August. That was the day he had started off on his journey – exactly three weeks ago . . . You're back where you started from. $Hell x 10n' (Ballard 2001: 37–8). In the postwar European labyrinth, time and space have formed a capitalist alliance based on confusion and incarceration.

Narratives of spatio-temporal, physical and psychological dislocation continue to inform Ballard's developing visions of Europe over the following decades. Published during the 1960s and early 1970s, the short stories that are collected in *Vermilion Sands* (1971) are set in another vast and vacuous European geography; namely, a '3,000 mile-long' city that 'stretches from Gibraltar to Glyfada Beach along the northern shores of the Mediterranean, and where each summer Europe lies on its back in the sun' (Ballard 1971: preface). The functionalist regime of 'The Concentration City' has mutated by this stage into a regime of leisure or, more specifically, a regime of leisure *as* work: 'work is the ultimate play, and play the ultimate work' (Ballard 1971: preface). Foreshadowing the psychopathology of work which *Super-Cannes* goes on to map out at length, however, the notion of 'play' in *Vermilion Sands* translates into a disconcerting form of suspended animation. Locked into a lifestyle of compulsive yet empty reiteration – events, characters, images and motifs repeat obsessively and relentlessly across the nine stories – the vagrant community of Vermilion Sands is as displaced as time itself.

Later short stories such as 'Having a Wonderful Time' (1978) and 'The Largest Theme Park in the World' (1989) extend the critical trajectories of *Vermilion Sands* by foregrounding the work/play dialectic in a number of related yet divergent ways. Narrated through a series of postcards written from the 'Hotel Imperial', 'Having a Wonderful Time' is a tale of State-engineered exile. The governments of Western Europe have conspired to relocate their 'unemployables' to a permanent holiday camp on the Canary Islands and, with the exception of a rogue insurrectionist (who eventually drowns), there is little resistance to this pan-Western European system of forced migration. Instead, any feelings of restlessness or homelessness are quickly blunted by the camp's exhaustive itinerary of social events and leisure pursuits.

In 'The Largest Theme Park in the World', Ballard explores the work/play dialectic from a slightly different angle when he presents an accelerated vision of self-imposed exile to the coastal resorts of Europe. By 1996, we learn, 30 million people have rejected 'the old Europe of frontiers and national self-interest' (Ballard 2001a: 1140) in favour of a new and united Europe which is underpinned by a philosophy of play. With the logic of the annual holiday taken to its logical conclusion, though, the 'passive regime of sun and sand' (Ballard 2001a: 1141) is soon rejected in favour of a communal lifestyle defined by structure and self-discipline. Turning their backs to the sun, the émigrés form a new Europe of 'quasi-fascistic' collectives, each boasting their own 'beach-führers', and each dedicated to the 'first totalitarian system based on leisure. From the sun-lounge and the swimming-pool, from the gymna-sium and the disco, had come a nationalistic and authoritarian creed with its roots in the realm of pleasure rather than that of work'. Notably, the story ends on a note of impending neo-imperial violence as the new Europeans, armed with their mantras of 'racial superiority', look to reinvigorate the 'tired blood' of old Europe with their very own brand of totalitarian play (Ballard 2001a: 1143).

Cocaine Nights (1996) and *Super-Cannes* (2000) are the latest stages in Ballard's fictional remapping of continental Europe. Set in semi-imaginary versions of Spain and France respectively, both novels engage in a wide range of urgent political and cultural debates: the impact of global capital-ism on physical and psychological landscapes, the transition of a Feder-alist Europe into a neo-imperial 'super-state', the resurgence of racist and political extremism, the rise in immigrant labour forces and the rapid growth of the sex industry within Europe's markets of 'free-trade'. Traditionally, Ballard's visions of Europe have been read within that extensive and diverse literary tradition of dystopian writing. Certainly, *Cocaine Nights*, *Super-Cannes* and the previous short stories do resonate with texts such as Aldous Huxley's *Brave New World* (1931) and George Orwell's *Nineteen Eighty-Four* (1948) which, born out of the historical and political contexts of World War I and World War II, present diver-gent yet equally hellish visions of the alliance of capitalist and state authoritarianism, the consequences of social engineering, and the cor-ruption of language for ideological ends. I want, however, to shift the focus and make a case for rereading Ballard's imaginary European geo-graphies as a series of what I would like to call 'nightmare utopias'. Meaning 'no place', utopia is an imaginary realm in which time, space and history are crucially absent. It is precisely within these kinds of ahistorical, apolitical and amoral spaces, I want to suggest, that new and insidious forms of power and violence can operate and flourish.

An important intertext for my reassessment of Ballard's European fictions is Georges Bataille's nightmarish account of interwar Europe, 'The Labyrinth' (1936). As T. J. Demos has noted, Bataille's version of the labyrinth describes 'a disorientating ontological and epistemologi-cal model of identity, structure and space, in which all are radically decentered' (2001: 103). An exploration, in part, of the relationship between language and Being, 'The Labyrinth' is also a meditation on the composition and decomposition of communities between the Wars. In this respect, Bataille's labyrinth designates a 'historically specific set of conditions and experiences relating to narratives of geopolitical displacement' (Demos 2001: 103). Indeed, the 'NOWHERE' (Bataille 1994b: 176) of Bataille's labyrinth not only represents a profoundly divided and 'disorientated Europe in the late 1930s and early 1940s' (Demos 2001: 103), but it also represents a Europe which lay 'abandoned to the secret paleness of death' by Fascism (Bataille 1994b: 177). Written in the face of Fascist ascendancy, 'The Labyrinth' posits an unflinching indictment of the totalizing and deracinating forces of Fascism as they colonize and petrify the physical and psychological landscapes of Europe. Within Bataille's critical imagination, Fascism manifests itself as a 'monstrous universal' given over to reducing a multiplicity of European nations and their people to a 'state of empty shadows' (1994b: 176–7).

Although written out of a post-Cold War context, *Cocaine Nights* and *Super-Cannes* resonate with Bataille's historico-political critique in a number of provocative ways. Bataille's version of the labyrinth not only provides a challenging paradigm for reconsidering some of the contextual trajectories of *Cocaine Nights* and *Super-Cannes*, but it also provides a way of thinking about the *form* of these two novels. More *why-* than *who-dunnits*, Ballard's mock-detective fictions do not really ask to be solved, for there is no definitive truth or reality to be recovered. Rather, like Bataille's labyrinth which has no solution, *Cocaine Nights* and *Super-Cannes* are literary riddles which demand a process of readerly investigation that is alive to the revealing powers of paradox, ambiguity and disorientation. By challenging us to enter into the labyrinth of contemporary European history and culture, Ballard challenges us to immerse ourselves in its deviant logics, its repressed histories and its emerging psychopathologies. This process of immersing oneself in the labyrinth is not only important for confronting difficult questions about agency, guilt and moral responsibility which these texts foreground. It also marks an integral and invariably disquieting process of self-reflection: to what extent are we, the readers, implicated in, or complicit with, the criminal horrors of contemporary history?

Into the Labyrinth: reading *Cocaine Nights*

> Hidden perspectives turned Estrella de Mar into a huge riddle. *Trompe-l'oeil* corridors beckoned but led nowhere . . . A flight of worn stone steps climbed from a corner of the square to the plaza, but in my present mood, I would soon transform it into an Escher staircase.
>
> (Ballard 1996: 151)

Depicting endless winding staircases and snaking corridors which recede into infinity, M. C. Escher's labyrinths are apt visual metaphors for the process of reading *Cocaine Nights*. Charles Prentice has arrived in the fictional resort of Estrella de Mar where his younger brother, Frank, has pleaded guilty to a deadly arson attack. Convinced of his brother's innocence (no incriminating evidence exists and even the local police believe Frank's overzealous admissions of guilt to be part of an elaborate performance) Charles sets himself up as an amateur detective who will cast his outsider's gaze on this mysterious set of circumstances. Throughout the course of his enquiries, however, Charles encounters repeated forms of linguistic resistance – elliptical responses, enigmatic asides – which impede his investigation. Most frustrating are Frank's own attempts to conceal the details of his role in the Hollinger murders: 'If I explained what happened it would mean nothing to you' (Ballard 1996: 24). Hinting at alternative systems of meaning in Estrella de Mar, Frank's enigmatic reply also sets the tone for a narrative of epistemological and hermeneutic obfuscation in which conventional assumptions and knowledges are increasingly eroded. Charles's persistent questions are deferred or silenced, for instance, by unhelpfully ambiguous responses: one character replies, 'Believe me, Estrella de Mar isn't the sort of place you're used to'; another is equally evasive: 'These questions you've asked – they may not be the sort of questions that have answers in Estrella de Mar' (Ballard 1996: 151, 174). At the same time that the mystery surrounding the Hollinger murders invites penetration, the process of narrative folding is so relentless that Charles and the reader are repeatedly blocked: 'I could sit all day spinning scenarios that proved Frank innocent, but threads unravelled the moment they left my fingers' (Ballard 1996: 151). In the absence of Ariadne's guiding thread, Charles and the reader are lost in a linguistic labyrinth of paradox, contradiction and confusion.

This culture of linguistic evasion is inextricably linked with the anomalous community of Estrella de Mar. Having turned its back on mass tourism, this curious enclave has undergone significant forms of social and cultural rejuvenation over recent years. In stark contrast to the vast, atomized leisure and retirement complexes which lack any 'sense of social structure', Estrella de Mar boasts a conspicuously strong sense of civic identity (Ballard 1996: 35). Against the 'monoculture of sun and sangria that becalmed the pueblo residents', Estrella de Mar is a hive of vibrant communal activity; its residents participate in miscellaneous social and cultural events ranging from art exhibitions, amateur dramatics and local council assemblies to church gatherings and school governors' meetings (Ballard 1996: 34–7). Furthermore, the 'true community' of Estrella de Mar prides itself on its allegiance to a more cohesive existence: 'Here there were no gangs of bored teenagers, no deracinated suburbs where neighbours scarcely knew each other and their only civic loyalties were to the nearest hypermarket and DIY store' (Ballard 1996: 66). However modestly, so the mantra of Estrella de Mar goes, 'a happier Twentieth Century had rediscovered itself in this corner of the Costa del Sol' (Ballard 1996: 66).

The secret behind Estrella de Mar's cultural cohesion resides in the controversial thesis that criminal violence is a legitimate corrective to social and psychological inertia. Beneath the polite surface of school festivals, tea parties and tennis club luncheons lurks a far less palatable reality; the entire resort is 'wired up to crime like a cable TV network' (Ballard 1996: 159). Bobby Crawford, the resident tennis coach and local psychopath, is the charismatic face of Estrella de Mar's criminal operations. An ambiguous figure who inspires a range of emotions in the residents and the reader, Crawford is presented as the 'saviour of the entire Costa del Sol' (Ballard 1996: 181), having discovered an ostensible antidote to the immobilizing forces of consumer capitalism:

> Our governments are preparing for a future without work [. . .] Leisure societies lie ahead of us [. . .] But how do you energize people, give them some sense of community? [. . .] Only one thing is left which can arouse people, threaten them directly and force them to act together [. . .] Crime and transgressive behaviour. (Ballard 1996: 180)

What's particularly notable about this moment of revelation is that Bobby Crawford's thesis for socio-cultural regeneration is delineated by Dr Sanger, the local psychiatrist and Crawford's long term-adversary. Sanger's act of ventriloquism not only gestures to the seductive nature of Crawford's philosophy, but it also demonstrates its pervasive nature. Indeed, for a man who appears infrequently throughout the first two-thirds of the narrative, Crawford wields an enormous amount of influence over the community of Estrella de Mar. His provocative language is seldom articulated in any explicit way, for instance, rather it is disseminated second hand through the resort's discursive networks – a veritable tissue of quotations drawn from Crawford's manifestos for socio-cultural transformation.

In this respect, the linguistic structures at work in Estrella de Mar share more than a passing resemblance to the way in which language operates within Bataille's labyrinth:

> In men, all existence is tied in particular to language [. . .] Each person can only represent his total existence [. . .] through the medium of words [. . .] Being depends on the mediation of words which cannot merely present it arbitrarily as 'autonomous being,' but which must present it profoundly as 'being in relation.' One need only follow, for a short time, the traces of repeated circuits of words to discover, in a disconcerting vision, the labyrinthine structure of the human being. (Bataille 1994b: 174)

By placing us 'in relation' to other beings, language emerges as a force for creating and sustaining a sense of community. The more the inhabitants of Estrella de Mar persist in reiterating Crawford's controversial theories the less they become aware of their own 'insufficiency', and the more 'sufficient' their community appears to become (Bataille 1994b: 172). As we are constantly reminded, without Crawford's regenerative regime of crime, 'Estrella de Mar would have sunk back into itself and turned into just another brain-dead town on the coast'

(Ballard 1996: 317). However, as Bataille's essay suggests, the linguistic relationships that form and connect us are so delicate and unstable that any notion of sufficiency, unity or belonging is ultimately illusory. Although the lack of stability within the labyrinth seems to be resisted to some degree by the formation of 'relatively stable wholes' (Bataille 1994b: 175) which attempt to order and organize fragile human relations, these fairly stable wholes remain, nonetheless, unstable. The myth of 'sufficiency' is precisely that, a myth of structure, completeness and cohesion; and in the place of an ordered centre, 'a network of endless waves that renew themselves in all directions' (Bataille 1994b: 177) comes into being.

In *Cocaine Nights*, 'community' emerges as something of a euphemism for a network of corruption and exploitation in which everyone, even Charles, is implicated: 'If Bobby Crawford was the young district officer, then David Hennessy and Elizabeth Shand were the agents of the trading company who dogged his heels, ready to rouse the docile natives with their guns and trinkets, beads and brummagem' (Ballard 1996: 230). The range of imperialistic metaphors embedded within the complex narrative of *Cocaine Nights* gestures to the colonizing ambitions behind Crawford's surface project of cultural and psychological decolonization. Boasting a history of racist brutality, Crawford reveals at one point how he rejuvenated the demoralized members of the Kowloon police force by initiating them into racially fuelled assaults on cross-border migrants: 'Believe me, there's nothing like a "war crime" to perk up the soldiery. It's a terrible thing to say, but war crimes do have their positive side' (Ballard 1996: 247). Exploiting the semantic and moral parameters of the euphemism 'war crime', Crawford's community project is more akin to a psychopathology of neo-imperialism founded on physical, linguistic and ethical violence.

It is evident in the shifting linguistic registers at work in Estrella de Mar which insist on categorizing violent sexual attacks on women and young children as '"good works" of a new kind' (Ballard 1996: 304) that Crawford's idiosyncratic form of colonization comes equipped with its very own lexicon of deviancy. Charles's move to excuse the hideous reality of paedophilia as a mere problem of demographics, for instance, not only smacks of gross delusion, it also gestures to an insidious process of ethical evasion through language: 'There's a problem in the Residencia – there are almost no children. People miss them, so sexual fantasies get mixed up with nostalgia' (Ballard 1996: 292). Disturbingly, this kind of moral postponement is reiterated on every level within the community: whilst Paula Hamilton denies all responsibility for her role in videoing a gang rape – 'The film took itself. I pressed the button. What does it matter? It was only a game' (Ballard 1996: 196) – Elizabeth Shand justifies sexual violation as a playful reminder to the prostitutes of their role in the consumer-capitalist machine: 'Rape? Awful I know. But it does keep the girls on their toes' (Ballard 1996: 133).

The proliferation of euphemistic and idiomatic phraseology through-out the discursive structures of Estrella de Mar means that language, meaning and morality are constantly on the move. It is precisely this absence of any kind of ethical, political or historical meaning which marks Estrella de Mar out as a 'nightmare utopia', a place which 'isn't anywhere' (Ballard 1996: 17). Complicit with the corrupt capitalist net-works that feed the resort, the community of Estrella de Mar refuses to confront its histories of paedophilia, racism and sexual violence. Instead, the community salves its conscience through a series of linguistic exchanges which block ethical and historical reflection and which ensure that any sense of culpability remains unexplored within endless proc-esses of linguistic deferral.

Even the community's attempts to justify the Hollinger murders within the framework of 'sacrifice', an act which would 'seal the tribe into itself' (Ballard 1996: 324) reveals itself to be another 'puerile but convenient illusion' (Bataille 1994b: 174):

> Why were they killed? For the sake of Estrella de Mar and all that Crawford had done for us. To stop everything falling apart when he left [. . .] A great crime was needed, something terrible and spectacular that would bind everyone together, seal them into a sense of guilt that would keep Estrella de Mar going for ever [. . .] The people of Estrella de Mar had to commit a major crime themselves, something violent and dramatic, up on a hill where everyone could see it, so we'd all feel guilty for ever [. . .] Still, he and Betty Shand were right – the fire and the deaths held everyone together and kept Estrella de Mar alive. Now they plan to do the same thing for the Resdiencia Costasol, with poor Sanger as the sacrifice. If Laurie Fox dies with him in his bed that makes it all the more lurid – no-one will ever forget it, and the bridge parties and sculpture classes will run for ever. (Ballard 1996: 317–18)

According to Bataille's studies of Aztec ritual sacrifice, the excessive sacrificial act is simultaneously cohesive and cathartic, serving to strengthen the current group and expiate any sense of guilt. This kind of anthropological approach to death doesn't quite fit the murderous ritu-als practised by the decentred community of Estrella de Mar, however. In his reading of Todorov's *The Conquest of America* (1984), Richardson notes that, although sacrifice is 'characterised by its openness' – 'Per-formed in public in full view of all, sacrifice testifies to the strength of the social fabric and takes place within societies founded around inti-macy and heterogeneity' – it is also, crucially, characterized by anonym-ity; because 'to name the victim would be to make the act criminal; it would become murder and therefore unacceptable' (Richardson 1994: 83–4). In *Cocaine Nights*, the past and future sacrificial victims are not only clearly identified, but the group's proleptic gesture to the killings of Sanger and Laurie Fox further suggests that 'sacrifice' operates as a euphemism for murder.

Notably, the community of Estrella de Mar does not regard sacrifice as a process of 'consumption that is concerned only with the moment' (Bataille 1988: 49). Rather, looking to the future, their murderous practises function as a form of neo-imperialistic expansion. In this sense, the killings in Estrella de Mar are closer to massacre than to sacrifice because they form a 'technical means of domination which assure[d] the growth of the group at the expense of the peripheral populations' (Durverger 1979: 233 quoted and translated in Richardson 1994: 82). Characteristic of communities which have 'a weak social fabric and [which] consequently tend to reduce themselves to homogeneity', massacre is the 'consequence of the determination to reduce everything to utilitarian value, to reduce the world to the nature of a thing' (Richardson 1994: 83–5).

Enter Charles, the hapless amateur sleuth who is duped into thinking that his role in Crawford's death is that of the noble and necessary scapegoat: 'Did he [Cabrera] already know, as he walked towards me, that I would take responsibility for the death?' (Ballard 1996: 329). The elusive narrative strands of *Cocaine Nights* unfold in this closing passage only to fold once more on themselves. Charles's immolation within the violent capitalist logic of Estrella de Mar is not, as he suspects, an expression of communality or social cohesion, but a statement of capitalist homogeneity in which he is reduced to the status of a productive and functional citizen. Indeed, with money being the only force that holds the decentred labyrinth of Estrella de Mar together, the naïve sleuth-cum-criminal is dispatched, without hesitation, in the name of capitalist corruption and neo-imperialist expansion.

Neo-fascist utopias or the horrors of homogeneity: reading *Super-Cannes*

In many ways a companion piece to *Cocaine Nights*, *Super-Cannes* continues to explore the relationship between capitalism, neo-imperialism and homogeneity within contemporary Europe. The coastal, leisure-based setting of Estrella de Mar has been superseded, however, by a land-locked empire of productivity. *Super-Cannes* is set in the fictional enclave of Eden-Olympia, modelled on the actual business park of Sophia-Antipolis, situated a few miles north of Antibes. A vast complex of multinational company offices (Mitsui, Siemens, Unilever, Sumitomo amongst others) and luxury apartments, Eden-Olympia is home to the highest earning 'professional caste in Europe, a new elite of administrators, énarques and scientific entrepreneurs' who are 'committed to the sanctity of the workstation and the pieties of the spreadsheet' (Ballard 2000: 5, 8). Signing up to the disciplines of the European corporate lifestyle are Paul Sinclair, an editor of an aviation magazine who is also recovering from a flying accident, and his wife Jane, a paediatrician who has been seconded to Eden-Olympia following the unexplained death of her predecessor and former lover, David Greenwood. While Jane integrates seamlessly into working life at the multinational business park, Paul is notably adrift from Eden-Olympia's defining ideology of labour. With no access to Eden-Olympia's corporate present, therefore, Paul decides to investigate the unsolved mystery of its past: David Greenwood, a mild-mannered children's doctor set out on a murder rampage one morning in late May, killing ten people (seven senior executives and three hostages) before turning the rifle on himself.

Initially, Paul's anomalous existence as an 'unemployable' means that he is alive to the insidious homogenizing forces that operate throughout Eden-Olympia. Psychological integration, he soon discovers, occurs at the level of physical space: upon closer inspection of Eden-Olympia's glamorous surface landscapes (a multi-complex of executive retail and leisure facilities which remain suspiciously unused) Sinclair uncovers a labyrinthine network of coercive psychogeographies – new and shiny corporate architectures which soothe the body and stimulate productivity. Enormous glass buildings and artificial lakes which are designed to give the illusion of space and freedom are, for example, memory-erasing architectures that sustain a kind of 'well-bred catatonia that only money can buy' (Ballard 2000: 20). Similarly, the simulated nature trails and ornamental pathways which promise moments of physical and psychological reprieve end rather abruptly when 'they are no longer visible from the road' (Ballard 2000: 37). Spending much of his time doubling back on himself or going round in circles – 'I circled the artificial lakes, with their eerily calm surfaces, or roamed around the vast car parks' (Ballard 2000: 37), Sinclair soon discovers that even if the 'maze' (Ballard 2000: 39) of Eden-Olympia was one from which its inhabitants wanted to escape, its many physical barriers would prevent that desire from ever materializing: 'the totalitarian systems of the future would be subservient and ingratiating, but the locks would be just as strong' (Ballard 2000: 133).

In 'The Psychological Structure of Fascism' (1933), Bataille stresses how social homogeneity, with its dominant characteristics of duty, discipline and obedience, is achieved and maintained by the exclusion of violent or excessive energies, social homogeneity 'must constantly be protected from the variously unruly elements that do not benefit from production' (Bataille 1994a: 139). On one level, we see how this translates into Ballard's neo-fascist utopia, a ruthless corporate workhouse in which human needs are carefully checked and balanced. As Wilder Penrose, the 'minotaur' (Ballard 2000: 13) at the centre of the labyrinth suggests, the 'human body [is] an obedient coolie, to be fed and hosed down, and given just enough sexual freedom to sedate itself' (Ballard 2000: 17). Interestingly, Penrose's use of the term 'coolie', which refers to unskilled and imported labour forces, gestures to another kind of heterogeneous presence, one which is simultaneously necessary *and* hostile to Eden-Olympia's continued homogeneity: the 'invisible' (Ballard 2000: 194) immigrant workforce. As Sinclair notes, the migrant labourers are not only vital to the harmonious workings of Eden-Olympia because they deal directly with middle-class waste – 'Portuguese cleaning girls [. . .] spent the days [. . .] wiping the last white crystals from the smeary table-tops, throwing out the condoms stuck in the toilet traps' (Ballard 2000: 178) – but their own role as foreign elements suggests that they too are waste products destined for expulsion.

Despite Penrose's claims that racism is absent from Eden-Olympia – 'There's nothing racist, by the way. We're truly international' (Ballard 2000: 19) – his fascist vision of a new Europe is predicated on a psychopathology of violence which is specifically racist in impulse, once again 'the mystical idea of race [affirms] itself as the imperative aim of the new fascist society' (Bataille 1994a: 155). Indeed, the name of Penrose's residence, 'Villa Grimaldi', is particularly resonant in this context. 'Villa Grimaldi' was the name of the largest detention and torture clinic run by the DINA (Directorate of National Intelligence) under General Pinochet's military dictatorship in Chile from 1973 to 1990 (O'Shaughnessy 2000: 66). A labyrinth of torture chambers, interrogation facilities and incarceration closets, Villa Grimaldi was a place of systematic execution where opponents of Pinochet, be they political group members or insurgent civilians, were subjected to a range of hideous physical and psychological abuse which included electric shock therapy, 'wet' and 'dry' asphyxiation and hanging (O'Shaughnessy 2000: 101).

In *Super-Cannes*, it is from Villa Grimaldi that Penrose exercises his very own brand of aggressive authoritarianism. Recalling Crawford's philosophy of violent rejuvenation in *Cocaine Nights*, Penrose rehabilitates the workforce of Eden-Olympia on a diet of cruelty: shackled all day to their workstations, the stressed executives unwind by committing atrocious acts (rape, murder, torture, arson) against immigrant and sex-trade workers. Extending Bataille's vision of fascist brutality as a form of violence directed exclusively 'toward foreign societies or toward the impoverished classes' (Bataille 1994a: 147), the emerging strain of neo-fascism in *Super-Cannes* is, in Ballard's words, a form of 'skilfully aestheticized racism' (Baxter 2004: 31–2). This sentiment is echoed fictionally when Penrose sanctions racial violence as a kind of weekend recreation for 'playgroup Nazis': 'You have to understand that these attacks are set tasks, assigned to them as part of a continuing programme of psychotherapy' (Ballard 2000: 250). Within Penrose's surface logic, the executives' need for violence equates to the vital act of expulsion. Heterogeneous waste energies must be dispelled if social homogeneity is to be maintained. In actuality, however, Penrose's therapy groups are closer to what Bataille defines as the 'imperative elements' of fascist homogeniety: 'the protection of homogeneity lies in its recourse to imperative elements that are capable of obliterating the various unruly forces or bringing them under the control of order' (Bataille 1994a: 139).

Through socially legitimated forms of violent excess, the 'imperative forces' of Eden-Olympia practice a regime of ethnic cleansing, 'an act pure in direction but sadistic in form' (Bataille 1994a: 146), and specifically racist in flavour.

Penrose's latent racism manifests itself on a number of levels throughout *Super-Cannes*. It is not coincidental that the therapy groups' mounting attacks on immigrant workers are known as 'ratissages'. Francis Baring points out the bloodied history of the term: 'ratissage' is 'an old French Army term from the Algerian war – thinning out the fedayeen' (Ballard 2000: 210). Furthermore, the geographical location of Villa Grimaldi reinforces the trajectory of Penrose's racist ideology: 'It has a superb view – on a clear day you can practically see Africa, the next best thing to for ever' (Ballard 2000: 246). The African geography within Penrose's sights is Algeria, the former French colony and the site of a violent war of independence (1954–62) which saw the decimation of its national territories and its people (Ruedy 1992: 156–94). Ballard draws on the violent history of Algeria in order to forge a critique of resurgent forms of political and racial extremism in contemporary Europe. The political climate of Eden-Olympia is, as one character reveals, 'so right-wing it's off the scale' (Ballard 2000: 193). Whilst its security personnel are identified as 'members of the Front National, especially active among the *pied-noir* in the South of France' (Ballard 2000: 59), Sinclair discovers that Robert Fontaine (one of Greenwood's victims) used to decorate the walls of his 'political office' with photographs of his dead victims – 'Blacks, yellows, browns. Anything except pinko-grey' (Ballard 2000: 193).

Within Penrose's puritanical vision, racial diversity is an irritating reminder of the contingent world; it is as intolerable to him as 'a drifting leaf', 'a passing rain shower' or 'bird shit on the sleeve' (Ballard 2000: 19). Echoing Pinochet's declaration of power over every fibre of Chilean society – 'Not a leaf moves in Chile if I don't move it, let that be clear' (O'Shaughnessy 2000: 123) – Penrose's neo-fascist sentiment is utterly totalitarian in its drive towards order, rationality and productivity. Yet, its tone is also paranoid. This arises, if we follow Bataille's model, out of Penrose's own heterogeneous function within Eden-Olympia's strict economy:

> [F]ascist leaders are incontestably part of [a] heterogeneous existence [. . .] that disrupts the regular course of things [. . .] The affective flow that unites him with his followers [. . .] is a function of common consciousness of increasingly violent and excessive powers that accumulate in the person of the leader and through him become widely available. (Bataille 1994a: 143)

Another aspect of the fascist leader's paranoia speaks to the fact that, while he 'makes an appeal to sentiments traditionally defined as exalted and noble and tends to constitute an authority as an unconditioned

principle, situated above any utilitarian judgement', Penrose is unable
to give a rational account for 'his nature as something other' (Bataille
1994a: 145). This form of ambivalent authoritarianism translates, towards
the end of *Super-Cannes*, into a complex power struggle which is led,
somewhat ironically, by Halder, the black German security guard who
is very much part of the contingent world that affronts Penrose's neo-
fascist sensibilities. By carefully stage-managing a series of heterogeneous events – 'Trashed cars, a few house fires and office break-ins'
(Ballard 2000: 378) – Halder deliberately upsets Penrose's regime of
unity, order and cleanliness: 'Eden-Olympia can fight off a billion dollar
take-over, but a little dog shit on the shoe leaves it helpless' (Ballard
2000: 378). Against expectation, however, Halder's resisting energies are
not part of a wider project of multicultural reassertion. The immigrant
employee does not act on behalf of the dispossessed and dislocated
migrant collective of Eden-Olympia, we slowly realize, because his
intention is not to eradicate the homogenizing forces of Fascism once
and for all, but to expose and demote the leader in a bid for corporate
take-over: 'Along with a few friends. I'm climbing to the top, Mr Sinclair,
in my own way' (Ballard 2000: 378).

Enter once more the hapless amateur detective. Just as Penrose encouraged Sinclair to investigate the violent history of David Greenwood's
death in the name of pseudo-scientific enquiry, so Halder experiments
with Sinclair's unconscious desires and ambitions in the name of moral
responsibility. Now under Halder's direction, Sinclair resolves to expose
the secret history of Eden-Olympia and extricate himself simultaneously from the network of crime with which he has become so complicit.
His decision to 'put Eden-Olympia on trial' (Ballard 2000: 352) is less an
autonomous move to install moments of ethical and historical reflection
within this amoral and ahistorical realm, however, and more another
heterogeneous act of resistance which has been meticulously stage-
managed by Halder. Clutching the 'pump-action shotgun' (Ballard
2000: 390) (which Halder has rather conveniently provided for him),
Sinclair's determination to 'finish the task that David Greenwood had
begun' (Ballard 2000: 392) merely promises to imprison him further
within the relentless and all-consuming maze of multi-capitalist corruption that is Eden-Olympia. Still going round in circles, Sinclair's final
gesture reveals that there is no physical or psychological way out of the
postwar labyrinth.

Situating the Violence of J. G. Ballard's Postmillennial Fiction: The Possibilities of Sacrifice, the Certainties of Trauma

PHILIP TEW

Chapter Summary: Detecting a homicidal compulsion at work in *Super-Cannes* (2000), *Millennium People* (2003) and *Kingdom Come* (2006), this chapter explores representations of violence, sacrifice and community in Ballard's postmillennial fictions. Tew considers the sense of communal unease and violent aggression which dominates these works and investigates the cultural implications of recurrent patterns and motifs of violent trauma.

Key Words: *Crash; Concrete Island; Cocaine Nights; Super-Cannes; Millennium People; Kingdom Come*; violence; sacrifice; community; René Girard; trauma; detective fiction; perversions; murder; complicity.

In the first 6 years of the twenty-first century J. G. Ballard published three interrelated novels, *Super-Cannes* (2000), *Millennium People* (2003) and *Kingdom Come* (2006). Each novel is marked by a group – or perhaps more accurately a cult – which is committed to different forms of widespread violent social behaviour without any motive of financial gain. In turn, each group is peculiarly radicalized, and their actions impact unexpectedly upon the life of a centrally situated (in narrative terms) professional male in the throes of a profound (mid-life) identity crisis. Across all three narratives the loose correlation of crucial elements is so notable as to appear, in aesthetic terms, either reductively repetitive or deliberately uncanny. In all three novels, for instance, troubling events become associated both in thought and action with the death of an individual who is socially adjacent to the protagonist (the putative former lover of a wife in *Super-Cannes*, a former wife who has remarried in *Millennium People*, and an estranged father in *Kingdom Come*). This trilogy thus reproduces the plot dynamics first seen in *Cocaine Nights* (1996), a more conventional murder mystery and exploration of the meanings of murderous violence. Certainly a homicidal compulsion informs all of Ballard's postmillennial fiction to date, but what differentiates *Cocaine Nights* from the subsequent fictions is its exploration of crime as a motive for specific monetary gain. In contrast to *Super-Cannes*, *Millennium People* and *Kingdom Come*, the earlier text is less concerned with what one might term a radical sense of evil.

Set in Estrella de Mar, *Cocaine Nights* engages with the concealment of an essentially banal act which is intended to scare off criminal rivals but which *accidentally* kills them along with three members of the Hollinger family (Ballard 1996: 20–1). This central event precedes the novel's opening, when Charles Prentice arrives to visit his recently arrested brother, Frank. Hence most of the salient dynamics are retrospective, another aspect shared with Ballard's postmillennial narratives. Upon discovering that his sibling has confessed to the firebombing which kills five, Charles takes on the role of amateur detective and sets out to investigate the incident (Ballard 1996: 29). He soon discovers that the lives of the local ex-patriot criminal community revolve around the Club Nautico, a place where, shortly after his arrival, Charles encountered a violent rape which went ignored by some of the club's members. This collective indifference highlights a conspiratorial and alienated mood within the community. Towards the novel's end, though, some of the partially regretful conspirators responsible for the firebombing confess to Charles. Although the narrative concludes with a further moment of sacrificial confession, it trivializes any sense of *ennui*. The central mystery, it transpires, is underpinned by an organized criminality rather than a random or subversive pathology. It is these essentially conservative coordinates which make *Cocaine Nights* distinct from Ballard's other writing about sacrifice.

Andrzej Gasiorek distinguishes between *Cocaine Nights* – which he groups with *Super-Cannes* – and *Millennium People*, seeing in the first pair an 'angle of vision, locating this destructiveness in the social realm itself and then tracing its corrupting effects on the lives of those caught up within it' (Gasiorek 2005: 21). In contrast, he situates *Millennium People* as part of an 'apocalyptic imaginary' (Gasiorek 2005: 21). Although a hint of the apocalyptic prevails, something far more fundamental and self-evident marks out the postmillennial texts. From the pan-European corporate elite in *Super-Cannes*, to the radicalized, fashionable west

London upper middle classes in open revolt in *Millennium People*, to the 'estuary' *nouveau riche* along the M25 periphery in *Kingdom Come*, Ballard's cults are all distinctly bourgeois. Another prominent aspect, only incidentally present in *Cocaine Nights* is a structure of sacrifice emerging from Ballard's sense of trauma. More vertiginous than their predecessor, all three novels possess an unfocused yet ineluctable sense of unexpected mourning shared by those who are not otherwise in any sense intimate. As Francois Flahault has suggested in *Malice* (2003):

> The process of mourning is not only about the bond between oneself and the deceased person. It is just as much about the relationship one maintains with one's own boundlessness. A death which one has not mourned thus holds the same power to invade as the object of an impossible and passionate lover. (2003: 47)

Ballard's three postmillennial novels exhibit both sacrificial violence and curious experiences of loss which undermines conventional ideas of mourning and selfhood.

Let's reconsider what occurs in a general sense in these texts. First, in *Super-Cannes* Paul Sinclair, a recuperating amateur pilot, travels to the Côte d'Azur where his younger wife, Jane, has been appointed as a company doctor at Eden-Olympia, a bourgeois business enclave where cultish middle class gang violence ferments among the villas. Reflecting on his wife's new place of work, Sinclair reveals how: 'Her predecessor, a young English doctor named David Greenwood, had a tragic and still unexplained death after running amok with a rifle' (Ballard 2000: 3). Unexpectedly, the life and death of this distant love rival begin to obsess Sinclair. Second, in *Millennium People*, a middle class revolt erupts in Chelsea Marina, London. Through the actions of Richard Gould (a disillusioned paediatrician), this leads to a more radical revolution or terror campaign in which David Markham's former wife, Laura, is killed in an explosion in Terminal Two at Heathrow airport. Laura's violent death precipitates Markham's compulsive involvement in the Chelsea Marina revolution, a revolution 'so modest and well behaved that almost no one had noticed' (Ballard 2003: 3). Although Markham is obsessed with the circumstances of his first wife's death, he is soon drawn to the perverse power inherent in such violent acts. Indeed, they evoke for him the transgression of the Hungerford massacre in which a 'new kind of violence had been born, springing from nothing' (Ballard 2003: 279). Gould goes on to kill a number of individuals, including an obscure television presenter, and he also plots a failed assassination attempt on a cabinet minister. As Jean Baudrillard has observed in *Symbolic Exchange and Death* (1993), such acts signify both literally and symbolically:

> [I]t matters little whether death is accidental, criminal, or catastrophic: from the moment it escapes 'natural' reason, and becomes a challenge to nature, it once again becomes the business of the group, demanding a collective and

symbolic response; in a word, it arouses the *passion for the artificial*, which is at the same time sacrificial passion [. . .] We, for our part, no longer have an effective rite for reabsorbing death and its rupturing energies; here remains the phantasm of sacrifice, the violent artifice of death. Hence the intense and profoundly *collective* satisfaction of the automobile death. (2003: 165)

As the obsessive staging of violent collisions between man and machine in *Crash* (1973) suggests, the quasi-sacrificial is a familiar enough propensity in Ballard's earlier work. In *Millennium People* Markham reflects:

In his despairing and psychopathic way, Richard Gould's motives were honourable. He was trying to find meaning in the most meaningless times, the first of a new kind of desperate man who refuses to bow before the arrogance of existence and the tyranny of time-space. He believed that the most pointless acts could challenge the universe at its own game. (Ballard 2003: 292)

There is, however, another aspect to such ritualized deaths (which appeases a sense of self antagonized by fate) and to the 'failed' Chelsea revolt: 'Only by cutting short their exile and returning to the estate could they make it clear that their revolution was indeed meaningless, that the *sacrifices* were absurd and negligible. A *heroic* failure redefined itself as a success' [My italics] (Ballard 2003: 292–3). The offering up of innocent victims, of minor celebrities in particular, expresses another perverse conjunction of the concepts of the sacrificial and the heroic. *Kingdom Come* begins with a short paragraph that Ballard has described as representing the essence of the novel: 'The suburbs dream of violence, asleep in their drowsy villas, sheltered by benevolent shopping malls, they wait patiently for the nightmares which will wake them into a more passionate world' (Ballard 2006: 3). In a fictional summer evoking the nationalism exhibited in Britain during the 2006 World Cup, hordes of the lower middle classes wear England football shirts and sport the St. George's flag. Ballard contextualizes these details in his conversation with Toby Litt:

JGB: [W]e see uneasy, sort of, tremors fluttering all those St George's flags. I mean, had you come here a week ago, every bloody shop in Shepperton had a large St George's flag. Many of the houses around here had flags fluttering. Every other car had more than one flag. You know, you can't help but think the excitement over the World Cup was about more than mere sport, I feel . . . I don't say that it's the first sign of a fascist takeover. But –

TL: I beg to differ.

JGB: Maybe it is. I mean, the point is that people are obviously bored and they are very dissatisfied with their lives, and I think it only would take a small push, and something rather unsettling might begin to happen. (Ballard cited in Litt 2006)

Richard Pearson, an unemployed advertising executive, travels to the suburb of Brooklands where his father has been shot by a gunman who apparently ran amok in a shopping mall (Ballard 2006: 4). Witnessing a racist attack and a display of support for thuggish marshals of sports clubs within days of arriving in Brooklands, Pearson reflects how 'violence and hate, as always, were organizing themselves' (Ballard 2006: 191). Ballard thereby concedes a disturbing balance recognized critically by Flahault: 'Being decent, just and benevolent is a way of existing. Being malicious is equally a way of existing' (2003: 167). As Flahault insists, malevolence and conflict (even when subdued) underpin all human existence. This is evident in the dead father's diary entries which reflect a desire for collectivity. He is drawn to the psychopathology of the crowd, observing that, despite its violent responses, this mass has no leadership: 'Everything I've read about the Nazi leaders shows that their followers didn't fear disaster but actively welcomed it' (Ballard 2006: 195). Although he fears a messianic figure will harness this latent energy, he is nevertheless drawn to the group. Paradoxically, his death almost supplies the necessary messianic element by inducing the curiosity and ongoing presence of his son.

Each of the three postmillennial narratives teases out a series of perverse, violent events. Yet, as René Girard has argued in *Violence and the Sacred* (1988): 'The borderline between rational discrimination and arbitrary persecution is sometimes difficult to trace' (1988: 19). There remains something akin to a paradoxical rationality in these contexts, a sociologically inscribed if perverse logic revealed beneath the apparent mysteries. In *Kingdom Come*, the authorities are relatively unperturbed, concerning themselves only with sustaining their overall hegemonic logic through media propaganda and consumerism. Initially, at least, they are indifferent to the spontaneity of individual acts of violence. Note how the narrative reflects on the consumers' awareness of the mediated reality of Brooklands:

> They knew they were being lied to, but if lies were consistent enough they defined themselves as a credible alternative to truth. Emotion ruled almost everything, and lies were driven by emotions that were familiar and supportive, while the truth came with hard edges that cut and bruised. They preferred lies and mood music, they accepted the make-believe of David Cruise the firefighter and defender of their freedoms. Consumer capitalism had never thrived by believing the truth. Lies were preferred by the people of the shopping malls because they could be complicit with them. (Ballard 2006: 204)

A further key characteristic of these novels is their representation of scapegoats. In 'Generative Scapegoating', Girard distinguishes various types of scapegoating. 'Psychosocial meaning', which is the populist usage for 'the victim or victims of unjust violence or discrimination' (Girard 1987: 73–4) only superficially applies to Ballard's texts. More interestingly, Ballard's work does evoke Girard's notion that not only does collective violence represent 'a contagious belief' (Girard 1987: 81), but it plays out an impulse and dynamic motivated by belief, since as Girard indicates, 'Scapegoating is not effective unless an element of delusion enters into it' (Girard 1987: 74). In *Super-Cannes* gangs of executives attack the immigrant poor in order to establish a reflexive conviction concerning their collective, superior selfhood. *Kingdom Come* deploys a similar example of this logic, underpinned as it is by various references to Nazi Germany. Before knowing his father was attempting to infiltrate what he imagines is a far right grouping, Pearson explores the evidence in his father's flat of a life he had hardly encountered. He is confronted by the man's apparent neo-fascist obsession to which his workstation is an 'altar' (Ballard 2006: 55). Pearson also finds books on fascist politicians and dictators alongside 'an illustrated guide to Nazi regalia and the ceremonial uniforms of the Third Reich' (Ballard 2006: 55). Hence a historical scapegoating haunts the text, and this becomes increasingly relevant as the persecution of ethnic minorities emerges among the middle-class sporting clubs of the Metro Centre.

All three novels are further interconnected by what Girard refers to as 'the logic of mobs on the rampage', a 'collective rage' which is causally simplistic or flattened (1987: 85). Each scenario involves a regression to what Girard describes as 'the very unyielding intensity of mimetic rivalry' a characteristic of early man which Girard believes is still to be found in the mob's ability to focus on 'a single target' (1987: 125–6). This is bleak subject matter which foregrounds trauma and violence. The temptation is to read their topographical significance. As I seek to demonstrate one needs a precise typology, seeing the innate qualities of both, the possibilities of their change, a shifting signification. Moreover, in this context it is easy to ignore a prominent feature of Ballard's fiction, the bleak humour. For his novels can be situated within the comic tradition which James Wood identifies in *The Irresponsible Self* as: 'This comedy, or tragicomedy, of the modern novel [which] replaces the knowable with the unknowable, transparency with unreliability' (2004: 10). All three postmillenial novels are sombre manifestations of 'the secular and comic nature of modern fiction' (Wood 2004: 18).

Many critics use Ballard's own traumatic childhood to biographically and critically enframe him. Gasiorek, for instance, states that, early in life, Ballard positions himself so as to exhibit and take advantage of

> an edgy aggressiveness [. . .] a sense of intellectual autonomy, and a non-conformist mind-set. Ballard the writer has been refusing to conform ever

since, adopting a libertarian and anarchic stance *vis-à-vis* social life, which is related in complex ways not only to the exacerbation of an already febrile imagination under the unsettling conditions of a prisoner-of-war camp, but also to the unbalancing of perspectives and frameworks that such conditions can bring about. (2005: 1)

Importantly for any critical reception of Ballard, Gasiorek situates Ballard's initial aesthetic in terms of his understanding of England as a foreign country expressed as a propensity towards the disturbance and hybridizing of genres. Foregrounding interpretatively the literary field, Gasiorek concludes that

[u]neasiness characterises Ballard's relationship with his adopted country and with all the literary modes he has deployed. He has repeatedly expressed his disapprobation of the prevailing literary culture of the 1950s, and he has heaped scorn on the overt moralism associated with the then hegemonic Leavisite tendency. (2005: 2–3)

For Iain Sinclair, the underlying dynamics and disposition of Ballard's work in the 1960s and 1970s involve:

A vocabulary that lurches between Victorian circumlocution and forensic exactitude. Ballard was in exile in Shepperton, a returned colonial; a time-traveller trying to recreate, through cabbalistic rhythms and repetitions, the Proustian excitement of scenes witnessed in childhood [. . .] Nobody could be expected to act on these instructions, they were magical and potentially threatening to the fabric of the received world. (1999: 8–9)

Rather than superficially evoking the familiar idea of the psychopathic consciousness, I will focus upon the subtleties of the ritualistic and transformative possibilities underlying Sinclair's abutment of the psychopathological with Ballard's transitional landscape (Sinclair 1999: 43) and his charming perversity (Sinclair 1999: 85). For as Ballard has commented to Sinclair: 'I think the suburbs are more interesting than people will let on. In the suburbs you find uncentered lives. The normal civic structures are not there. So that people have more freedom to explore their own imaginations, their own obsessions' (Ballard cited in Sinclair 1999: 84).

Within the contexts of my discussion, *Concrete Island* (1974) can be used to exemplify certain well-established Ballardian characteristics. After a front-tyre blow-out, an isolated and increasingly paranoid professional male protagonist, Maitland, finds himself trapped in the detritus of an isolated traffic island: 'The sequence of violent events only micro-seconds in duration had opened and closed behind him like a vent of hell' (Ballard 1992: 7). In the first ten chapters Maitland's feverish consciousness distorts the island in ways which are both troubling and manic. After his apparent initial rescue, injured, yet relatively immobile, Maitland is manipulated by a sexually suggestive young female, Jane, and a demented tramp of limited intelligence, Proctor. In this reworking of Shakespeare's *The Tempest* Maitland exhibits an insistent desire, a 'will to survive, to dominate the island and harness its limited resources' (Ballard 1992: 47).

On partly recovering, Maitland exhibits an increasingly Prospero-like self-assertion, becoming increasingly aggressive towards the others. His initial quest is to escape his *ad hoc* captors and to rejoin his apparently civilized life as an architect. However, in the events that lead to Proctor's death Maitland adapts to his *demi-monde* with its stark relationships, rejecting 'strains in his character, qualities irrelevant to the task of coming to terms with the island' (Ballard: 1992: 126). Proctor is sacrificed, albeit inadvertently, but he seems too incoherent and inconsequential to represent much of a loss. Proctor's final position is one of reductive abjection whilst Maitland's concluding sense of self is one of dominion (Ballard 1992: 126).

Interpretatively, Gasiorek conjoins *Concrete Island* with *High-Rise* (1975) because of the isolation of the protagonists who, by being denied action, are forced to understand their dilemmas psychologically. He historically situates the pair of fictions as 'belong[ing] to a particular socio-cultural period, the interregnum between the end of the "old Labour" project begun in 1945 and the beginning of the Thatcher era in 1979. The air of stasis hangs over these works' (2005: 107). As these texts demonstrate, Ballard perceives elements of cultural change. In his dialogue with Sinclair, for instance, Ballard identifies a suburban culture transformed by television (Sinclair 1999: 84). In this earlier phase, the violence contributes to an economy of actions marked by a dialectic of the spectacular, of the voyeuristically libidinous, of the putatively traumatological as opposed to a traumatized consciousness, and a transcendent possibility punctuated by death. Importantly such deaths retain a strong element of the accidental. The protagonists are not entirely passive: they are active observers, if not participants, of a quasi-sacrificial fervour. And this is a significant structure of action and idea since, as Walter Burkert indicates in *Savage Energies* (1983): 'Sacrificial killing is the basic experience of the "sacred"' (1983: 3). In Ballard, the sacrificial impulse illuminates either a kind of regression (a reaching for that which is absent, lost and recollected dimly) or an archetypal sense of the self.

Another earlier moment of Ballardian sacrifice begins with the awfulness within the mundane, the oddly cruel and impulsive. In *Crash*, 'James Ballard' describes Vaughan's sideswiping of a large mongrel dog where: 'Already his acts of violence had become so random that I was no more than a captive spectator' (Ballard 1973: 12). James admits being drawn into Vaughan's economy of imaginary deaths 'and wholly accepting [of] his logic' (Ballard 1973: 190). He also stresses early in the novel

that, although death might be rehearsed for Vaughan, it is finally accidental. Vaughan had hoped to sacrifice Elizabeth Taylor in 'a coronation
of wounds he had staged with the devotion of an Earl Marshal' (Ballard
1973: 7), but he accidentally kills himself by crashing into a busload of
tourists (Ballard 1973: 7). Sinclair is correct to identify in the text 'another
tradition, metaphysical, occulted' with Vaughan a 'psycho and mystic'
(Sinclair 1999: 90, 92). As Maurice Blanchot has argued in *The Infinite
Conversation* (1993): 'Magic does not always require ceremony, a laying
on of hands or the use of relics. There is already magic when one individual acts in an imposing manner with regard to another' (1993: 230).
Blanchot continues, 'The onlooker in any psychiatric clinic whatsoever
is struck by this impression of violence; moreover, he adds to it by being
a spectator. Speech is not free, gestures deceive' (1993: 230). Such is the
perspective of the reader of this phase of Ballard, as uneasy and uncertain as Blanchot's account of Freud concerning transference, another
reanimation of 'a primary "event" that is individual and proper to each
history, a scene constituting something important and overwhelming,
but also such that the one who experiences it can neither master nor
determine it, and with which he has essential relations of insufficiency'
(Blanchot 1993: 231). Here lies the troubling nature of the narratives
and the inadequacy of our critical accounts, or own appropriations
and reanimations. At this critical moment, consider the apparently sacrificial impulse in the earlier fiction in terms of Girard's definitional
account of sacrifice where the ritual, although symbolic, is essentially
intersubjective, devious, and remains innately misunderstood, but is
fundamentally related to 'reciprocal substitution' (1998: 1) to protect a
community from its own violence. There exists in a sacrifice the 'common denominator [which] is internal violence – all the dissensions,
rivalries, jealousies, and quarrels within the community that the sacrifices are designed to suppress' (Girard 1988: 8). The premillennial sacrificial motifs lack these qualities, because of their ephemerality, their
location in the interstices of contemporary culture. Any apparently
sacrificial impulse is not predicated upon Girard's tenet of the concept
of sacrifice as 'an instrument of prevention in the struggle against
violence' (Girard 1988: 18). The insanities of these books speak rather
of an individualistic ethos, a presupposition of, and enmeshment in
modernity.

In the earlier Ballard there is not such much an *ennui* as a flirtatious
kind of madness which adopts the language of excess. Blanchot speaks
of living with affirmation in the midst of terror and of engaging with
violence in such a manner that in confronting itself death draws back
and is transformed into a site of a speech which:

> is infinitely hazardous, for it is encompassed by terror. Radical violence is
> its fringe and its halo; it is one with the obscurity of the night, with the
> emptiness of the abyss, and so doubtful, so dangerous that this question

incessantly returns: why the exigency of such a language? What have we to do with it? (Blanchot 1993: 187)

Certainly Ballard's earlier work and its penumbra of violence evokes this logic, but it remains marginal and, when aestheticized, finally ephemeral, exhibiting a perverse beauty. The synthesis veers towards the triumphalist, expressing a confident elitism. The ritual that concludes *Crash* is one of scarring and insemination, a cathartic and ennobling vision of sacrifice which mixes blood and semen to create 'the first constellation in the zodiac of our minds' (Ballard 1973: 224). My contention is that the postmillennial fiction is more doubtful and differently nuanced. It is intensely pessimistic, exploring existential *ennui*. Sacrifice in these novels is structured so that the initial fervour predates the action in each case, so much so that the mystery or detective element is introduced with each protagonist tracking down the facts of the case. This echoes a tradition of genre fictions that both mediate the awful physical realities of the violent act while simultaneously and paradoxically centring them. The celebrants – which is to use a term of Girard's that seems so appropriate for these fictions – demonstrate precisely the 'misunderstanding' which Girard situates as central to the sacrificial movement; namely, the desire to 'restore harmony to the community, to reinforce the social fabric' (Girard 1988: 8). The celebrants imagine they have selected victims so that 'they can be exposed to violence without fear of reprisal. Their death does not automatically entail an act of vengeance' (Girard 1988: 13).

Bracketing *Super-Cannes*, *Millennium People* and *Kingdom Come* as a discreet Ballardian phase helps us to recognize that all three are explicitly centred upon an underlying malaise not individual or private, but communal, involving a series of collectively significant violent and aggressive impulses. For Freud, any traumatic situation expresses a neurotic symptom and in a somewhat optimistic fashion returns us to childhood experience (Freud 1964: 58), although he admits of their '*compulsive* quality' (Freud 1964: 76). When considering trauma in Ballard's postmillennial fiction, I would suggest that the explicit combination of the elements of the scapegoat and the sacrificial militate towards a perverse centring (that is as far as the rational logic of enlightened modernity is concerned) that recovers, as if archeologically, the roots of violent sacrifice as the basis of human society (Cousineau 2004: 16). Arguably, this goes far deeper than the latency Freud uses to suggest the sexual nature of the traumatized individual (Freud 1964: 77–8). Ballard says of *Kingdom Come* that: '[W]hat people are looking for is their own psychopathology. They're looking for madness as a way out' (Ballard cited in Litt 2006). In the postmillennial novels this is as true of the protagonists as the groups from which these forensic individuals initially appear to be excluded. Ballard adds:

[W]hat [I] see as threatening about the all-pervasive and all-powerful consumer society is that it's not any specific individual who is responsible for anything nasty that may happen in the future. This is a collective enterprise. All of us who are members of consumer society – all of us are responsible, in a way. I think that these are sort of almost seismic movements that drift through the collective psyche and which facilitate the emergence of ultra-right wing groups like the Nazis and the fascists in Italy. Or even the communist regime under Stalin. There you have extremely threatening political organizations which come to power with the complicity – that's the extraordinary thing – with the complicity of the populations they rule. (Ballard cited in Litt 2006)

The protagonist as outsider in each novel is drawn towards the inner workings of a particular sense of disturbance and unease, encountering, in a localized sense, and through a symbolic violent killing, a social condition which Piotr Sztompka has described as 'traumatogenic social change' (Sztompka 2004: 158). This condition can be initiated variously by sudden and rapid occurrences such as war and terrorist attack, or radical shifting dominant values and conditions so it remains surprising and shocking for an individual to comprehend and assimilate (Alexander et al. 2004: 159). However, this social revelation then unravels and allows a perception of an inner depravity or an innate universal complicity with the central traumatological act, that is to the sacrificial moment they have pursued seeking a notion of justice. In this way, one may situate the state of mind of Ballard's postmillennial protagonists, understanding that they are far less insouciant than their predecessors. They recognize the duality of suffering, both its evil and redemptive possibilities. Moreover, they partake of the kind of 'mimetic desire' (1987: 121) that Girard sees in Freud's *Totem and Taboo* and which not only draws upon a primeval 'mystique of collective violence' (Girard 1987: 120), but is 'a symmetrical, reciprocal process because it is mimetic' (Girard 1987: 123). The deaths partake of an innate paradox not simply because of the, at times, vicarious, and, at other times, active complicity of the victims in the sacrificial and scapegoating processes. Rather, as Girard indicates, the death of the sacrificial victim generates a pacification of the previously controlled mimetic urge (1987: 127–8). Such a past is explicitly invoked in passing; as Pearson reflects when order breaks down with the occupation of the Metro-Centre, and he is reminded of an earlier age and set of impulses: 'I felt my way past the counters, surrounded by hundreds of knives, saws and chisels, their blades forming a silver forest in the darkness. A more primitive world was biding its time' (Ballard 2006: 226).

Significantly, Ballard's three novels are very much akin to the modernist narratives categorized by Thomas Cousinaeu in *Ritual Unbound*, for 'their narrators tend to defend the designated victims in ways that ironically produce a *remystification* of sacrifice' (2004: 17). 'While taking the side of these victims against their persecutors', he continues, 'they often encourage the community of readers assembled around them to direct its own scapegoating impulses against other targeted figures' (Cousineau 2004: 17). Unlike Cousineau's account of the overturning of the 'mythic' core and 'sacrificial cause' (2004: 29) in key, multiply-centered modernist texts (such as *The Turn of the Screw* and *Heart of Darkness*), each by simultaneously creating 'an implicit, demystifying countertext that will be available to readers who have successfully resisted the narrator's sacrificial misreadings' (2004: 33), Ballard leaves its possibilities extant. *Kingdom Come* ends with the destruction of the shopping centre that has been at the heart of the peripheral unease circling the M25, and as the tumult subsides: 'The once real possibility of a fascist republic had vanished into the air with all the vapourizing three-piece suites and discount carpeting' (Ballard 2006: 279). Yet echoing elements of the ending of Nathanael West's *The Day of the Locust* (1939), Pearson concludes:

> I watched the spectators around me, standing silently at the railing. There were no St George's shirts, but they watched a little too intently. One day there would be another Metro-Centre and another desperate and deranged dream. Marchers would drill and wheel while another cable announcer sang out the beat. In time, unless the sane woke and rallied themselves, an even fiercer republic would open the doors and spin the turnstiles of its beckoning paradise. (Ballard 2006: 280)

So finally, why does Ballard repeat his pattern in these stories, varying only the location and the victimage/victimhood, and reiterating the underlying and relentless logic of perverse emotion, of an emotional dialectic of order/disorder, and the sacrificial urge, all spiced with his traumatological recognition of many lurking dangers? To co-opt Flahault's terminology, Ballard is demystifying the 'unequalled intensity' invested since the Enlightenment in the West in the very idea of the individual, thereby 'losing the self-idealization to which we attached our sense of worth, and losing the wholeness from which we derived a narcissistic satisfaction' (2003: 166). As Ballard has already suggested, 'I am not offering a grand answer to all society's problems. I leave that to others. I'm issuing warnings' (Ballard cited in Litt 2006). Perhaps Ballard's very repetition in the postmillennial novels itself suggests something beyond the contracted space of a singular signification, reinforcing the concept of an inner compulsion however unpalatable it might seem. What else might explain his repeated postmillennial economy of traumas? First, perhaps, because Ballard understands, much like Blanchot, that, 'The disaster is related to forgetfulness – forgetfulness without memory, the motionless retreat of what has not been treated – the immemorial, perhaps' (Blanchot 1993: 3) and that, 'There is disaster only because, ceaselessly, it falls short of disaster. The end of nature, the end of culture' (Blanchot 1986: 41). Second, Ballard reiterates the underlying threat and reality, the ambiguity at the heart of the sacrificial and the tragic tradition, for as Burkert says of certain classical rites: 'in the sacrificial feast the joy of the festival and the horror of death interpenetrate' (2001: 11). Ballard's books re-inhabit both a reality and such a fundamental otherness, hoping to acquire the energy and meta-symbolic vocabulary of that which both permeates and breaches reason, animating sacrificial energies so as to acknowledge 'that dark, "negative", depressing ideas can exert an irresistible seductive power over us' (Flahault 2003: 88).

Afterword

Toby Litt

I'd like to propose another thought experiment: We have got J. G. Ballard wrong. The whole lot of us. One hundred per cent wrong. J. G. Ballard isn't, truth be told, a writer at all – not in the sense we might commonly understand it. He writes, yes, that has to be admitted, hundreds of thousands of remarkable words, words worthy of close academic scrutiny, but that isn't the focus of his life, and never has been. Here is the secret. All J. G. Ballard's literary activity is a monumental diversion, an autobiographical smokescreen, in the creation of which he has only a passing interest. He can write as he does without ever giving his whole self to it; perhaps he gives 10 to 15 per cent of his attention, sometimes. He puts the words down extremely fast, his mind often elsewhere; he is impatient to get back to his true vocation. Because James Graham Ballard (born 15 November 1930 in Shanghai) is not a novelist and short story writer. Not essentially. He is a tunnel-builder, a cohort of ants, moles, rabbits and badgers, and the narrator of Kafka's 'The Burrow'. Beneath the gloriously shabby house in Shepperton there exists a vast network of steel-lined passages, taking the form of a pyramid. Through this three-dimensional maze, for that is what it is, only Ballard knows his way. Only Ballard knows his way because, extravagant as it may seem, Ballard is the only human being ever to have entered these tunnels. The great pyramid-maze has been excavated single-handedly over the course of the past 47 years. Entered through a small padlocked trapdoor, located immediately beneath Ballard's desk, it is the reason Ballard moved to Shepperton in the first place; it is the reason – of course, there must be a reason – why he has never moved. Here is where the Spielberg wealth went. Here is the reason for the widening gaps between books. Here is the masterpiece. The first tunnel Ballard built reached from beneath his house to a secret location yards from the Thames' riverbank. This was a necessary; so that he would have somewhere inconspicuously to dispose of all the excavated soil and rock – without having to resort to *The Great Escape* trouserleg-tactics. Also, he could set up a small warehouse here, to which deliveries of equipment might be made. Since that initial earthwork was completed, around 1964, Ballard has been tunnelling obsessively. Work on the deepest floor of the pyramid only reached completion in early May of last year. And still no one knows about it, still Ballard remains silent on the subject of his greatest achievement. That his literary career has drawn so much attention to him is, almost, an embarrassment to Ballard – especially since what he wanted most of all from writing was a small income and plenty of free time. Because of his growing notoriety, Ballard-the-tunneller has had to build up a convincing cover story, psychologically convincing. To this end he has meticulously faked a lifelong obsession with all things aerial: pilots, flight, spacecraft etc. Whereas, as now becomes clear, his concerns have always been chthonic. If he could, picking one of the Verne-journeys, he would travel not to the moon but to the centre of the earth. He has no real interest in the over-head world nor, when it comes to it, in the surface-level world. At all costs, though, the pyramid-maze must be protected. So Ballard has had to fake a curiosity about what goes on in the overhead and surface-level worlds. Often, he has merely taken that which was closest to hand. He could not be bothered to put in the research that traditional literary writing would require – research, that is, into traditional literary writing. And so, he has used what was in front of his face. The places he could not help but go. The buildings illness and bureaucracy required him to enter. The roads which took him there and back. And, thus, the pyramid-maze has been protected. Between it and discovery stands Ballard-the-writer, Ballard-the-autobiographer, Ballard-the-bluffer. And what it contains, at the very centre, a point reached after two hours of intricate descents, traverses and climbs, in a steel-lined room standing over three stories high, is . . .

This, I'd suggest, is just about how wrong we may have got J. G. Ballard. And, perhaps, also, how wrong he's got himself. We think he's a writer when, in fact, he is a tunneller; he thinks he's a tunneller when, in fact, he's a writer. For me, the least interesting Ballard of all is Ballard's Ballard – a reduced, explicated, psychologically prompted character: a technological writer with no interest in technology; a profound psychopathologist with little knowledge of psychopathology; a humanist who couldn't care less about humanity; an Englishman who, in his own country, remains abroad. What is he, then, if not these things? I don't know. I do know, with absolute certainty, that I am likely to be as wrong about Ballard as anyone else.

Kingdom Come: An Interview with J. G. Ballard

Jeannette Baxter

Jeannette Baxter: Over the course of your literary career you have published 18 novels, a novella, nearly a hundred short stories, and over a hundred pieces of journalism. When and why did you first start writing, and what remains your motivation to write?

J. G. Ballard: I wrote a great deal of 'fiction' as a child, starting when I was seven or eight, short imitations of school texts that impressed me for some reason (*Westward Ho!* is one I remember), G. A. Henty, tales of the Spanish Main, American novels that my parents were reading, articles in *Readers Digest* and so on. But *not* the Arabian Nights Tales, which I found rather frightening, or the Grimm Brothers fairy tales with their weird sub-Beardsley, Pre-Raphaelite illustrations, close to the Surrealists but too airless and vaguely sinister. At the Cathedral School we were set lines for the smallest thing, and were expected to copy out five pages or more of some school text, Dickens or Kingsley. I discovered that rather than copying the text it was easier and quicker to make it up myself. The day after handing in the sheets the master, a Church of England clergyman, said severely: 'JGB, next time don't copy out some trashy novel!' My first review, as it were, and I remember feeling vaguely pleased (I must have been nine or ten). In my teens I was writing short stories, and by the time I became a medical student I already knew that I would be a writer, and that it would govern my life.

Why one is a writer at all is difficult to understand, and no doubt the neuro-scientists will explain it all one day soon. I suspect that it's close to the need that actors seem to have to act all the time (people who knew him say there was no 'real' Laurence Olivier). There's some defect in their sense of themselves that leads them to stress and extend the smallest gesture. Writers in a sense are rewriting their own existences, since there is no repertory of available roles to draw on – no Lady Macbeth, or Norma Desmond. There's an attempt to make sense of the world, especially if one feels a bit of a misfit, and few writers seem to have had happy childhoods. In my case the shock of coming to England in 1946 was the Big Bang, from which I've never recovered. It was such a strange place, shattered by the war (mentally more than physically), scarcely able to face the future, entangled in a maze of archaic social delusions.

The whole nation needed to be laid on the psychiatrist's couch. It needed to free itself, and it needed to Americanize itself (as Shanghai had been Americanized). It needed to discover its future, and realise what was really going on in the world. This led naturally to science fiction. The shock has sustained me for 50 years. Contrary to what many people think, there's a highly moralistic strain in my fiction. Too moralistic, I often think.

JB: To what extent would you say that your novels engage with what it is to be English? What qualitative shifts do you discern between our ideas of Englishness in the postwar period and in the present day?

JGB: I'm not sure that I have explored Englishness in the usual sense of social customs, manners, behaviour, dress and codes of conduct and so on, in a spectrum running from Mass Observation to Waugh and the whole U and Non-U business. I like to think that I've fled from all that and viewed it through the same exasperated eyes of any French or American visitor tired of having to decode our little ways. The behaviour of the characters in *High Rise*, *Crash*, *The Kindness of Women* or my last four novels has not been affected by their being English. *Crash* translated without any difficulty into Cronenberg's generic North America. Most Americans who have read *The Atrocity Exhibition* assume that it is set in the USA. Not so – it's mostly London and the Home Counties. Shanghai was not a British colony, and was nothing like Hong Kong or Singapore. It was a vast, polyglot international metropolis, 90 per cent Chinese and a 100 per cent Americanized – American cars, coca-cola, Hollywood films. I like to think that the 'England' and 'English' characters in my fiction have been internationalized in the same way, so that they can be themselves and not have to worry about whether they are wearing a brown suit or saying serviette (did anyone ever?). One reason why my novels have been published around the world is that Japanese or Polish or French readers can easily identify with the characters. I don't think there's much Englishness in *Kingdom Come*. There is England, the England of 2006 and the motorway towns, that new England of the retail park and CCTV camera that Thatcher and Blair both wooed. Once you get the specimen on the dissecting table, cut away the brown suit and throw the serviette into the pedal bin you can get down to exposing the real pathology, which is what I'm interested in, along with Drs Nathan, Vaughan, Wilder Penrose, Gould and Maxted. Brown suit or the best grey worsted, this man is dangerously drawn to a self-constructed madness. . . . Why, and is it perhaps to the good?

To answer your second question, there of course have been enormous shifts in notions of Englishness – higher expectations, better health and education, the serious prospect of an end to monarchy and the class system, but also a decline in patriotism and any sense of national purpose – in short, all the usual tick boxes. But they're not really my concern. England has changed enormously, but it now seems to be on the verge of becoming a country without a future – unlike the USA, France, China, India. What does the United Kingdom stand for? Nothing as far as I can see. It's a place that takes its cue from TV programmes. Big Brother is interesting because it suggests that we are drawn to the bizarre and sociopathic. The Blair premiership suggests that we will like being lied to, that we prefer promises that will never be kept. All this, I suspect, is preparing us for the ultimate adventure playground – a full-blown psychopathology that we will embrace with the eagerness that the Germans displayed when they embraced the Nazis. In the end, anything is better than being sane.

JB: Although much of your writing has been characterized as dystopian, it seems that your latest novel, *Kingdom Come*, explores the horror of the utopian, the horror of the 'no-place' in which time, history, politics and morality are absent. Could you elaborate on this?

JGB: I think you're right. It's an important point. People use the term dystopian about my fiction, but how true is that? Most of my so-called dystopias are rather pleasant places to live in. *Nineteen Eighty-Four*, *Brave New World*, Fritz Lang's *Metropolis* are clearly hell on earth, but my novels, from *Crash* onwards, show places where the main characters are perfectly happy. Vaughan and his sex-crashing chums, the *High Rise* inhabitants happily tearing apart their up-market world, the crime-wave enthusiasts in *Cocaine Nights* and *Super-Cannes*, the rebels of *Millennium People* and *Kingdome Come*, are all having a great time. Not only that, but the reader might suspect that the author rather approves of their 'deviant' new logic. Or does he? I think the whole of my fiction is poised on that balancing point. Sometimes it tilts one way, sometimes another. The 'no-place' where history, politics and morality are absent is certainly a special kind of nightmare utopia, and it's one we have been moving towards for the past century. We have fewer and fewer moral decisions to make, whether driving our cars or raising our children, treating our employees and ex-wives. In fact, one could live today without making any moral decisions at all – that part of our lives has been subcontracted to the DHSS and the Home Office. There is a huge vacuum in people's lives, and what will fill it?

JB: Your more recent novels appear to be increasingly concerned with questions of complicity, of responsibility, as they provoke the reader to make a number of unsettling connections between euphemistic language and ethical deferral. In *Cocaine Nights*, for instance, the word 'game' substitutes for acts of violent gang rape. Can you say a bit more about this?

JGB: Language today is almost devoid of meaning, especially in the public sphere. One could almost say that communication is the last role that language is intended to play. Its real task is to blur and obscure, to blunt and defuse, to mothball anything with sharp corners. This has been going on for a very long time, ever since politicians noticed the power of mass-circulation newspapers, but it was always denied. Now we have a situation where those who speak this non-communicating language are quite open about it, and the public at large like it that way. The more blurred and meaningless a message, the more they respond. A statement such as '"Bird-flu is spreading rapidly through the British Isles and - in three months, half of you will be dead"' – would not cause panic because no one would grasp its meaning.

JB: While the inhabitants of Brooklands worship at the temple of consumerism, orthodox religion exists merely as an expletive in *Kingdom Come*. Why is this? Do you anticipate a time ahead when fundamentalist religions might dissipate the forces of 'Secular Consumerism'?

JGB: England is largely a secular society today, and if the novel were set in the USA it would be very different. Huge numbers of Americans go to church, though Jesus is sold like a product and religion could be considered as a branch of consumerism. Years ago I used to be baffled by the Radio Church of God and similar radio churches in the USA that attracted hundreds of millions of dollars from American listeners. Why on earth did they send in their hard-earned dollar bills? The answer of course is that the money transaction authenticated the transfer of religious feeling from preacher to listener. Money alone had the power to do this, a power greater than mere faith.

It's impossible to look very far ahead, because the placid surface of English life could be severely shaken by scarcely understood events – bird-flu, some kind of nuclear war in the Middle East, the collapse of oil supplies and so on. But I can't see the English embracing any kind of fundamentalist religion, unless it's based on Big Brother or the Premier League or a weird combination of both.

JB: You have long been keeping an eye on the consumer-capitalist machine and, in many respects, *Kingdom Come* can be seen as an extension of those 1960s consumerist critiques which included 'The Subliminal Man', 'The Intensive Care Unit' and *The Atrocity Exhibition*. What do you think are the main differences between the postwar and postmillennial stages of consumercapitalism?

JGB: There are huge differences. The postwar English public was exhausted by years of rationing, had never experienced the wonders of cars, washing machines, supermarkets and the entire mass-psychology of consumerism. We were all grateful for this cornucopia of possibilities that consumer-capitalism was bringing into our lives. Now all those riches are taken for granted, and the possibility that it might all end or be interrupted no more occurs to people than it occurs to a teenage girl that her mother might one day refuse to iron her shirts and cook her supper. People aren't even upset by huge income disparities, the million-pound City bonuses that are driving the public-sector middle class out of London. Consumerism has shifted seamlessly into entertainment. Compare the cathedral-like atmosphere of 1950s Harrods with present-day Selfridges. In the latter you're clearly stepping into an entertainment venue. In a big shopping mall everything is infantilized into a series of treats, and the functional aspect of plasma TV screens and even kitchen equipment is played down. Consumer capitalism is immensely flexible, and can adapt itself to anything.

JB: In some respects, your representation of the crowd in *Kingdom Come* engages with a number of observations which Wilhelm Reich made in his study, *The Mass Psychology and Fascism*. What do you make of Reich's suggestion that fascism is not a specific characteristic of certain nationalities or political parties which is imposed on innocent people, but something resembling a tribal violence that is inherent in human nature?

JGB: Yes, I completely agree with Reich. All my experiences during the war and countless horrors since, from the Congo to Yugoslavia to present-day Iraq convinces me that human beings are deeply dangerous, and fascinated by violence and death (probably for sound evolutionary reasons). I'm sure that fascism wasn't imposed on the German people – they embraced it eagerly and seemed ready to pay the price, as Maxted suggests in *Kingdom Come*. The Nazi era was an act of willed insanity which allowed the Germans to break free from the anger and defeatism that followed the Great War and reassert themselves as the dominant people of Europe. Could it happen again? Yes, as the founders of the EU well understood when they tried to bind France and Germany together. Could it happen here, in the United Kingdom? Yes, though we don't go in for ranting *fuehrer* and jackboots. I can't help but feel that a new Dark Age is upon us. The lights are still on, but we are retreating into an inner darkness, a deep cave filled with new age superstition, strange pseudo-science obsessions, bizarre phobias about imaginary diseases and everything else that the hell's kitchen of the human psyche can dream up. Reason rationalizes reality for us, in the sense of providing a convenient explanation for things we would rather not look too closely in the face. But we're tired of reason, and the great 250-year Enlightenment project is beginning to sink below the horizon. Future generations may see something almost autistic in our obsession with reason and view us as a race of obsessive trainspotters who only incidentally came up with modern science.

JB: Although your work can be read as a sustained critique of the aestheticization of violence within contemporary history and culture, it would appear that there is a shift in direction, say from *Super-Cannes* onwards, towards exploring specifically racially motivated forms of violence. Could you say more about this?

JGB: I think this reflects the expanding size of the Asian and Black populations. Thirty-five years ago, when I wrote *High Rise*, a luxury apartment block for middle-class professionals would have had very few, if any, black or Asian residents. Today there would be a good number. The retirement complexes on the Costa de Sol were white only 10 years ago, and probably still are. Blacks and Algerians are now present in the South of France, and are targets of Le Pen's bully boys. Asians and East Europeans have spread out to the London suburbs, and there are big concentrations around Heathrow and the M4 that constantly provoke racist attacks. I think I have faithfully represented this. In some ways these attacks are slightly different from old-style racism. The white working class is re-tribalizing itself, using sport and the union flag as catalysts. Asians, but also Poles and Kosovans, are seen as belonging to other tribes. They need to be attacked to emphasize one's own tribal identity. Skin colour is a useful marker, but isn't an essential element.

JB: Can you elaborate on the idea of 'elective madness' in *Kingdom Come*? How does an advertising executive fit into this psychopathology?

JGB: The point about elective madness is that it is a bottom-up phenomenon, as in the Nazi era. In Brooklands no leader is needed, so the chief analyst of the phenomenon can be a more or less neutral observer, or an active member (Maxted) of the group trying to short-circuit the phenomenon, setting off bombs and staging a failed assassination attempt (the shooting that killed Pearson's father) which they hope will provoke the creation of a fascist republic and force the government to intervene. Pearson is the equivalent of the narrators of the first three books of the quartet (Crawford, Penrose and Gould). Pearson loathes the racist violence, but his father's apparent involvement with the rightist groups leads him to turn a blind eye to the racist attacks and concentrate on the positive features of the new regime – the self-disciplined and healthily glowing families, the sense of a revived community with a new confidence and purpose in life (in short, that 'accommodation' made by so many in the 1930s in England and Germany who should know better). Pearson is about to leave them to it when he stumbles across David Cruise, and he sees a heaven-sent opportunity to put into effect the 'bad is good' marketing scheme that he once devised as a desperate way of reviving a stagnant consumer economy. Cruise becomes an afternoon-TV *fuehrer* (all that we flaccid Brits can achieve). Then real violence breaks out, and the poison rapidly spreads through the motorway towns. Pearson is appalled, but the authorities intervene and the siege begins.

In effect, Pearson follows the same trajectory as the narrators of *Cocaine Nights*, *Super-Cannes* and *Millennium People*, outsiders beguiled into serving a regime that they dislike but which appeals to unsatisfied needs that they have long repressed.

JB: Walter Benjamin once identified the true face of Surrealism with '"the face of an alarm clock that in each minute rings for sixty seconds"'. This seems a particularly apt way of describing the obsessive and reiterative nature of your own form of Surrealist writing. Why has Surrealism been such an influential source for you as a writer? Do you think surrealism survives in the late twentieth and early twenty-first centuries?

JGB: Surrealism certainly survives, and exhibitions of surrealist painters are hugely popular. Dali retrospectives in particular attract huge audiences. People knew that the accepted view of the world as a realm governed by reason and largely explicable in terms set by rationality doesn't exactly match the facts. Anyone involved in even a modest disruption of reality – a small fire in an office building, the failure of a lift filled with shoppers trying to leave a department store – knows the feeling that a parallel world has briefly revealed itself. More serious disaster – planes and car crashes – can leave that sense of dislocation for months, if not years. War, of course, is the ultimate Surrealist dislocation – buses on top of bombed buildings, and so on. Is there an alternative logic running everything, revealing the kind of meanings found in poetry and certain very special moments in life? Watching the birth of a child – and I speak as a father who saw two of his children born – is a profoundly Surrealist experience. Afterwards, reality seems a pale imitation.

In my own case I assume that my wartime childhood drew me powerfully towards the Surrealist view of things. Even before the Japanese invasion in 1937 Shanghai was a pretty Surrealist place – the 50 Chinese hunchbacks lined up to greet the guests at the film premiere of *The Hunchback of Notre Dame*, and a 1,000 other examples. War and internment undermined the authority of my parents and the adult world who had failed to anticipate the disaster that had overwhelmed them. Given the world we live in, I have no doubt that Surrealism will survive and prosper in the C12st century as it did in the C20th, though it is puzzling that no great painters have taken the place of Ernst, Magritte, Dali and Delvaux. But then there are no great novelists either (at least in the English language), no great poets, philosophers or composers, despite a superabundance of universities and art schools, galleries and concert halls. I wonder why . . .

This is an edited version of an interview which was conducted by fax on 2 March 2007.

References

Works Cited by Contributors

Foreword

Works by J. G. Ballard:

Ballard, J. G. (1962). *The Drowned World*. Middlesex: Penguin.

—(1970). *The Atrocity Exhibition*. London: Jonathan Cape.

—(1971). *Vermilion Sands*. London: Jonathan Cape.

—(1973). *Crash*. London: Jonathan Cape.

—(1974). *Concrete Island*. London: Jonathan Cape.

—(2000). *Super-Cannes*. London: Flamingo.

Secondary reading:

Deleuze, G. and Guattari, F. (1986). *Kafka: Towards a Minor Literature*, Minneapolis: University of Minnesota Press.

Vale, V. (2005). *J. G. Ballard: Conversations*. San Francisco, CA: Re/Search.

Vale, V. and Ryan, M. (2004). *J. G. Ballard: Quotes*. San Francisco, CA: Re/Search.

Introduction

Works by J. G. Ballard:

Ballard, J. G. (1966). 'The Coming of the Unconscious', in *New Worlds*, 50: 164, pp. 141–46.

—(1970). *The Atrocity Exhibition*. London: Triad Granada.

—(1973). *Crash*. London: Jonathan Cape.

—(1974). *Concrete Island*. London: Jonathon Cape.

—(1976). 'Notes Towards a Mental Breakdown' *The Complete Short Stories*. London: Flamingo, pp. 849–55 (2001).

—(1977). 'The Index' *The Complete Short Stories*. London: Flamingo, pp. 940–5 (2001).

—(1984). *Empire of the Sun*. London: Flamingo.

—(1991). *The Kindness of Women*. London: Flamingo.

—(1995). *Crash*. London: Jonathan Cape.

—(1996). *Cocaine Nights*. London: Flamingo.

—(1996a). *A User's Guide to the Millennium*. London: Flamingo.

—(1996b). 'The Coming of the Unconscious' in *A User's Guide to the Millennium*. London: Flamingo, pp. 84–9. First published in *New Worlds*, 1966.

—(1996c). 'Fictions of Every Kind' in *A User's Guide to the Millennium*. London: Flamingo, pp. 205–7. First published in *Books and Bookmen*, 1971.

—(1996d). 'First Impressions of London' in *A User's Guide to the Millennium*. London: Flamingo, p. 185. First published in *Time Out*, 1993.

—(1996e). 'Hobbits in Space' in *A User's Guide to the Millennium*. London: Flamingo, pp. 14–16. First published in *Time Out*, 1977.

—(1996f). 'La Jetée' in *A User's Guide to the Millennium*. London: Flamingo, pp. 28–29. First published in *New Worlds*, 1966.

—(1996g). 'Myth Maker of the Twentieth Century' in *A User's Guide to the Millennium*. London: Flamingo, pp. 126–30. First published in *New Worlds*, 1964.

—(1996h). 'A User's Guide to the Millennium' in *A User's Guide to the Millennium*. London: Flamingo, pp. 17–22. First published in *American Film*, 1987.

—(1996i). 'Which Way to Inner Space' in *A User's Guide to the Millennium*. London: Flamingo, pp. 195–8. First published in *New Worlds*, 1962.

—(2000). *Super-Cannes*. London: Flamingo.

—(2003). *Millennium People*. London: HarperCollins.

—(2006). *Kingdom Come*. London: Fourth Estate.

—(2008). *Miracles of Life: Shanghai to Shepperton, An Autobiography* (2008). London: Fourth Estate.

Secondary reading:

Baxter, J. (2004). 'Reading the Signs: An Interview with J. G. Ballard'. *Pretext*, 9, pp. 27–35.

—(2009). *J. G. Ballard's Surrealist Imagination: Spectacular Authorship*. Aldershot; New York: Ashgate.

Cowley, J. (2001). 'The Ballard of Shanghai Jail', the *Observer*. November 4.

Gasiorek, A. (2005). *J. G. Ballard*. Manchester: Manchester University Press.

Luckhurst, R. (1997). *The Angle Between Two Walls: The Fiction of J. G. Ballard*. Liverpool: Liverpool University Press.

Oramus, D. (2007). *Grave New World: The Decline of the West in the Fiction of J. G. Ballard*. Warsaw: University of Warsaw Press.

Rushdie, S. (1997). 'Crash', *The New Yorker*. 15 September, p. 68.

Chapter One: The Geometry of the Space Age: J. G. Ballard's Short Fiction and Science Fiction of the 1960s

Works by J. G. Ballard:

Ballard, J. G. (1962). *The Wind from Nowhere*. London: Penguin.

—(1965). *The Drowned World*. London: Penguin.

—(1985). *The Atrocity Exhibition*. London: Triad Granada.

—(1985a). *The Crystal World*. London: Triad Granada.

—(1985b). *The Drought*. London: Paladin.

—(1988). *Running Wild*. London: Flamingo.

—(1994). *The Kindness of Women*. London: Flamingo.

—(1996). *Cocaine Nights*. London: Flamingo.

—(1996a). 'Fictions of Every Kind' in *A User's Guide to the Millennium*. London: Flamingo, pp. 205-7. First published in *Books and Bookmen*, 1971.

—(1996b). 'New Means Worse' in *A User's Guide to the Millennium*. London: Flamingo, pp. 189–91. First published in the *Guardian*, 1981.

—(1996c). 'Which Way to Inner Space?' in *A User's Guide to the Millennium*. London: Flamingo, pp. 195–8. First published in *New Worlds* 118, May 1962.

—(2000). *Super-Cannes*. London: Flamingo.

—(2001). 'The Concentration City' in *The Complete Short Stories*. London: Flamingo, pp. 23–38 (1957).

—(2001a). 'The Enormous Space' in *The Complete Short Stories*. London: Flamingo, pp. 1130–9 (1989).

—(2001b). 'Introduction' to *The Complete Short Stories*. London: Flamingo, p. ix.

—(2001c). 'Manhole 69' in *The Complete Short Stories*. London: Flamingo, pp. 50–67 (1957).

—(2001d). 'Memories of the Space Age' in *The Complete Short Stories*. London: Flamingo, pp. 1037–60 (1982).

—(2001e). 'Myths of the Near Future' in *The Complete Short Stories*. London: Flamingo, pp. 1061–84 (1982).

—(2001f). 'News from the Sun' in *The Complete Short Stories*. London: Flamingo, pp. 1010–36 (1981).

—(2001g). 'A Question of Re-Entry' in *The Complete Short Stories*. London: Flamingo, pp. 435–58 (1963).

—(2006). *Kingdom Come*. London: Flamingo.

Secondary reading:

Aldiss, B. W. (1973). *Billion Year Spree: The History of Science Fiction*. London: Weidenfeld and Nicolson.

Amis, K. (1961). *New Maps of Hell: A Survey of Science Fiction*. London: Victor Gollancz.

Bradbury, R. (1953). *Fahrenheit 451*. New York: Simon and Schuster.

Clute, J. and P. Nicholls (1999). *The Encyclopaedia of Science Fiction*. London: Orbit. Rev. edn.

Franklin, H. B. (1979). 'What Are We To Make Of J. G. Ballard's Apocalypse?' in T. D. Benson (ed.), *Voices for the Future*, vol. 2. Bowling Green OH: Bowling Green University Popular Press, pp. 82–105.

Gasiorek, A. (2005). *J. G. Ballard*. Manchester: Manchester University Press.

Hennessy, B. (1971). 'Interview with J. G. Ballard' in *Transatlantic Review*, reprinted in Vale, V. and Juno A, (eds), *Re/Search: J. G. Ballard, 8/9*. San Francisco, CA: Re/Search, p. 164 (1984).

Luckhurst, R. (2005). *Science Fiction*. Cambridge: Polity.

Pohl, F. and Kornbluth C. M. (1953). *The Space Merchants*. London: Digit, [n.d].

Pringle, D. (1979). *Earth is the Alien Planet: J. G. Ballard's Four-Dimensional Nightmare*. San Bernadino CA; The Borgo Press.

Punter, D. (1985). *The Hidden Script: Writing and the Unconscious*. London: Routledge and Kegan Paul.

Stephenson, G. (1991). *Out of the Night and Into the Dream: A Thematic Study of the Fiction of J. G. Ballard*. New York, Westport CT and London: Greenwood Press.

Suvin, D. (1979). *Metamorphoses of Science Fiction: On the Poetics and History of a Literary Genre*. New Haven, CT and London: Yale University Press.

Vonnegut, K. (1992). *Player Piano*. London: Flamingo. (1952)

Zoline, P. (1983). 'The Heat Death of the Universe', in M. Moorcock (ed.) *New Worlds: An Anthology*. London: Flamingo, pp. 48–159. First published in *New Worlds* 173, July 1967.

Chapter Two: Disquieting Features: An Introductory Tour to *The Atrocity Exhibition*

Works by J. G. Ballard:

—(1990). *The Atrocity Exhibition*. San Francisco, CA: Re/Search.

—(1985). *Crash*. London: Triad/Panther.

—(1966). 'The Terminal Beach' in *The Terminal Beach*. London: Penguin.

Secondary reading:

Ashcroft, B. (1999). 'The Rhizome of Postcolonial Discourse' in Luckhurst R. and Marks, P. (eds), *Literature and the Contemporary*. London: Longmans, pp. 111–25.

Baxter, J. (2009). *J. G. Ballard's Surrealist Imagination: Spectacular Authorship*. Aldershot: Ashgate.

Baudrillard, J. (1988). 'The Year 2000 Has Already Happened' in Kroker, A. and Kroker, M. (eds), *Body Invaders: Panic Sex in America*. Montreal: The New World Perspectives, pp. 35–44.

Carter, A. (1984). 'Weaver of dreams from the stuff of nightmares' [Guardian review 26-10-79] in Vale, V (ed.) *Re/Search: J. G. Ballard*. San Francisco, CA: Re/Search, p. 140.

Deleuze, G. and Guattari, F. (1991). *A Thousand Plateaus*. Minneapolis: University of Minnesota Press.

Lautreamont, Comte de (1966). *Les Chants de Maldoror*. New Directions: New York Ronnov-Jessen, P. (1984). 'Against Entropy' in *Literary Review*, 74 (August), pp. 28–31.

Luckhurst, R. (1997). *'The Angle Between Two Walls': The Fiction of J. G. Ballard*. Liverpool: Liverpool University Press.

Self, W. (1996). *Junk Mail*. London: Penguin.

Vale, V. (ed.) (2005). *J. G. Ballard Conversations*. San Francisco, CA: Re/Search.

Vale, V. and Juno, A. (eds), (1984). *Re/Search: J. G. Ballard*. San Francisco, CA: Re/Search.

Chapter Three: The Gothic, the Body, and the Failed Homeopathy Argument: Reading *Crash*

Works by J. G. Ballard:

Ballard, J. G. (1970). *The Atrocity Exhibition*. London: Jonathan Cape.

—(1973). *Crash*. London: Jonathan Cape.

Secondary reading:

Baudrillard, J. (1991). 'Crash' in *Simulacra and Simulation*, trans. by S. Faria Glaser. Michigan: University of Michigan Press, pp. 111–20.

—(1991a). *Simulacra and Simulation* trans. by S. Faria Glaser. Michigan: University of Michigan Press.

—(1993). *The Transparency of Evil* trans. by James Benedict. Verso: London and New York.

Carter, A. (1974). *Fireworks*. London: Quartet Books.

Castle, T. (1995). *The Female Thermometer: Eighteenth-Century Culture and the Invention of the Uncanny*. Oxford University Press: Oxford.

Chamisso, A. (1980). *Peter Schlemihls Wundersame Geschichte*. Reclam: Stuttgart.

Cixous, H. (1976). 'Fiction and Its Phantoms: A Reading of Freud's "Das Unheimliche"', in *New Literary History*, Volume 7, no. 3, pp. 525–48.

Dickens, C. (1998). *Great Expectations*. Oxford World's Classics: Oxford. First published 1861.

Hoffmann, E. T. A. (1990). 'Der Sandmann' in *Nachstucke*. Reclam: Stuttgart.

—(1990a). 'The Sandman' in *Tales Of Hoffmann*, trans. and ed. by R. Hollindale. Penguin: Harmondsworth.

Jakobson, R. and Halle, M. (1956). *The Fundamentals of Language*. The Hague and New York: Mouton.

Poe, E. A. (2000). 'William Wilson' in *The Collected Tales of Edgar Allen Poe*. Harper: London.

Sage, V. (1988). *Horror Fiction in the Protestant Tradition*. Macmillan: Basingstoke.

Shelley, M. (1998). *Frankenstein: or 'The Modern Prometheus'*. Oxford World's Classics: Oxford. First published 1818.

Filmography:

Cronenberg, D. (1996). *Crash*. UK/Canada.

Chapter Four: Death at Work: The Cinematic Imagination of J. G. Ballard

Works by J. G. Ballard:

Ballard, J. G. (1985). *Empire of the Sun*. London: Granada.

—(1990). *The Atrocity Exhibition*. San Francisco: Re/Search.

—(1992). *The Kindness of Women*. London: HarperCollins.

—(1993). *The Atrocity Exhibition*. London: Flamingo.

—(1995). *Crash*. London: Vintage.

—(1996). *A User's Guide to the Millennium: Essays and Reviews*. London: Flamingo.

—(2001 [1976]). 'The 60 Minute Zoom', in *The Complete Short Stories*. London: Flamingo, pp. 856–63.

Secondary reading:

Cappock, Margarita (2005). *Francis Bacon's Studio*. London: Merrel.

Deleuze, Gilles (1989). *Cinema 2: The Time-Image*. London: Athlone.

—(1992). *Cinema 1: The Movement-Image*. London: Athlone.

—(2003). *Francis Bacon: The Logic of Sensation*. London: Continuum.

Deleuze, Gilles and Félix Guattari (2004). *Anti-Oedipus: Capitalism and Schizophrenia*. London: Continuum.

— (2004a). *A Thousand Plateaus: Capitalism and Schizophrenia*. London: Continuum.

Delville, M. (1998). *J. G. Ballard*. Plymouth: Northcote House.

Ficacci, Luigi (2006). *Bacon*. Cologne: Taschen.

Godard, Jean-Luc (1986). *Godard on Godard*. New York: Da Capo.

Harrison, Martin (2005). *In Camera Francis Bacon: Photography, Film and the Practice of Painting*. London: Thames and Hudson.

Hendricks, Gordon (1975). *Eadweard Muybridge: The Father of the Motion Picture*. London: Secker and Warburg, pp. 114–16.

Kauffman, Linda S. (1998). *Bad Girls and Sick Boys: Fantasies in Contemporary Art and Culture*. Berkeley: University of California Press.

Luckhurst, R. (1997). *'The Angle Between Two Walls': The Fiction of J. G. Ballard*. Liverpool: Liverpool University Press.

Murray, Peter and Linda Murray (1997). *Dictionary of Art and Artists*, 7th Edition. London: Penguin.

Sellars, Simon. (2006). 'Thirsty Man at the Spigot: An Interview with Jonathan Weiss'. http://www.ballardian.com/weiss-interview. Accessed 8 February 2008.

Sinclair, Iain (1999). *Crash*. London: BFI.

Solnit, Rebecca (2003). *Motion Studies: Eadweard Muybridge and the Technological Wild West*. London: Bloomsbury.

Sylvester, David (1987). *The Brutality of Fact: Interviews with Francis Bacon 1962–1979*. New York: Thames and Hudson.Vale, V and Andrea Juno (1984). *Re/Search: J. G. Ballard*. San Francisco, CA: Re/Search Publications.

Weiss, Jonathan (2005). *The Atrocity Exhibition*. Amsterdam: Ree l23.

Filmography:

Cronenberg, D. (1996). *Crash*. UK/Canada.

Spielberg, S. (1987). *Empire of the Sun*. USA.

Truffaut, F. (1962). *Jules et Jim*. France.

Weiss, J. (2001). *The Atrocity Exhibition*. USA.

Chapter Five: Mind is the Battlefield: Reading Ballard's 'Life Trilogy' as War Literature

Works by J. G. Ballard:

Ballard, J. G. (1968). 'Comment to 'End-Game', in Harry Harrison (ed.), *Backdrop of Stars*. London: Dobson, pp. 79–81.

—(1979). *The Atrocity Exhibition*. London: Triad Panther.

—(1984). *Empire of the Sun*. London: Panther Books.

—(1992). *The Kindness of Women*. London: Grafton.

—(1996). *The User's Guide to the Millennium*. New York, Picador USA.

—(2008). *Miracles of Life: Shanghai to Shepperton, an Autobiography*. London: Fourth Estate.

Secondary reading:

Baxter, John (2004). *A Pound of Paper: Confessions of a Book Addict*. London: Bantam Books.

Benjamin, W. (1979). 'The Storyteller. Reflections on the Works of Nikolai Leskow' (1936), in *Illuminations* trans. by Harry Zohn. London: Fontana/ Collins, pp. 83–110.

Bényei, Tamás (2000). 'White Light: J. G. Ballard's *Empire of the Sun* as a war story', in *AnaChronisT* [yearbook], pp. 249–77.

Cortellessa, A. (1999). 'Sugli Schermi: Burri, Ballard, Cronenberg (parte II)', in *Ipso Facto*, I, 3 (January–April 1999), pp. 107–29.

Delville, M. (1998). *J. G. Ballard*. Plymouth: Northcote House.

Freud, S. (1985). 'Childhood Memories and Screen Memories' (1889), in *The Psychopathology of Everyday Life*, trans. by Alan Tyson. London: Penguin.

Fussell, Paul (1975). *The Great War and Modern Memory*. London: Blackwell.

Gasiorek, A. (2005). *J. G. Ballard*. Manchester: Manchester University Press.

Harvey, A. D. (1998). *A Muse of Fire: Literature, Art and War*. London: The Hambledon Press.

Isnenhgi, Mario (1970). *Il mito della grande Guerra (The Great War Myth)*. Bari: Laterza.

Luckhurst, R. (1997). *'The Angle Between Two Walls': The Fiction of J. G. Ballard*. Liverpool: Liverpool University Press.

Oramus, D. (2007). *Gave New World: The Decline of the West in the Fiction of J. G. Ballard*. Warsaw: University of Warsaw.

Rossi, U. (2007). 'Is the War Inside Your Mind?: War and the Mass Media in J. G. Ballard's "Theatre of War" and "War Fever"', in Kulavkova, K (ed.), *Interpretations – European Research Project for Poetics & Hermeneutics. Volume #1: Violence and Art*. Skopje: Macedonian Academy of Sciences, pp. 155–77.

Self, W. (1995). 'Conversations: J. G. Ballard', in *Junk Mail*. London: Penguin, pp. 329–71.

Smith, S. and Watson, J. (2001). *Reading Autobiography: A Guide for Interpreting Life Narratives*. Minneapolis: University of Minnesota Press.

Chapter Six: From Shanghai to Shepperton: Crises of Representation in J. G. Ballard's Londons

Works by J. G. Ballard:

Ballard, J. G. (1985). *Empire of the Sun*. London: Grafton.

—(1985a). *High-Rise*. London: Jonathan Cape (1975).

—(1991). *The Kindness of Women*. London: Flamingo.

—(1994). *Concrete Island*. London: Vintage.

—(1995). *Crash*. London: Vintage.

—(1996). 'First Impressions of London', in *A User's Guide to the Millennium*. London: Flamingo, pp. 129–30.

—(2003). *Millennium People*. London: Flamingo.

—(2008). *The Drowned World*. London: Harper Perennial.

Secondary reading:

Baudrillard, J. (1994). *Simulacra and Simulation*, trans. by Sheila Faria Glaser. Ann Arbor: University of Michigan Press.

Deleuze, G. and F. Guattari (2002). *A Thousand Plateaus: Capitalism and Schizophrenia*, trans. by Massumi, B. London and New York: Continuum.

—(2004). *Anti-Oedipus*, trans. by Hurley, R., Seem, M., and Lane, H. London and New York: Continuum.

Foucault, M. (2002). *The Order of Things: An archaeology of the Human Sciences*. London: Routledge.

Goux, J. (1994). *The Coiners of Language*, trans. by Curtiss Gage, J. Norman and London: University of Oklahoma Press.

Groes, S. (2005). 'An Interview with Iain Sinclair', in *Pretext*, Autumn, 2005. Norwich: Pen & Inc.

Lefebvre, H. (1991). *The Production of Space*, trans. by Nicholson-Smith D. Oxford: Blackwell.

Luckhurst, R. (1997). *The Angle Between Two Walls: The Fiction of J. G. Ballard*. Liverpool: Liverpool University Press.

Moorcock, M. (1988). *Mother London*. London: Secker & Warburg.

Sennett, R. (1994). *Flesh and Stone: The Body and the City in Western Civilization*. London: Faber.

Chapter Seven: Visions of Europe in *Cocaine Nights* and *Super-Cannes*

Works by J. G. Ballard:

Ballard, J. G. (1971). *Vermilion Sands*. London: J. M. Dent.

—(1996). *Cocaine Nights*. London: Flamingo.

—(2000). *Super-Cannes*. London: Flamingo.

—(2001). 'Having a Wonderful Time' in *The Complete Short Stories*. London: Flamingo, pp. 968–971.

—(2001). 'The Concentration City' in *The Complete Short Stories*. London: Flamingo, pp. 23–38 (1957).

—(2001a). 'The Largest Theme Park in the World' in *The Complete Short Stories*. London: Flamingo, pp. 1139–44 (1989).

Secondary reading:

Bataille, G. (1933). 'The Psychological Structure of Fascism' in (1994) *Visions of Excess: Selected Writings, 1927–1939*. Ed. Allan Stoekl, trans. Allan Stoekl with Carl R. Lovitt and Donald M. Leslie, J. Minneapolis: University of Minnesota Press (first published 1985), pp. 137–60.

—(1994 [1935]). 'The Labyrinth' in (1994) *Visions of Excess: Selected Writings, 1927–1939*. Ed. Allan Stoekl, trans. Allan Stoekl with Carl R. Lovitt and Donald M. Leslie, J. Minneapolis: University of Minnesota Press (first published 1985), pp. 171–7.

—(1988). *Theory of Religion*, trans. by Robert Hurley. New York: Zone.

Baxter, J. (2004). 'Reading the Signs: An Interview with J. G. Ballard', in *Pretext*, Number 9, Spring/Summer, pp. 27–35.

Demos, T. J. (2001). 'Duchamp's Labyrinth: First Papers of Surrealism, 1942', in *October* 97, Summer, pp. 91–119.

Durverger, C. (1979). *La Fleur létale: économie du sacrifice aztèque*. Paris: Seuil. Trans. and cited in Richardson, M. (1994) *Georges Bataille*. London and New York: Routledge.

O'Shaughnessy, H. (2000). *Pinochet: The Politics of Torture*. New York: New York University Press.

Richardson, M. (1994). *Georges Bataille*. London and New York: Routledge.

Ruedy, J. (1992). *Modern Algeria: The Origins and Development of a Nation*. Bloomington: Indiana University Press.

West, N. (2000). *The Day of the Locust*. London: Penguin.

Chapter Eight: The Possibilities of Sacrifice, the Certainties of Trauma: J. G. Ballard's Postmillenial Fiction

Works by J. G. Ballard:

Ballard, J. G. (1973). *Crash*. London: Jonathan Cape.

—(1992 [1974]). *Concrete Island*. London: Jonathan Cape; London: TriadGrafton.

—(1996). *Cocaine Nights*. London: Flamingo.

—(2000). *Super-Cannes*. London: Flamingo.

—(2003). *Millennium People*. London: Flamingo.

—(2006). *Kingdom Come*. London: Fourth Estate.

Secondary reading:

Alexander, Jeffrey C., R. Eyerman, B. Giesen, N. J. Smelser, and P. Sztompka. (2004). *Cultural Trauma and Collective Identity*. Berkeley, Los Angeles and London: University of California Press.

Baudrillard, J. (1993). *Symbolic Exchange and Death*, trans. Ian Hamilton Grant. London and Thousand Oaks: Sage.

Blanchot, M. (1993). *The Infinite Conversation*, trans. Susan Hanson. Minneapolis and London: University of Minnesota Press.

Burkert, W. (1983). *Homo Necans: The Anthropology of Ancient Greek Sacrificial Ritual and Myth*, trans. Peter Bing. Berkeley, Los Angeles and London: University of California Press.

—(2001). *Savage Energies: Lessons of Myth and Ritual in Ancient Greece*, trans. Peter Bing. Chicago and London: University of Chicago Press.

Cousineau, T. J. (2004). *Ritual Unbound: Reading Sacrifice in Modernist Fiction*. Newark: University of Delaware Press.

Flahault, F. (2003). *Malice*, trans. Liz Heron. London and New York: Verso.

Freedman, A. (2003). *Death, Men, and Modernism: Trauma and Narrative in British Fiction from Hardy to Woolf*. New York and London: Routledge.

Freud, S. (1964). *Moses and Monotheism: An Outline of Psycho-Analysis and Other Works. The Standard Edition of the Complete Psychological Works. Volume XXIII (1937–1939)*. trans. James Strechey et al. London: Hogarth Press and the Institute of Psycho-Analysis.

Girard, R. (1987). 'Generative Scapegoating,' and 'Discussion,' in Burkert, W. R. Girard, and J. Z. Smith. *Violent Origins: Ritual Killing and Cultural Formation*. Ed. Robert G. Hamerton-Kelly. Stanford, CA: Stanford UP, pp. 73–105; pp. 106–45.

—(1988). *Violence and the Sacred*, trans. Patrick Gregory. London and New York: Continuum.

Litt, T. (2006). 'J. G. Ballard: unedited transcript' [Interview with J. G. Ballard, 10 July 2006]. http://www.tobylitt.com/ballardinterview.html. Accessed 14:06, 25th April 2007.

Sinclair, I. (1999). *Crash: David Cronenberg's Post-mortem on J. G. Ballard's 'Trajectory of Fate'*. London: BFI Publishing.

Sztompka, P. (2004). 'The Trauma of Social Change: A Case of Postcommunist Societies' in Alexander, Jeffrey C., R. Eyerman, B. Giesen, N. J. Smelser, and P. Sztompka, *Cultural Trauma and Collective Identity*. Berkeley, Los Angeles and London: University of California Press, pp. 155–95.

West, N. (2000). *The Day of the Locust*. London: Penguin.

Wood, James. (2004). *The Irresponsible Self: On Laughter and the Novel*. London: Pimlico.

FURTHER READING: J. G. BALLARD

What follows is a complete bibliography of works by J. G. Ballard and a list of key selected works on J. G. Ballard.

I. Works by J. G. Ballard

The details of J. G. Ballard's works given below are of the first edition published in the United Kingdom.

(1962). *The Wind from Nowhere*. Middlesex: Penguin.

(1962). *The Drowned World*. Middlesex: Penguin.

(1963). *The Four-Dimensional Nightmare*. London: Victor Gollancz.

(1963). *Passport to Eternity*. London: Dent.

(1964). *The Terminal Beach*. London: Victor Gollancz.

(1965). *The Drought*. London: Jonathan Cape.

(1966). *The Crystal World*. London: Jonathan Cape.

(1967). *The Day of Forever*. London: Panther.

(1967). *The Disaster Area*. London: Jonathan Cape.

(1970). *The Atrocity Exhibition*. London: Jonathan Cape.

(1971). *Vermilion Sands*. London: Jonathan Cape.

(1973). *Crash*. London: Jonathan Cape.

(1973). *Concrete Island*. London: Jonathan Cape.

(1975). *High-Rise*. London: Jonathan Cape.

(1976). *Low-Flying Aircraft and Other Stories*. London: Jonathan Cape.

(1977). *The Best of J. G. Ballard*.London: Futura.

(1978). *The Best Short Stories of J. G. Ballard*. New York: Holt, Rinehart, Winston.

(1979). *The Unlimited Dream Company*. London: Jonathan Cape.

(1980). *The Venus Hunters*. London: Panther.

(1981). *Hello America*. London: Jonathan Cape.

(1982). *Myths of the Near Future*. London: Jonathan Cape.

(1984). *Empire of the Sun*. London: Victor Gollancz.

(1988). *Running Wild*. London: Hutchinson.

(1987). *The Day of Creation*. London: Collins.

(1990). *War Fever*. London: HarperCollins

(1991). *The Kindness of Women*. London: HarperCollins.

(1994). *Rushing to Paradise*. London: Flamingo.

(1996). *Cocaine Nights*. London: Flamingo.

(2000). *Super-Cannes*. London: Flamingo.

(2001). *The Complete Short Stories*. London: Flamingo.

(2003). *Millennium People*. London: HarperCollins.

(2006). *Kingdom Come*. London: Fourth Estate.

(2008). *Miracles of Life: Shanghai to Shepperton, An Autobiography*. London: Fourth Estate.

Non-fiction

(1996). *A User's Guide to the Millennium: Essays and Reviews*. London: HarperCollins.

II. Critical Material

Book Length Studies

Baxter, J. (2009). *J. G. Ballard's Surrealist Imagination: Spectacular Authorship*. Aldershot: Ashgate.

Brigg, P. (1985). J. G. Ballard [*Starmont's Reader's Guide. 26*]. *Mercer Island*, WA: Starmont House.

Delville, M. (1998). J. G. Ballard. Plymouth: Northcote House.

Gasiorek, A. (2005). J. G. Ballard. Manchester: Manchester University Press.

Goddard, J. and Pringle, D. (1976). J. G. Ballard: *The First Twenty Years*. London: Bran's Head.

Luckhurst, R. (1997). *The Angle Between Two Walls: The Fiction of J. G. Ballard*. Liverpool: Liverpool University Press.

Oramus, D. (2007). *Grave New World: The Decline of the West in the Fiction of J. G. Ballard*. Warsaw: University of Warsaw Press.

Pringle, D. (1979). *Earth is the Alien Planet: J. G. Ballard's Four-Dimensional Nightmare*. [*The Milford Series: Popular Writers of Today*, Volume 26]. San Bernadino, CA: Borgo Press.

Sinclair, I. (1999). *Crash: David Cronenberg's Post-Mortem on J. G. Ballard's 'Trajectory of Fate'*. London: BFI Publishing.

Stephenson, G. (1991). *Out of the Night and into the Dream: A Thematic Study of the Fiction of J. G. Ballard*. London: Greenwood Press.

III. Select Book Chapters and Journal Articles Discussing Ballard's Work

Book Chapters

Adams, P. (2000). 'Death Drive', in Grant, M. (ed.), *The Modern Fantastic: The Films of David Cronenberg*. Westport, CT: Praeger, pp. 102–22.

Aldiss, B. (1971). 'The Wounded Land: J. G. Ballard', in Clareson, T. D. (ed.), *SF: The Other Side of Realism. Essays on Modern Fantasy and Science Fiction*. Bowling Green, OH: Bowling Green U. Popular Press, pp. 116–30.

Benison, J. (1985). 'In Default of a Poet of Space: J. G. Ballard and the Current State of Nihilism', in Vos, L, de (ed.), *Just the Other Day: Essays on the Suture of the Future*. Intrepid Reeks. 11. Antwerp: EXA, pp. 405–25.

Brower, C. (2002). 'J. G. Ballard', in Harris-Fain, D. (ed.), *British Fantasy and Science-Fiction Writers Since 1960*. Detroit, MI: Gale, pp. 46–62.

Brown, B. B. (2007). Violence Can Be Subtle: Enthymemes Shape an Anti-War Message in *Empire of the Sun*', in Wright, W. and Kaplan, S. (eds), *The Image of Violence in Literature, Media, and Society II*. Pueblo, CO: Society for the Interdisciplinary Study of Social Imagery, Colorado State University-Pueblo, pp. 215–21.

Caserio, R. L. (1990). 'Mobility and Masochism: Christine Brooke-Rose and J. G. Ballard', in Spilka, M., and McCracken-Flesher, C. (eds), *Why the Novel Matters: A Postmodern Perplex*. Bloomington, IN: UP, pp. 310–28.

Diedrick, J. (2006). 'J. G. Ballards "Inner Space" and the Early Fiction of Martin Amis' in Keulks, G. (ed.), *Martin Amis: Postmodernism and Beyond*. New York: Palgrave Macmillan, pp. 180–96.

Dowling, T. (1977). 'Alternative Reality and Deviant Logic in J. G. Ballard's Second "Disaster" Trilogy', in *Science Fiction: A Review of Speculative Literature*, 1:1, pp. 6–18.

Franklin, H. B. (1979). 'What Are We to Make of J. G. Ballard's Apocalypse?', in Clareson, T. D., *Voices for the Future: Essays on Major Science Fiction Writers, Volume 2*. Bowling Green, OH: Popular, 1979, pp. 82–105.

Gasiorek, A. (2006). 'J. G. Ballard' in Malcolm, C. A. and Malcolm, D. (eds), *British and Irish Short-Fiction Writers, 1945-2000.. Dictionary of Literary Biography 319*. Detroit, MI: Thomson Gale, pp. 3–11.

Gordon, A. (2002). 'Steven Spielberg's *Empire of the Sun*: A Boy's Dream of War' in Silet, C. L. P. (ed.), *The Films of Steven Spielberg: Critical Essays*. Lanham, MD: Scarecrow, pp. 109–26.

Gormlie, F. (2002). 'Ballard's Nightmares/Spielberg's Dreams: *Empire of the Sun*' in Silet, C. L. P. (ed.), *The Films of Steven Spielberg: Critical Essays*. Lanham MD: Scarecrow, pp. 127–38.

Greenland, C. (1983). 'The Works of J. G. Ballard', in *The Entropy Exhibition: Michael Moorcock and the British 'New Wave' in Science Fiction*. London: Routledge, Kegan Paul, pp. 92–121.

Jones, M. (1996). 'J. G. Ballard: Neurographer', in Littlewood, D. and Stockwell, P. (eds), *Impossibility Fiction: Alternativity, Extrapolation, Speculation.. Rodopi Perspectives on Modern Literature*. 17. Amsterdam, Netherlands: Rodopi. pp. 127–45.

Kutzbach, K. (2007). 'The Two- . . ., One- . . ., None-Sex Model: The Flesh(-)Made Machine in Herman Melville's "The Paradise of Bachelors and the Tartarus of Maids"and J. G. Ballard's *Crash*', in Kutzbach, K. and Mueller M. (eds), *The Abject of Desire: The Aestheticization of the Unaesthetic in Contemporary Literature and Culture*. Amsterdam, Netherlands: Rodopi, 2007, pp. 181–96.

Lutz, R. (1989). 'The Two Landscapes of J. G. Ballard's Concrete Island', in Slusser, G. E. and Rabkin, E. S. (eds), *Mindscapes: The Geographies of Imagined Worlds*. Carbondale: Southern Illinois University Press, pp. 185–94.

Mota, J. M. (1987). 'Media, Messages, and Myths: Three Fictionists for the Near Future', in Slusser, G. E., Greenland, C. and Rabkin, E. S. (eds), *Storm Warnings: Science Fiction Confronts the Future*. Carbondale: Southern Illinois University Press, pp. 84–93.

Punter, D. (1985). 'J. G. Ballard: Alone Among the Murdering Machines' in *The Hidden Script: Writing and the Unconscious*. London: Routledge and Kegan Paul, pp. 9–27.

Rossi, U. (2007). 'Is The War Inside Your Mind? War and the Mass Media J. G. Ballard's 'Theatre of War' and 'War Fever'', in Kulavkova, K. (ed.), *Interpretations: European Research Project for Poetics & Hermeneutics, Volume I: Violence & Art*. Skopje, Macedonia: Macedonian Academy of Sciences and Arts, pp. 157–76.

Taylor, J. S. (2002). 'The Subjectivity of the Near Future: Geographical Imaginings in the Work of J. G. Ballard', in Kitchen, R. and Kneale, J. (eds), *Lost in Space: Geographies of Science Fiction*. London: Continuum, pp. 90–103.

Wolfe, Gary K. (1992). 'The Dawn Patrol: Sex, Technology, and Irony in Farmer and Ballard', in Ruddick, N. (ed.), *State of the Fantastic: Studies in the Theory and Practice of Fantastic Literature and Film*. Westport, CT: Greenwood, pp. 159–67.

Wager, W. W. (1982). 'The Excluded Self', in *Terminal Visions: The Literature of Last Things*. Bloomington, IN: Indiana University Press.

Journal Articles

Baker, B. (2000). 'The Resurrection of Desire: J. G. Ballard's *Crash* as a Transgressive Text', in *Foundation: The International Review of Science Fiction*, 29:80, pp. 85–96.

Baudrillard, J. and Evans, A. B. (1999). 'Ballard's *Crash*', in *Science-Fiction Studies*, 18:3 [55], pp. 313–30.

Baxter, J. (2007). 'The Surrealist Fait Divers: Uncovering Violent Histories in J. G. Ballard's *Running Wild*' in Ades, D., Lomas, D. and Mundy, J (eds), *Papers of Surrealism*, Issue 5. [Electronic Publication]

—(2008). 'Radical Surrealism: Rereading Photography and History in J. G. Ballard's *Crash*, in *Textual Practice*, Volume 22, Issue 3, September 2008, pp. 507–28.

Botting, F. and Wilson, S. (1998). 'Automatic Lover', in *Screen*, 39:2, pp. 186–92.

Brigg, P. (1994). 'J. G. Ballard: Time Out of Mind', in *Extrapolation: A Journal of Science Fiction and Fantasy*, 35:1, pp. 43–59.

Brottman, M. and Sharrett, C. (2002). 'The End of the Road: David Cronenberg's *Crash* and the Fading of the West', in *Literature/Film Quarterly*, 30:2, pp. 126–32.

Brown, M. R. (2004). 'Dead Astronauts, Cyborgs, and the Cape Canaveral Fiction of J. G. Ballard: A Posthuman Analysis', in *Reconstruction: Studies in Contemporary Culture*, 4:3, Summer [no pagination].

Bukatman, Scott (1991). 'Postcards from the Posthuman Solar System', in *Science-Fiction Studies*, 18:3 [55], pp. 343–57.

Burgess, H. J. (2004). 'Futurama, Autogeddon: Imagining the Superhighway from Bel Geddes to Ballard', in *Rhizomes: Cultural Studies in Emerging Knowledge*, 8, [no pagination].

Butterfield, B. (1999). 'Ethical Value and Negative Aesthetics: Reconsidering the Baudrillard-Ballard Connection', in *PMLA: Publications of the Modern Language Association of America*, 114:1, pp. 64–77.

Chaudhuri, S. (2001). Witnessing Death: Ballard's and Cronenberg's Crash', in *Strategies: A Journal of Theory, Culture, and Politics*, 14:1, pp. 63–75.

Colombino, L. (2006). 'Negotiations with the System: J. G. Ballard and Geoff Ryman Writing London's Architecture', in *Textual Practice*, 20:4, pp. 615–35.

Crary, J. (1986). 'J. G. Ballard and the Promiscuity of Forms', in *Zone*, 1:2, pp. 159–65.

Craven, R. J. (2000). 'Ironic Empathy in Cronenberg's *Crash*: The Psychodynamics of Postmodern Displacement from a Tenuous Reality', in *Quarterly Review of Film and Video*, 17:3, pp. 187–209

Davis, N. (2000). 'An Unrehearsed Theatre of Technology': Oedipalization and Vision in Ballard's *Crash*', in Seed, D. (ed.), *Imagining Apocalypse: Studies in Cultural Crisis*. Basingstoke, NY: Macmillan-St. Martin's, pp. 136–50.

Day, A. (2000). 'Ballard and Baudrillard: Close Reading *Crash*', in *English: The Journal of the English Association*, 49:195, pp. 277–93.

Dowling, T. (1997). 'Alternative Reality and Deviant Logic in J. G. Ballard's Second "Disaster" Trilogy', in *Science Fiction: The Review of Speculative Fiction*, 1:1, pp. 6–18.

Emerson, G. (1986). 'The Children in the Field', in *TriQuarterly*, 65, pp. 221–8.

Finkelstein, H. (1987). '"Deserts of Vast Eternity": J. G. Ballard and Robert Smithson', in *Foundation: The Review of Science Fiction*, 39, pp. 50–62.

Firsching, L. J. (1985). 'J. G. Ballard's Ambiguous Apocalypse', in *Science-Fiction Studies*, 12:3 [37], pp. 297–310.

Foster, D. A. 'J. G. Ballard's *Empire of the Senses: Perversion and the Failure of Authority*', in *PMLA: Publications of the Modern Language Association of America*, 108:3, pp. 519–32.

Francis, S. (2006). 'J. G. Ballard's *The Unlimited Dream Company* as Self-Reflexive Fantasy', in *Foundation: The International Review of Science Fiction*, 35:97, pp. 70–84.

Guidotti, F. (2001). 'J. G. Ballard and the Absent Paradigm of Science Fiction: A Reading of *Crash*', in *Textus: English Studies in Italy*, 14:1, pp. 69–86.

Gundman, R. (1997). 'Plight of the Crash Fest Mummies: David Cronenberg's *Crash*', in *Cineaste: America's Leading Magazine on the Art and Politics of the Cinema*, 22:4, pp. 24–7.

Hardin, M. (2002). 'Postmodernism's Desire for Simulated Death: Andy Warhol's Car Crashes, J. G. Ballard's *Crash*, and Don DeLillo's *White Noise*', in *Lit: Literature Interpretation Theory*, 13:1, pp. 21–50.

Hayles, N. K., Porush, D., Landon, B. and Sobchack, V. (1991). 'In Response to Jean Baudrillard and J. G. Ballard', in *Science-Fiction Studies*, 18:3 [55], pp. 321–9.

Hollington, M. (1985). 'Great Books and Great Wars: J. G. Ballard's *Empire of the Sun*', in *Meanjin*, 44:2, pp. 269–75.

Latham, R. (1997). 'The Modern World Is an Enormous Fiction: J. G. Ballard and the Millennium' in *New York Review of Science Fiction*, 9:7 [103], pp. 1, 8–12.

Luckhurst, R. (1994). 'Petition, Repetition, and "Autobiography": J. G. Ballard's *Empire of the Sun* and *The Kindness of Women*', in *Contemporary Literature*, 35:4, pp. 688–708.

—(1995). 'Repetition and Unreadibility: J. G. Ballard's *Vermilion Sands*', in *Extrapolation: A Journal of Science Fiction and Fantasy*, 36:4, pp. 292–304.

Lutzkanova-Vassileva, A. (2002). 'Trauma, Media Technology, and Psychic Restoration in the Contemporary British Novel: The Testimonies of J. G. Ballard's *The Atrocity Exhibition*', in *CLA Journal*, 45:3, pp. 388–404.

Malzberg, B. N. (1991). 'The Cloud-Sculptor of Terminal X', in *New York Review of Science Fiction*, 29, pp. 1, 8–9.

McCarthy, P. (1997). 'Allusions in Ballard's *The Drowned World*', in *Science Fiction Studies*, 24:2 [72], pp. 302–10.

McKee, A. (1993). 'Intentional Phalluses: The Male "Sex" in J. G. Ballard', in *Foundation: The Review of Science Fiction*, 57, pp. 58–68.

McNamara, L. (2002). 'The Ruse of the Social: Human Waste and the Gated Community' in *Reconstruction: A Culture Studies eJournal*, 2:3 [Electronic publication].

Nicholls, P. (1975). 'Jerry Cornelius at the Atrocity Exhibition: Anarchy and Entropy in "New Worlds" Science Fiction 1964–1974', in *Foundation*, 9, pp. 22–44.

Nicol, C. (1976). 'J. G. Ballard and the Limits of Mainstream SF', in *Science-Fiction Studies*, 3, pp. 150–7.

Noys, B. (2007). 'La Libido reactionnaire?: the recent fiction of J. G. Ballard', in *Journal of European Studies* 37.4, pp. 391–406.

Oramus, D. (2006). 'The Persistence of Memory: Surrealism and Science Fiction in *Vermilion Sands* by J. G. Ballard', in *Foundation: The International Review of Science Fiction*, 35:97, pp. 59–69.

Orr, L. (2000). 'The Utopian Disasters of J. G. Ballard', in *CLA Journal*, 43:4, pp. 479–93.

Perry, N. and Wilkie, R. (1973). 'The Undivided Self: J. G. Ballard's *The Crystal World*', in *Riverside Quarterly*, 5, pp. 268–77.

—(1975). 'The Atrocity Exhibition', in *Riverside Quarterly*, 6, pp. 180–8.

Platzner, R. L. (1983). 'The Metamorphic Vision of J. G. Ballard', in *Essays in Literature*, 10:2, pp. 209–17.

Pocobelli, A. (2004). '"Pre-Uterine Claims": Cultural Contexts and Iconographic Parallels in Ballard's *The Atrocity Exhibition*', in *New York Review of Science Fiction*, 17:2 [194], pp. 18–21.

Pordzik, R. (1999). 'James G. Ballard's *Crash* and the Postmodernization of the Dystopian Novel' in *Arbeiten aus Anglistik und Amerikanistik*, 24:1, pp. 77–94.

Pringle, D. (1973). 'The Fourfold Symbolism of J. G. Ballard', in *Foundation: Review of Science Fiction*, 4, pp. 48–60.

Punter, D. (2002). 'Postmodern Geographies', in *SPAN: Journal of the South Pacific Association for Commonwealth Literature and Language Studies*, 52, pp. 3–20.

Rossi, U. and Philmus, R. M. (1994). 'Images from the Disaster Area: An Apocalyptic Reading of Urban Landscapes in Ballard's *The Drowned World* and *Hello America*', in *Science-Fiction Studies*, 21:1, pp. 81–97.

Ruddick, N. (1992). 'Ballard/*Crash*/Baudrillard', in *Science-Fiction Studies*, 19:3 [58], pp. 354–60.

—(1997). 'Falling between Two Walls' in *Science Fiction Studies*, 24:3 [73], pp. 483–8.

Schuyler, W. M., Jr. (1993). 'Portrait of the Artist as a Jung Man: Love, Death and Art in J. G. Ballard's *Vermilion Sands*', in *New York Review of Science Fiction*, 5; 5:9 [57]; 10 [58], pp. 1, 8–11; 14–19.

Scott, J. K. L (1996). 'Missing the Modern: Hervé Guibert and J. G. Ballard', in *French Studies Bulletin: A Quarterly Supplement*, 58, pp. 1–3.

See, F. (2004). 'Steven Spielberg and the Holiness of War', in *Arizona Quarterly: A Journal of American Literature, Culture, and Theory*, 60:3, pp. 109–41.

Sellars, S. (2000). 'Freefall in Inner Space: From *Crash* to Crash Technology', in Sawyer, A. and Seed, D. (eds), *Speaking Science Fiction: Dialogues and Interpretations*. Liverpool: Liverpool University Press, pp. 214–31.

Smith, J. A. (2005). 'Evolution of a Moralist: J. G. Ballard in the Twenty-First Century Smith', in *New York Review of Science Fiction*, 17:8, pp. 17–19.

Springer, C. (2001). 'The Seduction of the Surface: From Alice to Crash' in *Feminist Media Studies*, 1:2, pp. 197–213.

Tsai, J. (2006). 'Traversing beyond Pleasure and Knowledge: The "Metallized Elysium" in J. G. Ballard's *Crash*', in *Taiwan Journal of English Literature*, 3, pp. 79–96.

Wagar, W. W. (1991). 'J. G. Ballard and the Transvaluation of Utopia', in *Science-Fiction Studies*, 18:1 [53], pp. 53–70.

Wright, A. J. (1976). 'Allegory of the Ruin: J. G. Ballard's "The Drowned Giant"', in *Notes on Contemporary Literature*, 6:4, pp. 14–15.

Ziegler, R. (1999). 'Reader-Text Collisions in J. G. Ballard's *Crash*', in *Notes on Contemporary Literature*, 29:2, pp. 10–12.

—(2000). 'Mediation as Violence in J. G. Ballard's *Running Wild*' in *Notes on Contemporary Literature*, 30:1, pp. 2–4.

IV. Selected Interviews

Barber, Lynn (1970). 'Sci-Fi Seer'. *Penthouse* 5:5, pp. 26–30.

—(1991). 'Alien at Home'. *Independent on Sunday* 15 Sept., pp. 2–4.

Baxter, Jeannette. (2004). 'Reading the Signs: An Interview with J. G. Ballard'. *Pretext*, 9, pp. 27–35.

Blow, David. (1991). 'Bloody Saturday and After'. *Waterstone's Book Catalogue*, Winter, pp. 35–7.

Bresson, C. (1982). 'J. G. Ballard at Home'. *Métaphores*, 7, pp. 5–29.

Burns, Alan and C. Sugnet. (1981). *The Imagination on Trial: British and American Authors Discuss Their Working Methods*, pp. 16–30.

Di Fillipo, Paul. (1991). 'Ballard's Anatomy: An Interview with J. G. Ballard'. *Science Fiction Eye*, 8, pp. 66–75.

Frick, T. (1984). 'The Art of Fiction: J. G. Ballard'. *Paris Review*, 94, pp. 133–60.

Goddard, J. and Pringle, D. (1976). 'An Interview with J. G. Ballard' in J. Goddard and D. Pringle (eds). *J. G. Ballard: The First Twenty Years* (Hayes, Middlesex: Bran's Head, 1976): pp. 8–35.

Hennessy, Brenden. (1971). 'J. G. Ballard'. *Transatlantic Review* 39, Spring 60–4.

Juno, A., and V. Vale. (1984). 'Interview with J. G. Ballard'. *Re/Search*, 8/9 (San Francisco, CA: Re/Search, 1984): pp. 6–35.

Lewis, J. (1991). 'An Interview with J. G. Ballard', in *Mississippi Review*, 20:1–2, pp. 27–40.

Pickering, P. (1991). 'Out of the Shelter'. *The Sunday Times*, 22 Sept., p. 5.

Pringle, David. (1982). 'From Shanghai to Shepperton'. *Foundation: The Review of Science Fiction*, 24, pp. 5–23.

—(1987). 'J. G. Ballard'. *Interzone* 22, pp. 13–16.

Revell, G. (1984). 'Interview with J. G. Ballard'. *Re/Search: J. G. Ballard*, 8/9 (San Francisco, CA: Re/Search, 1984), pp. 42–52.

Self, W. (1995). 'Conversations: J. G. Ballard' in *Junk Mail*. London: Penguin, pp. 329–71.

Thompson, Ian. (1991). 'A Futurist with an urge to Exorcise'. *The Independent*, 21 September.

Whitford, F. (1971). 'Speculative Illustrations: Eduardo Paolozzi in Conversation with J. G. Ballard and Frank Whitford'. *Studio International*, 183, pp. 136–43.

V. Filmography

Cronenberg, D. (1996). *Crash*. UK/Canada.

Spielberg, S. (1987). *Empire of the Sun*. USA.

Weiss, J. (2001). *The Atrocity Exhibition*. USA.

VI. Websites

Ballardian.com

Published and edited by Simon Sellars, Ballardian.com is an excellent online resource which includes interviews, essays and reviews by and about J. G. Ballard. The site also offers several useful links and includes a comprehensive bibliography. http://www.ballardian.com/. Accessed 12 June 2008.

Jgballard.com

This unofficial site includes a very useful archive of interviews by Ballard together with reviews of his work. http://www.jgballard.com/index.php. Accessed 2 April 2008.

Yahoo/J. G. Ballard Discussion Forum

A Yahoo group devoted to discussing J. G. Ballard's work and other Ballardian-related matter. http://groups.yahoo.com/group/jgb/. Accessed 11 August 2007.

Wikipedia

The Wikipedia entry for J. G. Ballard provides several useful links and includes a comprehensive bibliography and a list of all works by Ballard adapted for film and cinema. http://en.wikipedia.org/wiki/J. G. Ballard. Accessed 27 May 2008.

Index

Aldiss, Brian 12
Algeria
   War of Independence (1954–62) 105
Amis, Kingsley
   New Maps of Hell 13
Antonioni, Michelangelo
   L'Aventurra 52
Asimov, Isaac 13
autobiography 68–70
'autofiction' 70

Bacon, Francis 58–62
   *After Muybridge: Woman Emptying
    a Bowl of Water and Paralytic Child
    on All Fours* 59
   Three Studies of the Human Head 58
Ballard: works by
   'The 60 Minute Zoom' 50
   The Atrocity Exhibition 2, 5, 7, 12,
    18, 32–3, 38, 41–3, 47–8, 51, 52,
    53–60, 67
   Cocaine Nights 95, 96, 97–102, 107,
    108–9
   The Complete Short Stories 21
   'The Concentration City' 14, 15,
    94–5
   Concrete Island 8, 107–8, 113–14
   Crash 1, 2, 5, 7, 8, 41–9, 53, 60–2,
    80, 86–90, 110, 114, 116
   The Crystal World 17–21
   The Drought 11, 19
   'The Drowned Giant' 12
   The Drowned World 78, 80, 84–6, 87
   Empire of the Sun 1, 5, 53, 62–5, 66,
    70–1, 79, 83–4
   'End-Game' 75
   'The End of My War' 75
   'The Enormous Space' 15
   'Having a Wonderful Time' 95
   High-Rise 79, 114
   'The Illuminated Man' 17
   'The Index' 8–9

The Kindness of Women 62, 66,
   69–72, 75–7, 79
Kingdom Come 107–12, 116, 118
'The Largest Theme Park in the
   World' 95
'Manhole 69' 15
'Memories of the Space Age' 16
Millennium People 2, 8, 80, 89,
   107–10, 116
*Miracles of Life: Shanghai to
   Shepperton, An
   Autobiography* 66–77
'Myths of the Near Future' 16–21
'News From the Sun' 16–17,
   19–21
'Notes Towards a Mental
   Breakdown' 8–9
'The Object of the Attack' 16
'Prima Belladonna' 6
'A Question of Re-Entry' 16
'The Subliminal Man' 14
Super-Cannes 8, 95–7, 102–9, 112, 116
'The Terminal Beach' 12
Vermilion Sands 95
War Fever 22
'Which Way to Inner Space?' 4,
   11–12, 16
The Wind From Nowhere 15
Barnes, Djuna 83
Bataille, Georges 94
   'The Labyrinth' (1936) 96–7,
    99–102
   'The Psychological Structures of
    Fascism' (1933) 103–6
Baudrillard, Jean 51
   'Crash' 41–8
   hyperreality 31–2, 46
   simulation 47
   Symbolic Exchange and Death 109
   The Transparency of Evil 34–8
   'The Year 2000 Has Already
    Happened' 31

Beckett, Samuel 83
Benjamin, Walter
'The Story-Teller' 72
Bergson, Henri
Matter and Memory 52
Bradbury, Ray 15
Fahrenheit 451 13
Brunner, John 12
Bunuel, Louis
Un Chien Andalu 24

Campbell, John W. 13
Camus, Albert 41
capitalism 82–3, 87, 89–90, 92, 95,
96, 100–2
and language 83–5
Carnell, E. J. 'Ted' 11–12, 22, 68
Carter, Angela 38
Chamisso, A
*Peter Schlemihl's Remarkable
Story* 35–7
Christopher, John 13, 15
chronophotography 53–6
Clute, John, and Peter Nicholls
Encyclopaedia of Science Fiction 12,
22
Cocteau, Jean 65
comic tradition 112
community 96, 98–102 *see also*
sacrifice
and language 99–100
Conrad, Joseph
Heart of Darkness 85, 118
Cronenberg, David
Crash 1, 41–2, 46–8, 51, 61
The Fly 62
Videodrome 62

Dali, Salvador 41
Deleuze, Gilles 29
Cinema 2: The Time-Image 52
The Logic of Sensation 59
Deleuze, Gilles and Guatarri, Félix
*Capitalism and Schizophrenia:
Anti-Oedipus* 51, 88
*Capitalism and Schizophrenia: A
Thousand Plateaus* 51, 88
depth-psychology 12, 14, 20
Deren, Maya
Meshes of the Afternoon 24

Directorate of National Intelligence
(DINA) 104
DuChamp, Marcel 41
dystopian writing 96

Eliot, T. S. (Thomas Stearns) 3
Enlightenment 35–7
Ernst, Max 41
Escher, M. C. 97
Euclid 39, 42
Evans, Christopher 59
evolutionary biology 13, 16–21

Fascism 96–7, 103–6
heterogeneity 103–5
homogeneity 102–4
Foucault, Michel
*The Order of Things:
An Archaeology of the Human
Sciences* 82–3
Franklin H. Bruce
'What Are We To Make of J. G.
Ballard's Apocalypse?' 14
French 'New Wave' Cinema 5
Freud, Sigmund 116
fugue state 17–19
screen memories 77
transference 115
the 'uncanny' 37, 39

Gernsback, Hugo 13
Girard, Réne *Violence and the
Sacred* 111–19
'Generative Scapegoating' 112,
117–18
Gloeckner, Phoebe 27–8
Godard, Jean-Luc
Alphaville 5
Pierrot le fou
Gold H. L. 13

Heinlein, Robert 13
Heller, Joseph 48
Hoffman, E. T. A.
'The Sandman' 36
humour 8, 40, 42
Huxley, Aldous
Brave New World 96

inner space 4, 15–17

James, Henry
  The Turn of the Screw 118
Jarry, Alfred 41
Joyce, James 3, 83

Kleist, Heinrich von 45

labyrinth 94–106
life narrative 69–72
life-writing 66, 68–70
Loy, Mina 83
Lumiere, August and Louis
  Cinématographe 52

'malerisch' 60–2
Marey, Etienne Jules 54, 58
Marker, Chris
  La Jetée 5, 57
metaphor 40, 43, 44
metonymy 40, 45, 48
mimetization 47–9
Moorcock, Michael 11–12
Muybridge, Eadweard 54–9
  Animal Locomotion 58
  Zoopraxiscope 55–6, 59

National Aeronautics and Space
  Administration (NASA) 16–17
New Wave science fiction 4
  literary experimentation 12–14, 24
New Worlds 4, 6, 11–16, 22, 68

Orwell, George
  Nineteen Eighty-Four 96

Paolozzi, Eduardo 6
paratext 32–3, 56
parody 37, 42, 43, 46
Pinochet, Augusto 104
Poe, Edgar Allen
  'William Wilson' 38
Pohl, Frederick and Kornbluth, Cyril M.
  The Space Merchants 13
Pop Art 5, 6
pornography 43–4, 46
psychopathology 39–41

Reagan, Ronald 41, 56
Resiner, Alan
  Last Year in Marienbad 24, 57

rhizome 29–31
Robbe-Grillet, Alain
  the French novel 41–2
Rosellini, Roberto
  Europe 51

sacrifice 101–2, 108–10, 114–18
  and trauma 109, 112, 114, 116,
  117
Science Fantasy 11
Science Fiction Adventures 11
Shakespeare, William
  The Tempest 113
Shelley, Mary
  Frankenstein 37
short story form 21–2
signification 79–93
sign system 80, 88–9
Sinclair, Iain 61, 78
space 80, 82, 87–8, 90–1, 93
space-time continuum 16–17
Spielberg, Steven
  Empire of the Sun 1, 51,
  63–4
Stanford, Leland 55
subjectivity 13–17 *see also* time
  repetition 25–7
Surrealism 5, 6–7, 27–33, 41
Suvin, Darko
  novum 13

'This is Tomorrow' Exhibition (1956)
time 16–21
  and narrative 32–3
  and subjectivity 32
traumatological 114, 117, 118
Truffaut, François
  Jules et Jim 56

Vonnegut, Kurt
  Player Piano 48

Warhol, Andy 24
Weiss, Jonathan
  The Atrocity Exhibition 51, 57–8
Wells, H. G. 13, 20
West, Nathaniel
  The Day of the Locust 118
Wölfflin, Heinrich 60
Wyndham, John 13